I am
IndesTructible!

ROB MARLAND is the author and editor of several books about Oscar Wilde, including *Oscar Wilde's First Tragedy: The Composition, Production, and Reception of Vera; or, The Nihilists* (2026) and *Oscar Wilde: The Complete Interviews* (2022). He is a member of the editorial board of *The Wildean*, the journal of the Oscar Wilde Society.

I am IndesTructible!

Selected Interviews with Oscar Wilde

edited by ROB MARLAND

Little Eye

First published in 2026 in Jena, Germany, by Little Eye

Introduction and editorial matter © Rob Marland 2026

A CIP catalogue record is available from the British Library.

Hardcover ISBN 978-3-982413-48-8
Paperback ISBN 978-3-982413-49-5

Set in Equity A 10/13 (typeface by Matthew Butterick)

Front cover: Oscar Wilde on the Isle of Wight by Jabez Hughes & Mullins (1884).

For errata and updates see https://robmarland.co.uk/wildeselints

Links to third party websites are provided in good faith and for information only.

*TO
HANNAH*

CONTENTS

 Selected Interviews with Oscar Wilde

Contents

ix

Introduction

NOBODY GOES TO see a performance of Oscar Wilde's masterpiece, *The Importance of Being Earnest*, for the plot. It is the language that has kept audiences enthralled – and in stitches – since 14 February 1895. Yet Wilde's friends insisted that even the best of his writing was but a pale reflection of his brilliant conversation, and those who had heard him speak were disappointed when they read his books. The epigrams that are strewn like so many jewels through Wilde's 'trivial comedy for serious people' originated in his own seriously trivial talk. For Wilde, conversation was 'the bond of all companionship', 'the only proper intoxication', and 'among the supreme aims of life'. During his self-imposed exile in France after serving two years' hard labour for what English law termed gross indecency, Wilde reminisced over his days of 'laughter and delight', when he had 'tired many a moon with talk, and drank many a sun to rest with wine and words'. What a tragedy, then, that his greatest work – the work to which he gave not only his talent but his genius – is lost to us.

Except, it isn't.

On the evening of 2 January 1882 five men rowed out over the choppy grey waters of New York's Upper Bay to the SS *Arizona*, a steamer anchored at quarantine a quarter of a mile off Staten Island. They clambered up an icy rope ladder and went in search of the ship's most famous passenger. They found him in the captain's room.

'How do you like America, Mr Wilde?'

Wilde burst out laughing in a succession of broad 'haw, haw, haws'. He didn't think it politic to answer: all he had seen of the country was an oil lamp flickering on the horizon.

A twenty-seven-year-old Wilde had come to America to lecture on art, not because he was an expert on the subject but because he was a prominent devotee of the so-called aesthetic movement, a fashionable fad for blue-and-white-china, sunflowers, and peacock feathers. W. S. Gilbert and Arthur Sullivan had written *Patience*, a comic opera lampooning the aesthetes, and their manager hit upon the idea of bringing one of London's velvet-clad nincompoops across the pond to advertise the opera's American tour. Wilde would create a demand for tickets for Gilbert and Sullivan's caricature, and audiences for *Patience* would flock to see the genuine article.

The scheme worked. Wilde became a phenomenon. His photographs and book of poetry sold in stacks. A constant stream of stories about him flooded the press. Newspaper readers wanted to know more about the real Oscar Wilde, and to meet this desire editors sought interviews with the 'Apostle of Aestheticism'.

At first Wilde was unprepared for all this attention. He confided in the magazine proprietor Mrs Frank Leslie that he had 'turned his back' on New York's 'horrible reporters'; she reminded him that it was their business to interview as it was his to lecture, and that he would be better off giving them something to print, else they would be liable to turn on *him*. Wilde was usually averse to good advice, but he took Leslie's.

Many American interviewers, primed by *Patience*, expected to meet a buffoon or huckster. Instead they found Wilde charming, and all but the most hostile were compelled to admit that his conversational powers and the range of his expertise and interests were impressive. He was polite, engaging, and above all amusing. The interviewers transcribed what Wilde said and left behind an invaluable record. These interviews are the best evidence we have of Wilde's opinions on a range of topics from architecture and fashion to the politicians, authors, actors, and artists of his day. What's more, they reveal how Wilde talked rather than how he wrote, and reading them is the closest any of us will ever come to joining one of history's greatest raconteurs in conversation. We hear him at his brilliant best and occasionally see the mask slip. He hones rationales for his various philosophies, tests anecdotes, trots out favourite phrases, and airs pet peeves.

What did Wilde think of the newspaper interview? He told one interviewer that 'some of the brightest hours' he had passed in America had been with 'the gentlemen of the press', and that he found them 'among the most intelligent men' he had encountered west of Ireland. The interview was 'a capital feature of the paper', and gave an interviewee 'an opportunity of saying and explaining things which he could not do as satisfactorily in an ordinary speech'. He had certainly grown to enjoy the experience, boasting that, in America, 'I used to have them (interviewers) coming to my rooms five or six times a day, and I rather liked it'. But he declined to return to the States in the early 1890s to promote his society comedies because he did not want to be mobbed by 'inquisitive reporters, who make no allowances for moods'.

In Europe Wilde would occasionally agree to chat with American correspondents or with young British and French journalists anxious to emulate their enterprising transatlantic peers. In London he complained to interviewers about the censorship of his controversial Biblical play *Salomé*, in Dunfermline he tussled with a correspondent from Alabama on 'the race question', and on a beach in Brittany he warned a reporter to 'beware of women who wear mauve'.

One of Wilde's chief delights was annoying the Philistine middle-classes by telling 'beautiful lies' and expressing opinions that were not really his own. He told interviewers that he had curled his hair in imitation of history's greatest tyrant, the Roman emperor Nero, when in reality he was following a Parisian fashion. And he claimed to dislike intelligent women, even though he edited a women's magazine that was written for and by women of culture and learning. He recognised that 'recreation, not instruction, is the aim of conversation', and that the liar is a far more civilised being than the 'blockhead' who points out that a tale told to amuse is untrue. Readers of the interviews should therefore exercise caution before trusting anything Wilde says, and remember his maxim: 'Between two truths, the falser is truer.'

⁎⁎⁎

Wilde's complete works were first published in 1908; collections of his letters began to appear in the first decades of the twentieth-century and culminated in the *Complete Letters* in 2000. In contrast, Wilde's interviews have rarely been reprinted. In 1979 E. H. Mikhail included about thirty (the number depends on how one defines an interview) in *Os-*

car Wilde: Interviews and Recollections, and in 2010 Matthew Hofer and Gary Scharnhorst collected forty-eight in their *Oscar Wilde in America: The Interviews*. But these are selections based on an incomplete survey. They omit many of the more fascinating interviews simply because, until recently, most of Wilde's interviews were unknown even to the most dedicated of Wilde scholars. This is perhaps inevitable given the ephemeral nature of the daily press. The newspapers in which Wilde's interviews first appeared – often in major cities but sometimes in small towns – were bought, read, and discarded. Even for scholars able to travel to far-flung libraries, the prospect of poring over heavy, bound volumes of fragile, yellowing newsprint, or spooling through microfilms on clunky machines, was hardly appealing. It is only thanks to the rise of newspaper digitisation, which allows scholars to run dozens of searches through thousands of titles in a single day, that many of Wilde's interviews have been rediscovered. But archival research remains a fruitful endeavour: one afternoon at the British Library I was leafing through a scrapbook compiled by the manager of Wilde's lecture tours and found pasted into its pages four previously undocumented interviews with Wilde, three of which had been snipped from newspapers not preserved by any library.

Some of these 'new' interviews are surprising for what they reveal about Wilde's preoccupations. For example, who thinks of Wilde as an environmentalist? Yet again and again he steered his interviews onto the problem of pollution. In the rapidly industrialising United States and Canada, there were few restrictions on burning factory waste or dumping it into rivers. Wilde was appalled by the 'filthy cloud' that hung over Cincinnati, and the Ottawa River, which was 'choked with sawdust'. He repeatedly asserted that '[i]t is quite impossible to have any art unless you have good air, good water, and clean cities'. His comments provoked ridicule at the time, but he was willing to wait for the judgement of posterity. That judgement has now found him to be entirely in the right.

Wilde was often interviewed in the comfort of his hotel rooms (he would recline on a sofa spread with a fur rug and an old gold shawl), but he also spoke to interviewers while strolling down New York's Broadway or London's St James's Street, in restaurants and lobbies, in train carriages and railway stations, and even at a 'lunatic asylum'.

Astoundingly, an article that was unknown to scholarship until 2021 reveals that he agreed to be interviewed at Reading Gaol. This was as he was nearing the end of his sentence and he presumably hoped that, by giving in to the constant requests for interviews communicated to him via the sympathetic prison governor, he might dissuade reporters from pursuing him after his release. He was interviewed for the final time in the shabby Parisian hotel where on 30 November 1900, aged forty-six, he died of meningoencephalitis.

The interviews in this book have been chosen for their quality. These are the best of the more than 230 interviews Wilde is known to have given. Many interviewers, and especially those in America, wrote long accounts of Wilde's lectures. These and other digressions have been silently omitted from the present collection. The interviews are arranged in chronological order and cover the greater part of Wilde's adult life, from 1882 to 1900, when he played many roles: aesthete, husband and father, playwright, convict, and, finally, impoverished exile. Readers are encouraged to follow the advice that Wilde shared with an interviewer in Paris and dip in wherever they wish – to 'overhear' the book as one might overhear a conversation in the street – and to be lulled by what Wilde's most devoted disciple, Robert Ross, described as the hypnotic quality of his friend's golden voice.

THE INTERVIEWS

'Oscar Wilde in New York', *The Sun* (New York, NY), 3 Jan. 1882, 1

A drenched reporter of *The Sun* climbed from a small rowboat to the high deck of the *Arizona*, while she lay off Quarantine last evening, and sought Mr. Oscar Wilde, the apostle of aestheticism, among the passengers. He was met aft by a tall young man, who was coming out of the Captain's room, saying:

'Ha, ha, ha! Wishes to interview me, does he?'

Mr. Wilde's laugh and accent were remarkable. It was a loud laugh, full of indubitably good nature, yet seeming somewhat forced. He stood at least six feet two inches tall, with broad shoulders and erect carriage. He wore a long ulster, lined with two kinds of fur, patent leather boots, and had a small round fur cap set squarely on his head. He stood at ease with one hand thrust into his ulster pocket and the other, with a large signet ring on its little finger, idly holding a cigarette which he occasionally puffed vigorously. He wore his hair long. It is brown and falls somewhat lankly on his shoulders. He wore a collar that can only be described as low-necked, inasmuch as it opened so very far down on his chest. It was caught at the bottom with a brilliant bit of sky blue plush, which hung down negligently. His face, topped by the round fur cap and flanked by the falling hair, was that of a man about twenty-six years of age. He has small blue eyes that are rather expressive, and a straight nose. The face is very long, and terminates in a jaw of unusual size, which is the most prominent and striking feature of his countenance. He threw his head back occasionally when he talked, in a way that made the jaw doubly prominent and gave the face an expression of extraordinary strength. Mr. Wilde accented his words very oddly, with an entire disregard of the customary emphasis, and continually relapsed into his peculiar laugh, without any apparent reason.

'What is aestheticism, Mr. Wilde?'

Laughing again, he replied: 'Aestheticism is the science of the beautiful. It is a search for the secret of life. By the way, do you know, I was very much disappointed in the Atlantic Ocean. It was very tame. I expected to have it roar about and be beautiful in its storms. I was disappointed in it.'

'Do not the disciples of aestheticism exhibit marked peculiarities in costume in England?'

'Yes; the movement has brought out individualities, but it is because of its force. If a movement has not sufficient force to develop individual characteristics it is of little worth as a movement of improvement. What am I to do? I'm to lecture through the country if I find that I like lecturing, and intend to produce my play.'[1]

At the termination of the interview, as the reporter descended over the side of the steamship, a crowd of passengers chanted 'A pallid and lank young man,'[2] and screamed rough jibes about aestheticism.

1   Wilde's first play, *Vera; or, The Nihilists*, is a melodramatic tragedy set in Russia. In late 1881 Wilde had cancelled a scheduled performance of the play in London.
2   Lyrics from *Patience* describing Bunthorne, an aesthetic poet.

'A Six-Feet-Four Young Man', *The Evening Telegram* (New York, NY), 3 Jan. 1882, 3rd ed., 5

A chilled crowd of aesthetic human beings—the men nearly all wearing long hair, *a la* Tilton,[1] and low-necked shirts—beat their hands and stamped their feet on the deck of the Guion Steamship Company this morning while waiting for the *Arizona*—on which was their apostle, Oscar Wilde—to make her berth. The big ship left Quarantine at ten minutes after seven o'clock, but it was nine before she commenced wearing alongside of her wharf. She came in prow first and stuck fast on a bank of mud twenty feet from the dock. Tugs pushed and pulled, the *Arizona*'s engines worked vigorously, but mud was victor for a time. The battle raged over two hours before the steamship could be reached with a gangplank. While the fight between steam and mud was in progress the shivering mass of humanity on the dock greeted with round after round of applause a towering form on the *Arizona*'s deck.

It was that of a man, youthful in appearance. He stood six feet four inches. He has a smooth face and long flowing locks. An overcoat of bottle-green cloth, fur-lined and fur-collared, a sealskin cap, and yellow kid gloves made the man more conspicuous. It was Mr. Oscar Wilde, the poet and journalist.[2]

Oscar Wilde photographed by Napoleon Sarony as he appeared to New York's reporters on the deck of the *Arizona*.

'I am here to lecture and see the country,' he said with a hearty laugh as he extended his hand to the *Telegram* reporter. 'Will I stay long? Really I can't say. It depends upon circumstances. You see this thing is all new to me. I've made my first trip to America very pleasantly. It has been delightful on deck during the whole passage, with the exception of two days. My fellow-voyagers are splendid people.

'They have given me such glowing descriptions of the country that I am in love with it already. I want to see what there is in your great metropolis, and the Far West has attractions, unless it is misrepresented, that I must witness. And I am anxious to see something of Mexico.' Lighting a fresh cigarette, Mr. Wilde continued: 'Already I have experienced something of American courtesy. This gentleman (pointing to Mr. Frank Moseman, a Custom House officer) came on board at Quarantine and relieved me of all trouble concerning my baggage. Then a little steamer met us on the way up the harbor and brought on board an agent of the *International Review*, whose mission was to secure from me an article for that magazine. I had hardly heard the proposition before another steamer hailed us. She had on board Mr. Morse, the business manager of my agent, Mr. R. D'Oyly Carte.[3] I learn from him that our original plans must undergo a change. After lecturing in New York I shall proceed to Baltimore, Boston, Philadelphia and Washington.

'Do tell the people my honest age. I believe the *Telegram* will report me truthfully. I wish other papers of this city had done so. I was twenty-six last October,[4] and say, too, that I shall remain long enough to see what there is worth seeing in glorious America.

'What is it, steward?' The steward of the *Arizona* was waiting to speak to Mr. Wilde. 'An order for my lecture? Certainly.' The lecturer took a card from his card case and writing his name upon the back of it with the words, 'Pass bearer,' said, 'You are the only man in this country that has my autograph. If you can make any money by selling it I'll give you another.'

Mr. Wilde talked rapidly and laughed merrily several times while making the remarks given above. As he was about passing down the gang plank he turned to the *Telegram* reporter and said, while a shadow fell over his face:—'I have been misrepresented already, not through malice, I think, but I have come here determined to get acquainted with the big-hearted American people, and (pausing for a moment while his features again lighted up with a good-natured smile) I shan't return to Europe until I do.'

1   Theodore Tilton (1835–1907) was an American newspaper editor and poet. Like Wilde, he had collar-length hair.
2   Wilde had published a collection of poems in 1881. Although he had published a few articles in magazines, he was by no means a journalist.
3   Colonel William Francis Morse managed Wilde's American lecture tours on behalf of the British theatrical impresario Richard D'Oyly Carte (1844–1901). He later managed Wilde's first British lecture tours.
4   Wilde was twenty-seven. He habitually shaved a year or two off his age.

The Indianapolis Journal (Indianapolis, IN), 14 Jan. [1882]

Here, at 10 o'clock, comes Oscar Wilde, from a dinner at Mrs. John Bigelow's. There are murmurs of curiosity and craning necks to see him while he removes his plum-colored ulster in the reception-room; and the crowded guests surge aside to give passage as Mrs. Croly leads him up the parlors and presents him to Mrs. Alcott.[1] The apparition of him creates a ripple of not impolite amusement. Almost giantesque in stature and proportion, the eye naturally falls on his lower extremities, formerly known as 'legs,' encased above the knees in loose trunks of black doeskin, and below the knees in black silk stockings that fit snugly over a pair of very attenuated calves. I have seldom seen slimmer extremities, excepting those which Sarah Bernhardt displays in *Frou Frou*.[2] His body is clad in an ordinary swallow-tail coat, with a rim of white linen vest inside the collar, cut very low, leaving a vast expanse of shirt bosom, of fine pique, illuminated with a single pin of three enormous pearls. A large turn-down collar of pique completes the costume, and uncombed hair falls to his shoulders in the most negligent mood imaginable. A white silk handkerchief is stuck in the bosom of the vest.

After general curiosity was satisfied and introductions lapsed, I spoke with the Devotee of Beauty. 'How on earth did you and Mr. Ruskin come to break stones on the highway?' I inquired.

'Why, this is it,' he said, with spirit, evidently glad to escape from conventional questioning. 'One day, when we gathered to the lecture, Mr. Ruskin's audience was very small. It was shortly announced that they were gone to the boat-race. Mr. Ruskin said that exercise was good and necessary, but it seemed too bad that it could not be attained in some really beneficial pursuit. He said he would see if he could not propose something.'

'This was at Oxford?' I asked.

'Yes, at my college, Maudlin.'

'Maudlin?' I repeated, not remembering any such college.

'Yes,' he answered; "Magdalen," you call it, but we pronounce it "Maudlin."'

I did not ask him if it was named after Mary Maudlin, but he went on:

'Next day, Ruskin came to the class, and called our attention to the fact that there was no direct communication between two adjacent villages, and that the inhabitants of one could get to the other only by going far around. He said he was going at work to build a road across the swamp between the villages. He had located it, and was going to work next morning at break of day. If any of the class wished to join, he would cheerfully show them how to break stones and wheel a wheelbarrow.'

'Did you laugh at the proposition?'

'No, indeed. We never thought of its being at all fantastic. He was quite serious, and we had for him a feeling of admiration and respect only. Well, next day some forty of us luxurious sluggards got up at dawn and joined him over on the edge of the swamp. We had our hammers, our shovels, our crowbars, and our wheelbarrows, and we speedily learned how to use them. It is not very complicated. For three months we forty—a good part of the class—persevered and stuck together, and all that time Ruskin wheeled earth among us and kept up the most delightful conversation, or rather monologue, on art. It was a profitable season. And at the end of it there was a long mound of earth across that swamp which a lively imagination might fancy was a road.'

Just here, Mrs. Croly, who had been waiting for a chance, presented Judge Brady, Ex-Mayor Ely, Commissioner King and Mrs. King, Mary Mapes Dodge, Mrs. Rees, and others.

I was at the reception, on Friday evening, given by Mr. and Mrs. A. A. Hayes and Mr. and Mrs. W. F. Morse at the unique parlors of the former.[3] This was Mr. Wilde's first appearance in New York society. It was in the afternoon, and he appeared in a bright snuff-colored brown suit of melton—long frock coat and pantaloons.

The parlors were furnished in a style quite Oriental. Velvet carpets nearly covered with Turkish rugs; a variety of pretty chairs with no upholstery; no doors, but everywhere heavy portieres drawn aside; a white crape shawl laid over one sofa and an expensive afghan over another; a camel's-hair shawl of exquisite texture hung upon the wall like tapestry, and an enormous Chinese umbrella, ten feet across, opened in the corner, its great bamboo handle terminating under the table in the middle of the floor. The effect of the whole was that of a bazar. The absence of flowers was rather noticeable. 'Where are the flowers?' I said to Mr. Wilde.

'Ah,' he replied, 'I see very few flowers in America. I am fond of flowers, though not more so than thousands of others. Of course, we young fellows used to go to a ridiculous extreme in all these matters. My room used to be full of lilies. The special reason why we have made the lily and sunflower types, as it were, of our floral taste, is because they are so definitely beautiful, and because they lend themselves so readily to every sort of decoration. The lily is wonderfully graceful—all sorts of lilies—and the sunflower has an opulent gorgeousness and the true Oriental spirit as it moves and turns its face to the sun. I have seen hardly any flowers since I came here—in the shop windows, the hotels, or even the parlors of the wealthy. In this respect Europe is ahead.'

I asked him if his dress was his ideal of masculine attire?

'No,' he said. 'I think everybody should wear knee-breeches.'

'But,' I said, 'in regard to color. Your dress is mainly without color—not at all, in this respect, like the showy costume of George IVth. time.'

'I doubt if color is at present attainable,' he said; 'perhaps not even desirable. We must make haste slowly. Some slight change in form is nearly all that can be at present effected. We must go no faster than men will follow. Sharp colors would probably not be in good taste, anyhow; the quiet browns and claret colors are very beautiful. I usually wear claret colored velvet myself. Of course when the Brotherhood meet in London we indulge our individual tastes and go to all sorts of extremes.'

'What is your fundamental principle in regard to architecture and decorations?'

'That they should follow the suggestions of nature in her local aspects. The Doric porticos and Corinthian capitals on Fifth Avenue are meaningless. In the lands where they originated they were full of meaning, but here they are dead forms—mere mockery. Why should not there spring up in America a new continental architecture, based on golden rod, and asters, and dahlias, and wild azaleas, and daisies, and dandelions, and cactuses, and pines, and magnolias, and prairie flowers, and grasses? Why should not your architecture and all your household decoration be based upon your own flora instead of upon obsolete or arbitrary forms?'

The conversation was a good deal broken by interruptions, but the above is the gist of it.

1   The report is of a reception for the American novelist Louisa May Alcott (1832–1888) at the New York home of the American author and journalist Jane Cunningham 'Jenny June' Croly (1829–1901) on 8 January 1882.

2   Sarah Bernhardt (1844–1923) was a French actress and a friend of Wilde's. She was well known for her thinness. New Yorkers had seen her in *Froufrou* (1869), a play by French dramatists Ludovic Halévy (1834–1908) and Henri Meilhac (1830–1897), in 1880.

3   Augustus Allen Hayes, Jr. (1837–1892) was an American businessman and author of nonfiction works on travel.

'The Art of Dining', *The Cincinnati Commercial* (Cincinnati, OH), 14 Jan. 1882, 4

NEW YORK, January 10, 1882. Your correspondent called on Mr. Wilde this afternoon. He entered the drawing-room in a *negligee* costume of dark green. The short loose coat was buttoned high, showing a cravat of subdued cardinal. The coat was embroidered with green and cardinal cord, and there were a wide lapel and deep cuffs of quilted cardinal silk upon it. The trousers were long and full, and a round cord ran down the outside of the seams. He wore cardinal stockings and patent-leather pumps.

'What did you think of your audience last evening?'[1]

'I was really much interested. I felt so keenly that it was a privilege I had never had before of telling a sympathetic audience what some of us were trying to do in England. The people seemed so near me, and I saw so many interesting faces of young girls and young men in the gallery. In England one never has the opportunity to speak in public, only those in politics, and I think it a great educational exercise.'

'What do you think of American women?'

'I have the opinion that all sensible men have of American women. No sensible man ever tells that opinion.'

As to his peculiar theory and its rise Mr. Wilde said: 'My theory is that you cannot teach anybody what is beautiful. The true spirit of beauty must be revealed. In 1873 I went to Oxford and entered Magdalen College.[2] It was at this time that the theory of the effect of beautiful associations began to manifest itself in my mind. This town is by far the most beautiful I have ever seen and it had its effect upon me. Ruskin was there and I became a disciple of his, and his teachings gave an impetus to this thought.[3] In 1876 I visited Italy,[4] and went through all the churches, drinking in all of the beautiful in art. I came back to Oxford more confirmed than ever in my theories, and it was then I began to write my poetry and to gather around me a group of young men—an aesthetic clique. I had a beautiful house by the river-side, which I fitted up in consonance with my ideas. We were very enthusiastic young men, and insensibly we became extravagant in our expressions. Rumors began to reach us that this movement of ours had reached London, and one day we were startled by a minister saying in effect that when young men in the University, not in polished banter, but in sober earnest declared that they were striving to live up to their blue china, it was apparent that a form of heathenism had crept into these cloisters which they were bound to fight with all their power. On top of this came Du Maurier's first caricature in *Punch*, and we found ourselves famous.[5] In 1878 I went to London. My idea was to sweep away all barriers and bring the artist into direct communication with his patrons, and I was well received. The movement had its effect upon the drama, as you know, and through all the upper circles of English society. It tends to lessen cost in dress. The dresses of the aesthetics in *Patience* are not much exaggerated.'

'What will be the practical outcome of all this?'

'That depends more upon America than upon myself. The movement deals with two kinds of people; those who create art, handicraftsmen, and people who enjoy art but do not create it. To the handicraftsman it gives perfect joy in his work, and puts an end to all the discontent of the working classes; that is the great danger of Europe, and will give him his opportunity of expressing his life in the work. The spread of machinery has nearly made man a machine, quite as soulless as itself. Love of art and the power of design make every handicraftsman a man. People who do not work in art are influenced by the beautiful and simple things that are about them every day of their lives. It will not merely be a constant source of joy and delight, but they will find that art is not a mere luxury nor an object of trade, but one of the great elements in the creation of all nobility of life.'

'Do you expect to stay long in this country?'

'I never make plans. I hate plans. If it interests me so much as I expect and hope it will, I shall stay until the end of spring. I must go to Italy every year. I am eager to see your western country, the Indian Territory and Mexico. Our middle class wear frock coats and high hats. I want to see those people who live in open air, hunt, fish and shoot. I want to study their perfect freedom, and I wish to see your flowers. There are so many more flowers in this country than in ours. So many new forms and subjects for studies in color. This is the young, new country to which we look for the perfect development of our themes.'

Concerning the architecture of New York, Mr. Wilde said: 'It is not worse than the cities in England, and not better. There is not much Greek art on Fifth Avenue.'

1   Wilde gave his lecture 'The English Renaissance' for the first time on 9 January 1882 at New York's Chickering Hall.
2   Wilde began his studies at Magdalen in 1874.
3   John Ruskin (1819–1900) was the leading art critic of the Victorian era and, between 1869 and 1878, Slade Professor of Fine Art at Oxford University.
4   Wilde had visited Italy in 1875 and 1877.
5   *Punch* was a British satirical magazine. It had featured cartoons by George du Maurier (1834–1896) that lampooned the aesthetic movement. Some of the characters in these cartoons, such at the painter Maudle and the poet Jellaby Postlethwaite, were popularly supposed to be based on Wilde.

'Aesthete Wilde on Greek Plays', *The Evening Telegram* (New York, NY), 13 Jan. 1882, 4th ed., 1

Mr. Oscar Wilde, the poet and apostle of aestheticism, breakfasted this morning by appointment with Mr. R. D'Oyly Carte at the Hoffman House. To a representative of the *Telegram*, who met him shortly after the repast and requested an expression of his views in regard to the proposed performance, in this city in a few weeks, of the *Oedipus Tyrannus* of Sophocles,[1] he said—

'The first modern attempt to perform a Greek play was the introduction on the stage, a year and a half ago, at my suggestion, at Oxford, of the *Agamemnon* of Aeschylus.'[2] I did not take part in it myself, as I had then left Oxford, but it was performed by my undergraduate friends. The elocution of the young men in the delivery of this play was characterized by great sweetness and correct modulation of the voice, and one of the actors, who took the part of Clytemnestra, was so successful that he has since decided to adopt the profession of an actor.[3] The distribution of the parts, the selection of the dresses, and the arrangement of the scenery for this play were mine.[4] I believe this is the first instance of a Greek play being performed in England, although Latin plays are acted at Westminster School every Christmas.

'I regret much to learn that the *Oedipus*, when performed here, is to have only one actor who will speak the lines in Greek, while the other actors will make use of English. The effect of this will be to destroy the unity of the performance, and it will be rendered only curious, whereas it should be beautiful. The play is the best acting play of the Greek literature, and is mentioned by Aristotle as an absolute type of perfection in the dramatic art. I saw it performed in the Comedie Française in Paris last summer. The manager presented us with a good French translation of the *Oedipus* — so good that it was really worth listening to — and it struck me that not only in its plot, but in the construction, dramatic conception and effect, the *Oedipus* gives one an excellent motive for a modern play.'

After these remarks Mr. Wilde took his departure, buttoning closely about him his fur-lined ulster and placing upon his head a large sealskin cap. Altogether, the apostle of aestheticism today looked more like a Russian than a Britisher.

1   The play was performed at New York's Booth's Theatre on 30 January. Wilde would see it on the 28th, at the end of a week's run at Boston's Globe Theatre.
2   The play was staged at Balliol College in June 1880 and, later in the year, transferred to London for three performances.
3   Francis Robert 'Frank' Benson (1858–1939), who played Clytemnestra, did indeed embark upon a career as an actor. He founded his own company in 1883, managed the Stratford-Upon-Avon Shakespearean Festival for thirty years, and was knighted in 1916.
4   Wilde is exaggerating his involvement. Benson and William Napier Bruce (who played Agamemnon) were responsible for organising the production.

'A Talk with Wilde', *Philadelphia Press* (Philadelphia, PA), 17 Jan. 1882, 2

As a Pennsylvania ferry-boat swung into her slip at Jersey City at a few minutes before one o'clock yesterday afternoon, the crowd scattered about the dock exclaimed in subdued tones: 'There he is; see him, that's Oscar Wilde.' The tall figure of the apostle of Aestheticism, clad in his olive-green overcoat with its otter trimmings, and with his large face brightened by a smile and framed in long brown locks, blown about by the wind, was a conspicuous figure, as he stood in the very front of the crowd of passengers pressing against the gunwales of the boat. He had evidently been enjoying a breezy trip across the tawny Hudson, for his eyes sparkled and his face was flushed with pleasure as, with a long stride which kept him far in advance even of the eager rush with which a New York crowd escapes from a ferry, and which left his valet struggling hopelessly in the rear with a burden of baggage, he entered the Pennsylvania station, and passed to the waiting Philadelphia express. His sole companions were W. F. Morse, business manager for D'Oyly Carte, and a *Press* reporter. The party took seats in the smoking compartment of the Pullman car 'Jupiter,' and shrinking from curious eyes into a corner, Mr. Wilde alternately read *Fors Clavigera* and *The Poetry of Architecture*, until the train had fairly started.[1] Then, as he saw through the window the dismal marshes which skirt Jersey City, his eye became melancholy and he contemplatively puffed a cigarette. As the train sped on its way through New Jersey, he scanned the flitting landscape closely, sometimes smiling like a child at a glistening stream or a stretch of yet green meadow, and again seeming to find the sorrow of old age in the frequent expanses of brown country and dripping black undergrowth, made more dreary by the overcast sky. The truth is, the poet had not had his breakfast; and thus unfortified against the horrors of a New Jersey landscape on a rainy day, it was no wonder that he finally relapsed into a state of hopeless dejection. Incredible as it may seem, the most non-aesthetic object on earth, a way-station sandwich, restored his spirits enough for him to enter into an animated conversation with the *Press* reporter.

'I am very tired,' he said. 'I have been so kindly received in New York, and so cordially welcomed by so many lovely people, that of course I wanted to see many of them before I went away. I was up late last night dining at Mrs. Paran Stevens' and afterward going to a reception at Mr. S. L. M. Barlow's, and I was so late today that I had no time to breakfast.[2] Then I have been kept so busy answering letters. Why, it is strange how people seem to think I have nothing to do but answer letters.'

'This is your first railway ride in America, is it not?'

'Yes, this is the first time I have ever been in an American railway car. We go so swift—much faster than in England. There are but a few fast trains there—the Edinburgh and Liverpool trains. And then there isn't any such comfort as this. There are but two or three cars like this,' indicating the sumptuous Pullman with a sweep of the arm, 'in the country. I hate to fly through a country at this rate. The only true way, you know, to see a country is to ride on horseback.[3] I long to ride through New Mexico and Colorado and California. There are such beautiful flowers there, such quantities of lilies and, I am told, whole fields of sunflowers. Your climate is so much finer than that of England, so bright, so sunny, that your flowers are luxuriant,' said Mr. Wilde, with a polite disregard of the clouds, and with a delightful ignorance of how hothouses are robbed of their treasures to let him breathe an atmosphere of fragrance.

'You have reason to be pleased with your reception in the United States?'

'O, yes, indeed. Do you know, the night before I landed I was wondering how it would be—thinking of the cloud of misrepresentation that must have preceded me, and wondering whether the people would wait to know me for what I am. But a poet must be indifferent to blame, as he must be to praise. He deserves neither till long after he is dead. Not till then can he be judged. While one is living, one can only work for what is to be. Do you know,'—his face lighting up with a sudden smile while his eyes roamed reflectively,— 'our people in England took the greatest interest in my coming to America—No,'—in reply to a suggestion by the reporter,— 'no, they did not regard it at all as an aesthetic mission to a barbarous clime; but our artists wish very much to have their ideas planted and growing in America.'

'What are your plans for the development of aestheticism in America?'

'It is impossible to define them yet. In this, my first lecture, which I am now delivering, I endeavor to explain the *spirit* of our art theories. As for the particular form it may take I must wait to tell that in a second lecture after I have become acquainted with the country and have come to know something of its artistic materials and possibilities, and have learned to appreciate its national spirit. I must know something of your woods for ceilings, for example, and numberless things of that kind.

Art must differ with place and people. What would be quite right in England might be quite wrong here. It is only the general principles that I can teach now; their definite application must come later.'

Here the poet gazed thoughtfully out of the window, and the reporter suggested that his impressions of American scenery must be as yet very limited. 'Yes,' was the reply, 'but I enjoy very much what I have seen. But one cannot expect color in winter, when everything is so drear and brown. How dreadful those marshes are this side of New York. What a pity! and how unnecessary. They might plant them with something, so many beautiful things will grow in a marsh. Why, they might have great fields of callas growing there! Do you understand my line for lilies, and roses, and sunflowers? No? O, don't you know, there is no flower so purely decorative as the sunflower. In the house, it is perhaps too large and glaring. But how lovely a line of them are in a garden, against a wall, or massed in groups! Its form is perfect. See how it lends itself to design, how suggestive it is. So many beautiful, very beautiful wall papers have been designed from the sunflower. It is purely decorative,' and the sunflower worshipper became lost in reverie. Then, opening his eyes wide, his whole face radiant, he resumed: 'And the lily. There's no flower I love so much as the lily. That, too, is perfect in form, and purely decorative. How graceful, how pure, how altogether lovely its shape, its tender poise upon the stem. And you have such beautiful lilies in America. I've seen a new one that we do not have in England, that star-shaped lily. I always loved lilies. At Oxford I kept my room filled with them, and I had a garden of them, where I used to work very often. As for roses, they are so full of color, so rich, so passionate. They suggest the feeling where the others suggest the form. They richly fill what the others outline. Why do not people grow them everywhere? I was pleased with the Raritan back there, with its brown current and brown banks; but still, those banks ought not to be bare and bleak—cover them with hardy lilies. Did you ever see those wonderfully beautiful books William Blake published so magnificently illuminated? In one of those books, enclosed in a charmingly appropriate border, are three lovely poems—one on the Sunflower, one on the Lily, and one on the Rose. It is a page altogether exquisite.'[4]

'Do you hope to teach the "common people," even the abjectly poor, to find these beauties, and by them to elevate their lives?'

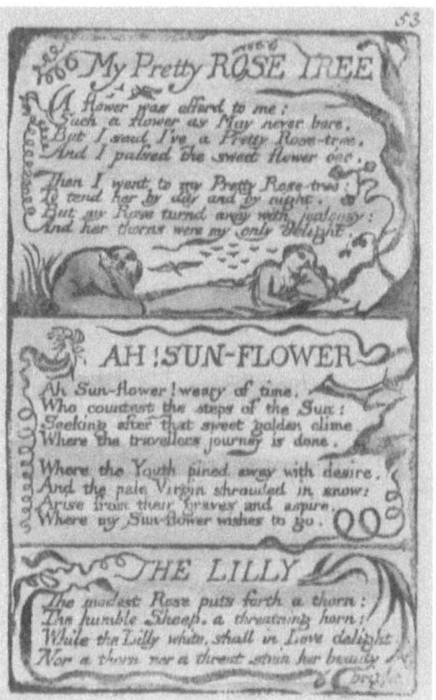

Songs of Innocence and of Experience, Plate 53,
by William Blake.

'The two classes we must directly work upon are the handicraftsmen
and the artists. As for the class between, the idle people, rich or poor,
it is useless to go to them, and tell them "you must do this, and you
ought to do that." There must be a great mass of handicraft produced,
before you can hope to affect the masses. And the handicraftsmen must
be directed by the artists, and the artists must be inspired with true
designs. It is only through those classes we can work.'

'Do you not hope to bring back picturesque dressing, as one of the
forms in which the spirit of your art will work itself out?'

'All that must take time. We have to move very carefully, you know.
Prejudice cannot be carried by storm. And, by the way, one of the
most delightful things I had in America is meeting a people without
prejudice—everywhere open to the truth. We have nothing like it in
England. But to return—we must get the women to dress beautifully
first; the men will follow. Velvet is such a beautiful material,—why do
not men wear it? Gray, or brown, or black velvet is always beautiful.'

'You have been quoted as saying that the women's dresses in *Patience*
are not exaggerated.'

'Oh, the embroidery and paintings on the dresses are made for stage
effect, and are larger than are worn in what is called good society. But

Lillie Langtry and Clara Morris.

in design they are correct. *Patience*, by the way, has done our cause no harm. Ridicule may be a serious weapon, but there should be that in a true poet or a genuine cause which is indestructible; and there is indestructibility in our cause. Oh, no; people understand that *Patience* is merely a burlesque. I enjoyed it very much. The music is delightful, and that is certainly on our side, even if the words are not.'

'Speaking of dresses—how do you like the beauty of their American wearers?'

'I am charmed with American beauty. They possess a certain delicacy of outline surpassing English women. And there is a charm about this curve here,' said Wilde, drawing his finger from cheek to chin, 'that is peculiarly fascinating. But the color of English women is richer and warmer, I think. I saw Clara Morris on the stage in New York one evening, and I was as delighted with her as with Sarah Bernhardt, who had told me very much about her charm;[5] and I have met many surpassingly beautiful young ladies since my arrival. Mrs. Langtry, I may tell you, is quite with me in all this movement.[6] She has an artistic house, deserves all her reputation for beauty, and sympathizes thoroughly with the aesthetic school.'

'What are your politics, Liberal or Conservative, Mr. Wilde?'

'O, do you know, those matters are of no interest to me. I know only two terms—civilization and barbarism: and I am on the side of civilization. It is very strange, that in the House of Commons you never hear the word "civilization." They spend night after night squabbling over petty things, when they ought to be working against barbarism. Then, in our country there is seldom a piece of legislation that does not benefit one class more than another; and that perhaps makes the wretched party spirit more bitter. But Gladstone is the greatest Prime Minister England ever had.[7] A short time before I came to America, he said to me that from the United States would come at once the greatest danger and the greatest good to civilization. The greatest danger in the vast accumulation of capital, and the greatest good in the perfect simplicity of American politics, and in the fact that the only reason for the passage of a great law over here is that it is for the good of the whole people. The personal control of capital, with the power it gives over labor and life, has only appeared in modern American life. We have as yet nothing like it in England. We call a man rich over there when he owns a share of Scotland, or a county or so. But he doesn't have such a control of ready money as does an American capitalist. He is often pressed even for a matter of fifty or sixty thousand pounds,' said Mr. Wilde, carelessly.

'What poet do you most admire in American literature?'

'I think that Walt Whitman and Emerson have given the world more than anyone else.[8] I do so hope to meet Mr. Whitman. Perhaps he is not widely read in England, but England never appreciates a poet until he is dead,' said Mr. Wilde with a trace of bitterness. 'I admire him intensely—Dante Rossetti, Swinburne, William Morris and I often discuss him.[9] There is something so Greek and sane about his poetry; it is so universal, so comprehensive. It has all the pantheism of Goethe and Schiller.[10] Poets, you know, are always ahead of science; all the great discoveries of science have been stated before in poetry. So far as science comes in contact with our school, we love its practical side; but we think it absurd to seek to make the material include the spiritual, to make the body mean the soul, to say that one emotion is only a secretion of sugar, and another nothing but a contraction of the spine. Why does not science, instead of troubling itself about sunspots, which nobody ever saw, or, if they did, ought not to speak about? Why does not science busy itself with drainage and sanitary engineering? Why does it not clean the streets and free the rivers from pollution? Why, in England there is scarcely a river which at some point is not polluted; and the flowers are all withering on the banks!' And Mr. Wilde again lapsed into melancholy.

'Do you think Mallock's *Romance of the Nineteenth Century* a correct picture of a section of English society?'[11]

'No novel can include England,' was the quick reply. 'I enjoyed reading that book, though it has its many faults. But I have repeatedly upheld it against attack, because it is the first attempt by an English novel-writer to grapple with English society as it actually is. I mean by that, it is the first attempt to picture lives that are themselves interesting. George Eliot has made perfect pictures of lives in the provinces, and so have others; but Dickens and Thackeray are our only novel-writers who have touched London life realistically.[12] We have nobody in English literature, for example, like Balzac, who has lived through so many changes of government and upheavals of society, and who mirrors all so exactly.[13] A novel-writer must himself first live what he portrays.'

At this point, the train reached Trenton, where Robert E. Winner joined the party, and the conversation became general. During the approach to Philadelphia, Mr. Wilde showed an eager interest in the many novel things he saw. He listened with wide-open eyes to an explanation of a long train of oil cars, but did not say whether he found any beauty in them. A glimpse of Fairmount Park brought back his happy smile, and he was greatly pleased with the ride over the elevated tracks and with the Broad Street station. As his conspicuous figure walked through the waiting room, many a whispered comment flew about; but the aesthete dived into a cab, and was whirled quickly away to his quarters at the Aldine Hotel.

1   These are works by John Ruskin.
2   Marietta Stevens née Reed (1827–1895) was a wealthy and influential socialite. Samuel Latham Mitchill Barlow I (1826–1889) was a lawyer, art collector, and Democratic Party power broker.
3   Wilde rode through Greece on horseback in 1877.
4   The poems are 'My Pretty Rose Tree', 'Ah! Sun-flower', and 'The Lilly'.
5   Clara Morris (1849–1925) was a Toronto-born American actress, famed

for her emotional performances.

6   Emilie Charlotte 'Lillie' Langtry née Le Breton (1853–1929) was a British socialite, 'professional beauty', and a friend of Wilde's.

7   William Ewart Gladstone (1809–1898) was a Liberal politician who served as Prime Minister of the United Kingdom for twelve years, spread between four terms, beginning in 1868 and ending in 1894.

8   Walt Whitman (1819–1892) was an American poet, a pioneer of free verse, and author of the frequently revised *Leaves of Grass*. Wilde met him on 18 January 1882. Wilde told his tour manager that he wished to meet American poet and essayist Ralph Waldo Emerson (1803–1882); Emerson died shortly after Wilde's arrival in America and before any meeting could be arranged.

9   Dante Gabriel Rossetti (1828–1882) was an English painter and poet. Algernon Charles Swinburne (1837–1909) was an English poet. William Morris (1834–1896) was an English designer and poet.

10 Johann Wolfgang von Goethe (1749–1832) and Friedrich Schiller (1759–1805) were German authors. Both were proponents of the Sturm und Drang movement, a precursor of the Romantic movement.

11 *A Romance of the Nineteenth Century* is an 1881 novel by English novelist William Hurrell Mallock (1849–1923).

12 George Eliot (1819–1880), William Makepeace Thackeray (1811–1863), and Charles Dickens (1812–1870) were English novelists, known for their realism and social criticism. Wilde described Eliot's style as 'far too cumbrous' and thought that 'Dickens has only influenced journalism'. He preferred Thackeray, whose 'delightful superficial philosophy, superb narrative power, and clever social satire have found no echoes'.

13 Honoré de Balzac (1799–1850) was a French novelist and playwright. Wilde would later describe him as France's 'one great genius'.

'Oscar Wilde in Boston', *Daily Evening Traveller* (Boston, MA), 28 Jan. 1882

Mr. Wilde was found by a representative of the *Traveller* soon after his arrival this morning at Hotel Vendome, who accepted the cordial invitation of the young poet to enjoy a little chat in his private parlor. The talk drifted naturally to topics of art and the peculiarities of the movement known as aestheticism in England. Mr. Wilde is an intelligent and highly-educated young man and an exponent of the best thought in artistic life. His views have long been quite widely misrepresented, he feels, by the American press, much of whose outpourings about him he characterises as mere foolishness. Referring to the misrepresentation he had suffered, the question was asked in what manner, to which Mr. Wilde replied that misrepresentation requires no definition. These personal discourtesies are, he confesses, largely matters of indifference to him, many journals having been notoriously unfair to him, and he regards the difference between the American and the English press to be that the former relies too much on imagination, while the latter is controlled by existing fact.

'My object in coming to America,' said Mr. Wilde, 'is to tell the American people what is the latest and most important movement of thought in England, wishing that all should exactly understand what in England we artists intend to do. Our object is to produce more concentration, more definite artistic movements of value than ever before.'

'Do you limit this movement to what are, distinctively, termed the "fine Arts," or do you also include the decorative, Mr. Wilde?' was questioned.

'No one art is finer than any other,' he replied. 'All true art is decorative art. The two finest paintings in Italy are those on ceilings in the palace of Pope Sixtus, from Michael Angelo.[1] There are in Venice decorations from Tintoretto,[2] and so I repeat that all pure art is decorative in its nature.

'The object of English aesthetes,' resumed Mr. Wilde, 'is to introduce beautiful designs in handicraft. It is not our primary object to procure more beautiful things for the rich to enjoy, but to teach the poor, the working people, to create beauty by educating them in designs and endow them with fine and permanent taste in handicrafts. To this end schools of design must be multiplied, and we have them in every city in England. The present movement is the most wonderful of anything that has taken place in the history of England within the last century. It is not to be called an imperceptible growth. All modern movements must have a definite form. We must know exactly what a movement means and what it intends. The aesthetic departure began with the Pre-Raphaelites. Ruskin has aided it enormously. It is, indeed, an inspiration introduced in life. You remember Goethe said, "Everything that is great promotes cultivation as soon as we are aware of it."'

'Practically, has the movement made a visible difference in England, Mr. Wilde?'

'It is widely noticeable,' he replied; 'yes,' smiling in answer to a half-spoken question, — 'yes, it is noticeable in ladies' dress, particularly in color. All beautiful color should be a gradation. The draperies, too, evince the education of the eye in form.

'Literature is, of course, a part of the movement. With the beautiful designs of Morris has gone the passionate and fervent eloquence of Ruskin; Rossetti, too, is not merely a painter but a poet also; Morris is not merely a designer, but the sweetest singer since Chaucer. As for a definition of aestheticism, the wider the definition, the more empty it is. Modern aestheticism is distinguished by its peculiar methods of approach. Philosophy used formerly to try to give a formula for beauty. We try rather to approach it always in its special manifestations. Every poem, every picture has a certain quality, certain virtues in it, and to disengage that particular quality, to discover that virtue, is the aim of the modern aesthetic critic. The truths of art cannot be taught. They are only revealed to natures that are receptive of beautiful impressions, and so we, in our aesthetic movement, want to create the artistic temperament which alone can discern the quality of aesthetic creation, and this is the reason of the immense importance we attach to what people call decorative art.

'The desire for beauty,' resumed Mr. Wilde, 'is the desire for life. It is the essential part of all great civilizations. Without it, civilization has, indeed, no meaning, because industry without beauty becomes barbarism.

'I hope,' he continued, 'that the newspapers of America will not mock what they should reverence, nor scorn what they should love. I can only hope that the American people will treat newspaper attacks on this movement with the indifference with which I treat them.' Of Burne Jones, the English poet said: 'I consider that Burne Jones possesses the loftiest spiritual imagination, of the most fervid type, a splendid range of vision, a beautiful and joyous power of color and a wonderful fertility of design.'[3]

'The supreme object of life,' said Mr. Wilde later, 'is to live. Few people live. It is true life only to realize one's own perfection, to make one's every dream a reality. Even this is possible.'

The above is merely a hasty resume, compelled by the exigencies of an evening paper, of a long and most interesting conversation with

Mr. Wilde. In manner the young poet well illustrates his own theories of the beautiful. With great refinement and courtesy he unites the perfect *savoir faire* of well-bred life and his running comments on current topics are full of insight. It is, indeed, the cheap wit that finds absurdity in all it does not understand and doubtless much of the misrepresentation of Mr. Wilde is owing to this cause. His lecture on Tuesday evening will be awaited with genuine interest.

1   The Sistine Chapel takes its name from Pope Sixtus IV, who restored it between 1473 and 1481. Michelangelo (1475–1564) painted the ceiling between 1508 and 1512 for Julius II and *The Last Judgement* between 1535 and 1541 for Clement VII and Paul III.
2   Tintoretto (1518–1594) was an Italian painter who worked in Venice. Wilde visited the city in 1875.
3   Wilde was Irish but was often described as English in the American press. Sir Edward Coley Burne-Jones (1833–1898) was a British painter and designer and, since 1880, a friend of Wilde's.

'Oscar Wilde', *Morning Journal and Courier* (New Haven, CT), 2 Feb. 1882, 2

Oscar Wilde, the poet and apostle of aesthetics, lectured last evening at Peck's Grand Opera House to an audience of four or five hundred. It included not a few distinguished citizens, most of whom were accompanied by ladies. The lecturer arrived at the hall a few minutes before 8 o'clock. Outside there were thirty or forty persons waiting to catch a glimpse of the lecturer. They were probably much disappointed at finding him attired in ordinary dress like any other gentleman—no knee breeches, nothing but a plain black suit. The lecturer was accompanied solely by his agent, Mr. Vale, and his colored waiting man. While Mr. Wilde was adjusting his toilet with an aesthetic, languid, composed air before the glass in the dressing room, Mr. Vale spoke with enthusiasm of Mr. Wilde's Boston success the evening before—a $3,000 house. Mr. Wilde having adjusted his long and flowing locks, which were parted duly in the middle and fell about his neck and collar, he was interviewed by a representative of the *Courier*. He bowed with the air of an Apollo and our reporter took mental cognizance of the six feet of aesthetic humanity before him, finding him very much like the photographs displayed in Peck's window yesterday, minus the fur lined overcoat. He was dressed in a conventional dress suit, the pantaloons cut without special attempt at shadowy legs, black vest cut low, displaying a vast expanse of highly polished shirt bosom, in the exact center of which reposed a single stud composed of a pair of beautiful pearls. His collar was a low turn over, his tie a white, flowing silk tie or handkerchief. A pair of massive watch seals dangled from a fob chain. The following conversation ensued:

Reporter—'How were you pleased with Boston?'

'Oh, very much, very much indeed,' said Mr. Wilde, his face assuming a happy, genial smile. 'I expected to be. Boston has indeed a great deal of culture, art and refinement.'

'Did you visit the prominent people and places?'

'Oh yes, and my experience was very delightful. I think it was one of my pleasantest stopping places. I was honoured with an interview with Longfellow and others of note there.[1] I had a charming time after my lecture at a party at Mrs. Julia Ward Howe's.[2] I also took a run over to Harvard College and visited that institution. Harvard reminded me much of our English universities,—of our own Oxford. I liked Boston so well that I shall return there before my departure for my home.'

'How long do you remain in America?'

'Oh,' said Mr. Wilde, with a heavenly expression rolling his eyes slightly upward, 'that depends somewhat. I have no fixed plan as yet.'

'Do you remain in New Haven tomorrow?'

'Yes, I shall remain awhile. Professor Whitney, whom I have had the pleasure of meeting, has kindly consented to show me Yale University, in which I shall take great pleasure.[3] I afterward go to Hartford, where I lecture in the evening.'

'Your poetry I see finds many American readers, and the newspapers have given many samples to their readers. Are any of your works published under your own direction in America?'

'Ah, they read my poems but through piracy. It is a pity that the author is not protected in his work, as to its reproduction in this country. Yes, it is pleasant,' and here the author looked the ineffable again, 'it is pleasant to be read, to have your thoughts read, to touch humanity in that way.'

'May I ask do you confine yourself strictly to your manuscript in lecturing?'

'Oh, no. I often diverge. If the spirit of the audience moves me aright I give expression to new thoughts that occur to me. The inspiration of the moment gives me new currents of thought.'

'You do not dress tonight in your regalia?'

'Oh, no; that is a matter in which I allow myself to be guided by circumstances and the weather. Knee breeches are a little cool for this evening. Dress should be aesthetic, not conventional. Beautiful colors should be considered in dress. I would allow liberality in the choice. My movement is to utilize the beautiful. Whatever is beautiful is a pleasure. So the beautiful should improve and grace the mind and add to the higher forms of feeling and life.'

Just here the audience began to stamp vigorously. 'What is that noise?' said Mr. Wilde, with a dreamy, far away expression.

'That,' replied the reporter, 'is your audience, who are impatient for your appearance.'

'Impatient,' said Mr. Wilde, dreamily. The reporter, with a good-night, withdrew, Mr. Wilde retiring to converse with his agent, after which he placed his manuscript under the gaslight and read over a page or two, after which he stepped out upon the platform and calmly arranging his manuscript waited for the burst of applause which greeted him to subside, when he began the lecture.

1	Henry Wadsworth Longfellow (1807–1882) was an American poet. Wilde visited him at his home in Boston on 30 January (see p. 64).
2	Julia Ward Howe (1819–1910) was an American poet and abolitionist.
3	Presumably William Dwight Whitney (1827–1894), an American linguist and lexicographer. He was Professor of Sanskrit at Yale.

'A Man of Culture Rare', *Rochester Democrat and Chronicle* (Rochester, NY), 8 Feb. 1882, 4

Oscar Wilde, his knee breeches, his business manager and his colored body servant arrived in the city late yesterday afternoon and were at once driven to the Osburn house, where rooms had been assigned them.

The great leader in modern aestheticism at once retired to his apartment and did not again make his appearance until half past 7 o'clock, when he rode to the Grand Opera house, where a blushing reporter of this paper was presented to him in the dressing room. There was certainly nothing limp nor languid in the hearty English grip with which he clasped the proffered hand, and had it not been for the singularity of his attire there would have been nothing in particular to distinguish him from an ordinary English gentleman. In appearance he was the typical Bunthorne of *Patience*. He was dressed in knee breeches, black silk stockings marvelously fitted, low patent leather pumps, regulation dress coat, low cut double-breasted white vest, shirt collar turned low with a voluminous white tie, and a broad expanse of shirt bosom, ornamented with a single stud, in which were set two pearls and a diamond. A fob with double seals jingled below his vest, and the only other article of jewelry visible was a large seal ring upon the third finger of his left hand. The effect was curious if not picturesque, and it was heightened by the remarkable face and head. Thick and heavy hair, parted in the middle, fell nearly to the shoulders on either side, enclosing a long, narrow and oddly marked face. The forehead is low, the cheek bones high, the eyes bright and full of expression, the mouth large and mobile, the lips full, and the chin giving the impression of unusual length. It is not a handsome face; it is not a strong face, but it is an exceedingly interesting face, made doubly so, perhaps, by a knowledge of the man's life and position. It is emphatically the face of a dreamer, intelligent and refined, but not the face that would inspire confidence in earnestness of purpose and vigor of execution. This is the first strong impression, but the judgment of the mind is wonderfully shaken by a brief experience with his conversational powers.

As the reporter perched gingerly upon the edge of a chair, Oscar Wilde inquired if art had gained any foothold in Rochester, which enabled the visitor with pardonable pride to refer to Powers' art gallery and the art exchange, never failing sources of inspiration. He admitted that the art exchange was good as far as it went, but that in reality nothing could be done until there was founded a school of design. 'You must teach the people to do artistic work,' he said, 'and then the movement will begin to assume form. It is not to the rich who can afford to be patrons, but the workers in art to whom we must look for development.'

Wilde photographed by Sarony in the costume he usually wore while lecturing in America.

'How about the treatment you have received from the newspapers in this country?'

'I have no complaints to make. They have certainly treated me outrageously, but I am not the one who is injured, it is the public. By such ridiculous attacks the people are taught to mock where they should reverence, to scoff at things to which they will not even listen. Had I been treated differently by the newspapers in England and in this country, had I been commended and endorsed, for the first time in my life I should have doubted myself and my mission. What possible difference can it make to me what the *New York Herald* says? You go and look at the statue of the Venus De Medici and you know that it is an exquisitely beautiful creation. Would it change your opinion in the least if all the newspapers in the land should pronounce it a wretched caricature? Not at all. I know that I am right, that I have a mission to perform. I am indestructible! Shelley was driven out of England, but he wrote equally well in Italy. It was not he who was injured, it was the people. I cannot expect,—I do not wish better treatment than Keats and Shelley received, and yet I must confess that I am surprised.[1] You have sent many Americans to us in England, and at least we have received them courteously. You have sent us a good many actors, some of them good, some of them very bad; but I do not think they can justly complain of rudeness on our part. How would it have appeared had we accused Booth of blackmail, as I was accused in Baltimore?'[2]

The listener gave expression to his vagueness and Mr. Wilde continued:

'We have many eminent men in our country, men eminent in art and letters, but they would not think for a moment of venturing here in a public capacity. They know well enough the treatment they would receive, the questionable courtesy I have experienced.'

'How were you pleased with the demonstrations of the Harvard students?'[3]

'There was nothing offensive in that. I understood well enough that it was meant as a good natured joke, and I entered into the spirit of it fully. It recalled to my mind many incidents of my life at Oxford.'

'As you do not read what the newspapers say about you, I suppose you know nothing of the thousands of paragraphs that are flying about the country about you. Most of them, I presume originated in the newspaper offices. For instance I read the other day that you were presented to a prominent society lady in Washington, and she exclaimed, "And so this is Oscar Wilde; but where is your lily?" The quick reply was, "At home, madame, where you left your good manners." I suppose, of course, that had no foundation in fact?'

'On the contrary, it is absolutely true, with the exception that it happened in London and that the lady was a duchess.'

'What did she do then?'

'She did what any duchess would do under the circumstances, I suppose—blushed and remained quiet.'

'Well, then there is another story in which the boot is on the other foot. It is said that you complained that there were no quaint ruins in this country, no curiosities, and a lady replied, "Time will remedy the one, and as for the curiosities, we import them."'[4]

'Yes, that is an excellent story. It was first told of Charles Dickens when he visited this country.[5] I find every community has its lady who is remarkably bright in her repartee and she is always credited with the latest *bon mot* going the rounds. Those two stories are following me all over the country, localised in almost every city.'

'Pardon the digression, but I would like to know your opinion, from a thoroughly artistic standpoint, upon the prize fight which took place today?'[6]

Mr. Wilde laughed and said, 'Even that has its artistic side. You know the ancient Greeks—'

At this point, Mr. Vale, the manager, made his appearance at the door and announced that it was 8 o'clock and time to go on. The lecturer at once sprang to his feet, excused himself, walked quickly to the back entrance, walked to the front of the stage, and without preface, commenced at once to deliver his lecture on 'The English Renaissance.'

1   John Keats (1795–1821) and Percy Bysshe Shelley (1792–1822) were English Romantic poets, both of whom Wilde idolised.
2   Edwin Booth (1833–1893) was an American tragedian. Wilde saw him perform in London in 1881. Wilde had been accused by a Baltimore paper of demanding a fee to attend a reception (see p. 75).
3   At Wilde's Boston lecture a large group of Harvard students entered wearing knee-breeches, colourful ties, and long wigs. Each carried a sunflower.
4   Wilde used this story in *A Woman of No Importance*: 'LADY CAROLINE. There are a great many things you haven't got in America, I am told, Miss Worsley. They say you have no ruins, and no curiosities. | MRS. ALLONBY. (*To* LADY STUTFIELD.) What nonsense! They have their mothers and their manners. | HESTER. The English aristocracy supply us with our curiosities, Lady Caroline. They are sent over to us every summer, regularly, in the steamers, and propose to us the day after they land. As for ruins, we are trying to build up something that will last longer than brick or stone.'
5   Dickens toured America in 1842 and 1867–1868.
6   On 7 February 1882 the American heavyweight bare-knuckle boxing champion Patrick 'Paddy' Ryan (1851–1900) lost his title to John Lawrence Sullivan (1858–1918) in a fight in Mississippi City.

'Utter Oscar', *Buffalo Morning Express* (Buffalo, NY), 9 Feb. 1882, 4

After the lecture a representative of *The Express* was introduced to Mr. Wilde, who was half-reclining in a large chair in one of the waiting-rooms just off the stage. On near inspection the disciple and expounder of aestheticism was found to be fully as masculine in his lineaments, sturdy in build, and genial in expression as he had seemed by the artificial lights. Sunlight pouring in a window illumined the long and heavy hair which has been particularly mentioned because of the outlandish, or rather aesthetical, way in which he wears it. It was not so dark as it had appeared viewed from the auditorium, but a genuine golden although dull hue—old gold, in fact. That just describes it. Old gold hair is just the thing for an aesthete, it may be presumed.

Mr. Wilde expressed much satisfaction with his reception here. He had felt that the audience were listening to him intently, and that many were interested in his subject.

'But I'm dreadfully tired,' said Oscar, in a manner that was languid but a voice that sounded jovial rather than otherwise. 'It isn't the lecturing, I delight in giving my lectures when I find there is interest in them, but it's the long distances. The traveling has nearly used me up. I haven't been used to it you know. At home I'd get up in the morning, have breakfast, do some writing, and then maybe start off for Egypt or some other distant part, but take my time about it all.'

The reporter ventured to ask if he didn't find the American means of travel more comfortable than in Europe?

'The English railroads,' replied Mr. Wilde, 'are as bad as they can be. The American railroads are just as bad. There is no comfort on them anyway. One can't read or write comfortably, and if you look out of the window to see if an object is a house or a tree it's three miles behind you before you can determine.'

Questioned as to what the extent of his tour of this country would be, he replied he hardly knew. He had wanted to visit California and Mexico. 'They speak of your country,' said he, 'why, you have a world. I had no just idea of it.' The scenery of the Hudson he referred to enthusiastically, and he was much interested in allusions made by the newspaper man to the mountain scenery on the Erie Railway and some of the Pennsylvania lines. Mr. Wilde had somehow conceived a great fancy for a Mexican visit. 'I should like very much to ride through Mexico,' said he. 'I should like also to visit many parts of your country. Your cities have no architecture; they are too new. But you have grand rivers and mountains.'

In the course of his conversation Mr. Wilde touched occasionally on the subject he holds nearest at heart, that of art improvement, and at such times he spoke enthusiastically, his big eyes full of light. 'It is the subject to which your country must devote herself. She has had her war, she is prosperous, and now she must give her attention to art if she would obtain permanent good. The young women of the country must be expected to do the most.

'You have a decorative Art Society here, I believe. The mission is a noble one. It is not for the rich that we want art promoted, but for the poor.'

Then somehow Mr. Wilde mentioned the newspapers. 'You're a newspaper man,' said he, 'but I can't help saying that I am astonished at the ridicule, the mockery with which the American press treats lofty and serious matters.'

Our representative could but admit that some American newspapers are a good deal given to levity.

'If in one of these papers an article were to be begun with a serious or noble expression of sentiment would the people take it for a joke?' asked Oscar.

The newspaper subject dropped, Mr. Wilde enumerated various things which had favorably impressed him.

'What is your opinion of American ladies, Mr. Wilde?'

'I have the same opinion of them that every sensible man must have,' he said. But just what that opinion was he did not elucidate. He had, he said, seen many very beautiful women in this country—many in Baltimore, and a great many in New York.

Mr. Wilde's geographical and some other ideas concerning the United States are yet in an early stage of development. As he journeys further and investigates deeper, he will no doubt become still more firmly fixed in the opinion that here is a great field for the cultivation of the true and the beautiful in art, as well as any other fairly paying crop.

Mr. Wilde's first intention was to remain in Buffalo over night, and in that event was invited by Mr. H. L. Meech to attend the Theatre in the evening, and subsequently the City Club. But on account of the little time at his command, Mr. Wilde late in the afternoon determined to pick up his grip-sack and start for Niagara Falls forthwith. He will do the Falls—aesthetically, as it is to be presumed, and will this evening start for Chicago, where he lectures next Monday.

'Storks and Lilies', *The Chicago Herald* (Chicago, IL), 11 Feb. 1882

Oscar Wilde arrived in the city last evening from Buffalo and went to
the Grand Pacific Hotel. He complained at first of being very tired, and
asked that he might not be disturbed. Later, however, he intimated that
he would see representatives of the press at half-past nine, at which
hour the reporter of the *Herald* presented his card and himself to the
hotel clerk who acted as the intermediary between them and the great
aesthete. The representatives of the other journals crowded after them.
This was more than the apostle of culture had bargained for, and he
sent word that he was not equal to the task of talking to more than, at
the most, two at once. In short he insisted on a two-two arrangement.[1]
His wishes were complied with, and the party was divided. When
the *Herald* reporter and his companion were ushered into the great
presence Oscar greeted them with effusion, treating each to a warm
hand-shake, and a polite invitation to be seated. He himself assumed a
recumbent position on a couch aesthetically covered with a bearskin
and a buffalo robe. Oscar is all that fancy paints him. He is tall. He is
lady-like. His flowing golden locks are parted in the middle and hung in
slightly waving masses down to his shoulders, framing a face which but
for the expressive eyes would be commonplace. Clad in gray trousers,
a mouse-colored velvet jacket, magenta necktie, red socks, and very
every-day, unaesthetic slippers, with the end of a red handkerchief
peeping from the breast pocket of his jacket, he presented a picture for
gods and men. He smokes. Asked how he liked his reception, he said:

'Personally—what I have come across in society—the reception I
have met with from your men and women has been most pleasant. You
mean, I suppose, your newspapers?'

Being informed that the question had especial reference to the manner in which his audiences received him, he said: 'If you mean those
scholars at Boston (laughing heartily), that was a bit of school-boy fun
not meant in any sort of malice. But it is different with the newspapers.'

'In what way?'

'Well, for this reason. In England, one knows from long study of the
English character, if one tries to create any new movement, to produce
any new work in poetry or painting, or to protest in any way against

the commonplace life of the modern English people—one knows that at once one loses all ordinary rights of a citizen, and that everything slander and folly and ridicule can do will be done; so, personally, I have long ago ceased to find any pleasure or to receive any pain from what anonymous newspaper writers choose to say of me. The harm that they have done in America has been to the public and not to me. America should be a country without prejudice. The newspapers seem to have raised again that mist of misrepresentation, that fog of folly which blinds people to all that is noble and simple and strong in a great movement. I feel, when I lecture, that for the first half of my lecture, at least, I am merely struggling against the misrepresentation that has preceded me. Whether, before I have finished my lecture, I am able to dispel that is not for me to say; I hope that I am. I do not think, however, that we in England would welcome any young American who had won any position in poetry or in art, who had something to say and would say it, in the way in which I have been welcomed. I acknowledge though that, as I have said, I steeled myself years ago against feeling pleasure or pain from that source. But I had an idea when I was coming to America that people would listen to what I had to tell them about the most concentrated art movement we have ever had in England, that they would judge me by what I said, and would not make up mere literary garbled folly against me. In Europe we are all so overweighted with prejudice, so trammelled by history, so old, that we always think of America as a country without any prejudice. When we think of you in Europe we think of you as a simple, practical, grand nation.'

Oscar was asked at this stage to favor his interviewers with a definition of his mission.

'I want to tell the American people what is the meaning of this movement in England, to which England is giving so much of its genius and so much of its youth. You have had the satire first; I think you should now hear the truth. We look to America in England for newer and more natural forms of art; we look to you for a school of sculpture particularly. "Man does not live by bread alone," and we feel that with your wonderful climate, the strong, healthy physique of your men and women, and the quick enthusiasm of life among you, you should have most noble art. Up to this you have had much to contend with; you have had to conquer nature and to conquer your own enemies. You have done both in a shorter time than any nation ever did it before. There comes now a period of peace with you—a period for production, for a more widely spread civilization than you have yet had time to produce. You have seen, more than any modern nation, that life without industry is barren—you must remember that industry without art is barbarism. All these wonderful material inventions that make life easier and lighter for you—the steam engine, the telegraph, and the like, are noble or not entirely in the spirit in which you use them. The problem of modern life is how, with all these wonderful inventions—far greater than any that Greek or Italian ever dreamed of—you can create a civilization greater, or even as great as theirs.'

'Then, Mr. Wilde, you regard the modern civilization as less perfect than the Greek?'

'Yes. Modern civilization has done nothing to compare with the achievements of the ancients. We owe to them the invention of let-ters—nothing has been in modern times to compare with that or with the discovery of the science of numbers. I know (laughing) that the Greeks, for instance, were remarkably more civilized than the English nation. It is very valuable to be able to speak through a telephone to a man at the antipodes, but the value entirely depends on the worth of what one has to say; it is very valuable to travel at sixty miles an hour, but the value entirely depends on how much the man who travels can gain from the places he sees and the things he visits. Most English people race over Italy in two weeks and bring back a memory of a bad dinner at Verona, or how their courier cheated them at Rome. To be content with merely material sub-stratum of civilization is as if a literary man were to be content with knowing all the letters of the alphabet and never care to combine them or to use them. There is a general idea that the artist has a supernatural horror of a steam engine. Let me assure you that nothing of the kind is the case. One of Turner's most beautiful pictures, hanging in the National Gallery in London, is a picture of an express train.[2] All that we feel about such inventions is that we want people to use them for the noblest purposes. Civilization has only one aim—to give every man the opportunity of realizing the perfection of his own nature. One must never mistake the means for the end.'

Asked what he thought about the natural features of the country through which he has passed since his arrival, the aesthete replied: 'I

Rain, Steam, and Speed - The Great Western Railway (1844) by J. M. W. Turner.

have only seen two things that were wonderful—the Hudson River and Niagara Falls.' Of the first he said: 'I should imagine its beauty is chiefly in autumn, when the trees are in their wonderful foliage; but even as I saw it, with the trees all brown and leafless, there was a wonderful beauty about it. As for Niagara,' he went on after a laugh at the insinuations of one of his too-too visitors that it may not have been arranged to suit him, 'one knows nothing of it till one is underneath the falls.'

'Were you not pleased with them as seen from the top?'

'I don't think that when one sees them first one at all realizes how sublime they are. The outlines are somewhat monotonous. But I don't think I ever realized so strongly the splendor of the beauty of the mere physical force of nature as I did when I stood by Table Rock. Another thing that interested me very much was the curious repetition of the same forms, of the same design almost, in the shapes of the falling water. It gave me a sense of how completely what seems to us the wildest liberty of nature is restrained by a governing law.'

'Mr. Wilde, they say that you were not pleased with the Atlantic.[3] May it be asked if that is true?'

'Oh, that unfortunate saying! It will become historic, I suppose,' and the long curls shook, and the whole frame of the aesthete quivered, as he enjoyed a hearty laugh. 'You know I wanted to see a big storm. I am very fond of the sea, and I have been at sea in very rough weather. I wanted to see the fury of an Atlantic gale. The grandest sight I ever saw in my life was a storm coming from Athens to Naples—a cyclone that came from the desert.'

The character of the conversation changed at this point, Oscar turning inquisitor and putting questions concerning the city, its resources, the great fire and the way the place was rebuilt, its art collections, etc. he expressed great admiration for the American character, which, he says, is remarkable for individualism, self-respect, and many other good qualities, and appeared much gratified to know that there are but few paupers in the country. He says that he goes from here to Fort Wayne and Detroit, where he lectures on Thursday and Friday, and will not extend his tour further west than St. Louis, returning East from that point. Talking of Ireland, he grew animated in describing her wrongs. 'Ireland,' he said, 'is the Niobe of nations.' On his return to New York he will superintend the production of his play, which will portray modern Russia, and which will not be so ornately mounted as New York papers have said. He declined to say just what its title is or who will produce it.[4]

1   A play on aesthetic slang ('too too'), but also accurate: Wilde spoke to two pairs of interviewers.
2   Joseph Mallord William Turner (1775–1851) was an English painter. His painting *Rain, Steam and Speed – The Great Western Railway* was first exhibited at the Royal Academy in 1844.
3   See p. 9. Wilde's opinion had been much discussed in the press.
4   *Vera; or, The Nihilists*. Colonel Morse had revealed the title in January.

'Weary Wilde', *The Chicago Times* (Chicago, IL), 11 Feb. 1882, 6

Oscar Wilde arrived in the city last evening, and was found at the Grand Pacific Hotel by a reporter of *The Times*. The public has had so many descriptions of him that another one is hardly necessary. It is sufficient to say that he is tall, looks very much as he is represented in his photographs in the shop-windows, wears his hair long, parted in the middle, and drooping down the sides of his face and over his neck, and was

Wilde photographed by Sarony in his usual interviewing posture: reclining on a sofa spread with a fur rug. He holds a copy of his *Poems* (1881).

dressed last evening in a light suit of English goods, with sack coat and pantaloons, light red necktie, with a handkerchief to match just protruding from the breast pocket of his coat, and low shoes. He was reclining leisurely on a sofa smoking a cigar, and greeted *The Times* representative cordially, speaking in a broad English accent. His face is long and extremely boyish,—in fact, he looks like a very much overgrown boy,—and his features, while thoughtful, are somewhat effeminate. The conversation began with a casual reference to the pleasant weather, and he replied that he had been traveling so long that it hardly seemed pleasant to him. He was asked how he liked the west, and replied that it was freer from prejudices than the east, which catches too many of the floating follies of Europe, which the people in the west have no time for, and are too distant from it to contract.

'What are your general impressions of America?' was queried.

'That is a difficult question to answer. I have seen only the towns, not the country. I have not seen in the east anything that is distinctively American. In the best cities there is very high cosmopolitanism, but in the lesser cities a curious provincialism. What interests me most in coming to the west is that here I shall see that type of civilization which is definitely American, created by yourselves and for yourselves.'

'What did you think of Niagara?'

'When I saw it, it was not so noble in outline and design as I had expected, perhaps, although the color was beautiful. All the most beautiful colors are those in motion; they are full of change. It was not till I stood under the cataract that I realized how enormous were the physical forces of nature amidst which I was standing.'

Coming to his favorite theme, the reporter enquired: 'What is the predominant idea of the philosophy which you teach?'

'The whole essence of this artistic movement in England is, on the one hand, a desire to discover in every city those men and women who have power of artistic design, to give them the best models and examples possible, to train them in the noblest surroundings, to produce the noblest work, and as regards the people who are not handicraftsmen, people who have not this power of design, nor the capacity for artistic creation, we want to produce in them that artistic temperament without which there is no understanding of art, no real joy of life; in a word, no civilization. There is only one way of producing this artistic temperament, and that is by accustoming them from their childhood to the abiding presence in their own houses of beautiful and joyous color and noble and natural design. We want to make art, not a luxury for the rich, but, as it should be, the most splendid of all the chords through which the spirit of any nation manifests its power. We want to make it part of the daily atmosphere in which people live.'

'What do you mean by art and artistic?'

'An artistic thing is anything which, irrespective of its practical use, pleases one by the beauty and delicacy of its form, wonder of its design, or the nobility of its color. A man who creates an artistic thing is a man who works not with his hands only, but with his heart and with his head.'

'Do you make art the chief end of life, then?'

'Life without industry is barren, and industry without art is barbarism.'

'You speak of civilization. Which, in your judgment, produces the greater civilization, an invention such as the telephone and the telegraph, or one of Michael Angelo's paintings?'

'If you mean which is the greater sign of civilization, the production of an Angelo or an Edison, I answer an Angelo. One Angelo is worth a hundred Edisons.[1] These modern inventions are not good or bad in themselves at all. They certainly increase one's wonder at the mysteries of nature, and one's admiration of the genius of man, but their use for civilization depends entirely on the spirit in which they are used. To give you an instance: a tramway is an exceedingly useful and economical means of conveyance, but in Oxford today they are pulling down one of the most beautiful old bridges of England in order to substitute in its place what they call in England a light and elegant cast-iron structure, to facilitate the running of a tramway. In this there is no gain to England at all—only the irreparable loss of stately and noble architecture.'[2]

'Which is the more important to civilization, beauty or usefulness?'

'Well, useful is a dangerous word. Useful for what? I deny that between the noblest usefulness and the noblest beauty there is anything but the completest accord and unity.'

'What do you mean by civilization?'

'Civilization is those conditions under which man most completely realizes the perfection of his nature. And so civilization, without art, is a contradiction entirely, and civilization without beauty is an impossibility.'

'What do you think of art in eastern cities as compared with art in England?'

'You want in this country to begin with the primary element of beautiful cities; that is, noble architecture. The old red brick houses that your Puritan fathers built are much more beautiful, much more simple and natural than the sham Greek porticoes, the Doric chimneys, and the Corinthian upper stories on fifth avenue. For domestic architecture, there is nothing more suitable than red brick.'

'Is age necessary to beautiful buildings?'

'Not at all. The beauty consists in the nobility of the architecture and the symmetry of design. Age often adds a charm, but it will never make an ugly building beautiful.'

Mr. Wilde will spend the next few days in looking about the city.

1   Thomas Edison (1847–1931) was an American inventor and businessman. Wilde and Edison met at Edison's New York offices, probably in late 1882.
2   Rumours that Magdalen Bridge would be demolished were unfounded. Tram tracks were laid over the bridge in November 1881.

'Oscar Wilde Has Come', *Chicago Daily News* (Chicago, IL), 11 Feb. 1882, 3pm ed., 1

'I am glad to see you,' said Mr. Oscar Wilde, the famous Irish aesthete, extending his hand to the reporter, and placing a chair in parlor 3, Grand Pacific hotel. And the voice was full of music, the striking face bright and genial, and the extended hand warm with feeling not to be mistaken.

'What do you think of America as a country?' the reporter felt along.

'It is not a country. America is a vast world by itself, full of wonders to the visitor with eyes, and full of surprises. I liked New York very much for its cosmopolitan features; I liked Boston for its many literary reminiscences. In Baltimore I found pretty women, and in Philadelphia literary men.'

'What is your theory on decorative art?'

'That it has been and will be done mostly by women. Men are so busy in the struggle for life and commercial supremacy that to the women must be relegated the task of sustaining and advancing decorative art; and this is proper and as it should be.'

'And your reception in America?'

'It has surprised me—that is, at first I could not understand it. But I very speedily became aware that this sort of thing resulted from gross misrepresentation by thoughtless and ignorant people and mismanagement of my business affairs. I feel it very bitterly and regret it to the utmost measure. When I begin my lecture I always feel that the first half of it is delivered in a mist of folly and misrepresentation; but if I can win over my audience by the time I finish, I am glad.'

'What do you think of the eastern people as a class?'

'It is self-evident that they have caught much of the tinsel and flimsy nothings of Europe. Of course there is more art in the east than in the west, but I would much rather speak to a people devoid of art than to a people bad in art.'

'You have an object in this new departure?'

'Well, yes; rather, perhaps, am I fully imbued with the Celtic love of rebellion. I am a rebel in art as many of my countrymen are rebels in politics. I am a rebel because I object to these crude forms and rules one dare not criticise. I imagine my mission to be that of a reformer, and I do not expect any more consideration from the general public than has been meted out to other reformers in the past—nothing more, but at the same time it shall not be less.'

'And in the future—'

'I expect to be recognized properly in good time.'

'What do you think of American newspapers?'

'They are particularly bright, but in many instances thoughtless. Why should a reporter—one of the calm, pleasant, polished fellows whom I delight to meet—call on me, receive my hospitality, and go out to his paper and causelessly and needlessly misrepresent me? Is that journalism? Is that the treatment a gentleman should receive from a gentleman? However, the time has long since passed when anything possible for a newspaper to print can make me glad or sad. One cannot pause to read and discuss and fret over everything about oneself in the prints—one might as well pause on the streets and dispute the right of thoroughfare with every urchin. Misrepresentation cannot have a lasting effect.'

'You will doubtless meet a large and respectful audience in Chicago.'

'I hope so. It will make me glad, and I am quite safe in thinking I shall leave friends here. I do not misrepresent myself, and hence the public will readily understand me and my work. Of all I have heard about Chicago, the good heart and intelligence of her people have been foremost.'

'Will the decorative in art become popular?'

'Yes, as all things beautiful become popular. The education of the eye produces precisely the same effect as the education of other organs or senses. Why should not a man or woman love that which adds charm to home and surroundings? Who will not turn about to gaze on a beautiful child, a beautiful picture or statue? Will not the people turn in love and admiration to that which is beautiful rather than cling to that which is uncouth and ill-shaped! 'Twould be strange indeed if the latter prevailed.'

'Then you are an educator?'

'Something of that sort. Your Morse had a difficult time in teaching the people to believe in his telegraphy; Fulton met many trials and disappointments in applying his steam to shipping, and your William Lloyd Garrison and Wendell Phillips were maltreated in the public halls of Boston because they ventured the opinion that slaves should be free; because they were rebels against prevailing custom and popular opinion. However, the men triumphed, and in the city where they were most scorned are they now most loved and revered. Is not this poetic justice?'[1]

'On the whole, what is your impression of America?'

'Favorable, sir; favorable. Had I known as much of America ere I sailed as I have since learned, my reception in New York and my tour through this country might have been very different. However, that is a matter of the past which it is useless to discuss.'

The reporter here withdrew and left Mr. Wilde to the consideration of a mammoth pile of mail. But the reporter left Mr. Wilde bearing away an impression far different from that with which he entered the aesthete's presence. To say that Mr. Wilde is a fascinating gentleman, polished and courteous in his manner and graceful in every movement, might not convey the desired idea of him. In form he is tall and well proportioned, and his face is one never to be forgotten—a long face, clear complexion, partially opened mouth displaying large, well-molded teeth, and, above all, a pair of wonderfully deep, clear, blue eyes, honest, generous and kindly in their expression. The only point about him differing materially from any other polished, elegant gentleman is the mass of brown hair partly shadowing the face. The hair is parted in the middle and hangs straight down to the neck, with never the suspicion of a kink or curl. So profuse is the hair that not a glimpse of the ears can be had. He was attired in a morning dress of modest brown, trimmed and faced on the coat lapels with dark crimson, a narrow cord of the same color running down the outside seams of ample pantaloons. Mr. Wilde's accent is decidedly English, but not of the cockney type. All in all, he is probably the most thoroughly misrepresented foreigner ever landed on American shores.

---

1   Samuel Finley Breese Morse (1791–1872) was an American inventor who was partly responsible for developing the technology that allowed tele-graphic messages to be sent over long distances. Robert Fulton (1765–1815) was an American engineer and inventor, credited with building the first commercially successful steamboat (1807). William Lloyd Garrison (1805–1879) was an American abolitionist and publisher of the anti-slavery news-paper *The Liberator*. Wendell Phillips (1811–1884) was an American lawyer, orator, and abolitionist. Wilde lunched with him in January 1882.

'Truly Aesthetic', *The Daily Inter Ocean* (Chicago, IL), 13 Feb. 1882, 2

Oscar Wilde sat in his room in the Grand Pacific last night, a room made bright and artistic with beautiful things. A large center-table was heaped with choice old books, some of them rare old curios, with precious broken binding and soulful mediaeval dogs' ears. In the window's embrasure was a beautifully intense writing desk, all-inlaid with pearl, quite Japanese and early English,[1] heaped with letters answered and unanswered. The bright coal blazed in the grate. The sofa, with its covering of skins of wild beasts and its further curtain of the old-gold silk shawl, with netted fringe, was drawn up to a comfortable angle with the fire, and upon the couch thus made reclined the aesthetic young man, this time smoking a cigarette. He was dressed in a quilted black silk smoking jacket with scarlet collar, lapels, and waistbands. He wore the same scarlet necktie, handkerchief, and socks, or at the least they were of the same color as upon the previous visit of *The Inter Ocean* reporter. His pantaloons were black, with a scarlet cord down the seams to match the trimming of the jacket. He greeted his visitor with languid grace.

'As my former interview with you was necessarily brief,' said the reporter, 'there were a few questions I should like to ask you.'

Mr. Wilde made a gesture of assent, and the reporter asked him what he thought of Chicago.

'That is a difficult question to answer,' he said. 'I don't pretend to have seen the city yet. I have been here too short a time; but from what I have seen I like it much better than New York. The streets are wider, cleaner, and there are not all the railways overhead and in the middle of the street, and that dreadful noise is not here. It is wonderful to think how you have built such a large city in so short a time, especially after such a great calamity as your great fire.[2] But of course it is a little sad to think of all the millions of money spent on buildings and so little architecture.'

This he said with a sigh, and glance out of the window upon the twinkling lights of the city.

'But that will come in time, no doubt.'

'Have you seen any art in Chicago?'

'I have seen one Chicago artist whose work is of the highest artistic

Electrotype copper plaque illustrating Wilde's poem 'Requiescat', by John Donoghue. Donoghue gave Wilde the clay original. Wilde later ordered five plaster casts and displayed a copper version in the drawing room of his Tite Street home.

quality, whose work is beautiful—more beautiful than the work of any sculptor I have seen yet, and of whom you should all be proud. I refer to Mr. Donoghue.'[3]

'Is Donoghue a sculptor?' asked the reporter.

'Do you tell me you don't know him? He is a native of Chicago, studied in Paris, has come back to his own city, having done beautiful work already, and prepared to do beautiful work for you if any of you care for it,' said Mr. Wilde, with ill-concealed sarcasm.

'Here is a plaque he designed for one of my poems—a figure of a girl—so simple, so powerful, so pretty. It is perfect.'

The reporter took his word for it.

'What do you think of the people of America?'

'In the Eastern cities the people are very cosmopolitan. I think this is strongly characteristic as regards the men and women. It was in the West of America that I expected to find real American life—life made by yourselves and for yourselves.'

'How have you liked your audiences?'

'At all important large cities I find the audiences intelligent, courteous, and sympathetic. In some of the small provincial towns which I have visited on my journey there have been attempts at disturbances. However, in all these cases the good sense and good feeling of the majority of the audiences entirely stopped any attempts of the kind.'

'You refer more particularly to Rochester?'[4]

'Yes.'

'How was it in Boston with the Harvard students?'

'What the young men did there was a mere piece of undergraduate high spirits. I received it in the same spirit, and my lecture at Boston passed off most brilliantly. It was not intended as an attempt to disturb my lecture, but merely a bit of school-boy fun. You don't suppose for a moment that a movement of any importance can be affected by sixty young men?'

'What do you think of athletic sports?'

'When I lectured in Boston I told these young men of Harvard that so far from their athletics being opposed to art, the best motives for the noblest sculptures would most probably be found on their running-ground, on the river, in the gymnasium. I reminded them that Greek sculpture never looked for any nobler motive than a young man starting for a race, tying his sandals before leaping, hurling the weight, and the like, and advised them to put up in their beautiful gymnasium a few casts of the best Greek statues of young athletes, so as to remind them that all their own physical perfection, and strength, and fleetness of foot and the like, might give to the artist beautiful subjects for his art.'

'Where does your lecture tour extend?'

'I lecture next week in Detroit, Fort Wayne, and Cleveland; after that in St. Louis, Cincinnati, and other cities.'

'Will you go south?'

'I do not know yet whether I can go to Canada or your own Southern States.'

'Will you go to the far West?'

'I don't think I shall have time to go to the far West. So many lectures to give, so much traveling to do. I am afraid I shall have to give up what I had looked forward to meeting in America—California in the spring, Colorado, and a ride in Mexico. I want to see Leadville immensely.'

'Those mining towns are quite a curiosity.'

'Yes; those new forms of life—new attempts at civilization that have sprung up in your mining cities—are objects of the keenest intellectual interest to us in Europe. In speaking of Rochester,' said Mr. Wilde, rising and helping himself to a fresh cigarette, 'I must say that I am trying to keep as good an opinion of your country as I can. Your great cities confirm me in my best opinion, while the pretty provincial villages are what such always are, entirely unimportant.[5] Let a young man go to England, and lecture on any subject he chooses, he will at least be treated with respect.'

'Are you satisfied with the results of your tour financially?'

Mr. Wilde mildly stared with surprise at such an outrageous question, but evidently thinking that this was a type of civilization 'created by ourselves and for ourselves,' he confessed that he had done pretty well.

'I have had large audiences,' he said. 'By the way, how much easier it is to speak to a thousand people than a few dozen. Wendell Phillips told me that it was a test of a true orator for him to interest an audience of twenty.'

'How much do you get a night?'

This was too much for Mr. Wilde. He pushed back his hair and threw his cigarette away. Finally he said:

'How much do your best lecturers get?'

'Some of them get $500 a night.'

'Well, I got $1,000 a night, in Boston, and shall get the same here. Of course, in little cities I don't expect so much. But it is merely filling in the time.

'I am extremely impressed by the entire disregard of Americans for money-making—'

Here the reporter was so surprised that he dropped his pencil.

' —as shown by the remarks made by many of the Western journals. They think it a strange and awful thing that I should want to make a few dollars by lecturing. Why, money-making is necessary for art. Money builds cities and makes them healthful. Money buys art and furnishes it an incentive. Is it strange that I should want to make money? And yet these newspapers cry out that I am making money!'

1   An allusion to *Patience*. Lady Jane suggests that the soldiers improve their uniforms by surmounting them 'with something Japanese – it matters not what – would at least be Early English!'

2   The Great Chicago Fire burned for three days in October 1871. It killed
      approximately 300 people; about 3.3 square miles or 9 km² of the city
      were razed.
3   John Talbott Donoghue (1853–1903) was born in Chicago. Wilde had
      visited Donoghue's atelier that afternoon.
4   At Rochester students had disrupted Wilde's lecture by turning down
      the gas and inducing an African American man to parade down the aisle
      imitating the supposed mannerisms of aesthetes.
5   The context suggests that Wilde may have said 'petty' rather than 'pretty'.

'Oscar Wilde', *The Chicago Daily Tribune* (Chicago, IL), 15 Feb. 1882, 3

A representative of *The Tribune* called at the Grand Pacific Hotel yesterday afternoon and requested one of the gentlemanly clerks to transmit a
bit of pasteboard bearing his name to the parlor of Mr. Oscar Wilde, the
celebrated esthete. A sable attaché of the hotel departed with the card,
and returned in a few moments with the pleasing intelligence that 'de
gemman would see de gemman.' The reporter started for the regions
above, and on the way his guide asked:

'Is dat man an actor?'

Supposing that he referred to Mr. Wilde, the newspaper man informed him that he was the noted Oscar Wilde.

'What opery-house am he a playin' at?'

'Oh, he's a lecturer, not an actor. He's an esthete.'

'Is he, dough? I thought he looked like one ob dem fellahs wat tum-
bles in a circus,' said the wise-looking African, and the reporter saw
that he had mistaken the great Oscar for an athlete.

The door of Parlor 3 was soon reached, and the scribe was solemnly
ushered into the presence of the prophet of the beautiful. He arose from
the sofa upon which he was reclining with a languid air, and allowed
his hand to be pressed by the lead-stained hand of the journalist. Mr.
Wilde is like unto the chameleon, as he has velvet coats of all hues.
On this occasion he wore one of a drab tint, and this, together with a
pair of baggy gray trousers, cloth-topped gaiters, a green necktie, and a
handkerchief of the same shade, completed the outer toilet.

The Chicago Water Tower, which Wilde criticised on aesthetic grounds.

After greeting the reporter he sank back upon the sofa, which was covered with buffalo-skins, and dreamily sipped a cup of tea. The newspaper man ventured a question.

'How were you pleased with your reception last evening,' he asked.

There was a soulful gurgle of fragrant Young Hyson in Mr. Wilde's throat, followed by a painful silence which suggested that a tea-leaf had lodged in the region of his larynx, and he said: 'I was much pleased at the way my lecture was received by a Chicago audience. Don't you know it is wonderful to think that one man can stand before such a vast audience and sway people with your voice. It seemed grand to me last night that I was able to do this.

'By the way,' he continued, 'your newspapers seemed to think that I was to deliver the same lecture I delivered in New York City. The *Times'* report amused me very much, as I could easily see from reading it that they had no reporter there. All they gave me was a meagre half column.'

'Mr. Wilde,' said the reporter, 'are you aware that you wounded the pride of our best citizens by referring slightingly to our water-tower?'[1]

'I can't help that. It's really too absurd. If you build a water-tower, why don't you build it for water and make a simple structure of it, instead of building it like a castle, where one expects to see mailed knights peering out of every part. It seems a shame to me that the citizens of Chicago have spent so much money on buildings with such an unsatisfactory result from an architectural point of view. Your city looks positively too dreary to me,' and the esthete closed his eyes as if to shut out the view of a flat across the street.

'Have you seen much of Chicago since you have been here?'

'Oh yes, quite as much as I care to see. I have driven through your parks, and viewed the principal objects of interest.'

'Of course, then, you have been to the stock-yards and seen them kill pigs?'

'No, indeed,' said Mr. Wilde, with a horrified look, 'such sights have no interest for me,' and he shrugged his broad shoulders so that the spoon in the tea-cup settled like a bean in a bladder.

'How have you been impressed with our first social circles?' asked the reporter, thinking to strike Oscar where he lived.

'I have been to one or two receptions,' he said, 'and I like your society people very much. They have all apologized to me for their newspapers, telling me that I mustn't mind what you reporters say.'

'That is surprising. Chicago's people always swear by their newspapers, and declare them the best in the world.'

'Oh, that's a bit of buncombe,' said Mr. Wilde with a laugh. 'Your newspapers are comic without being amusing. English papers are founded on facts, while American papers are founded on imagination. How long have you been a journalist?' he asked suddenly, turning the tables on the scribe.

'About three years.'

'I should think you young men of the profession would have some ambition. Why don't you take your newspapers out of the hands of the old fogies, and make an effort to revolutionize the world?'

The reporter suggested that a man could not revolutionize the world to any great extent on $20 per week, and Mr. Wilde said with a laugh that he guessed that was a fact.

Here he reached for a box of Turkish cigarettes which reposed on the mantel, and the reporter posed himself for a bow of acknowledgement;

but Mr. Wilde selected one cigarette, lit it, and replaced the box on the mantel, leaving the newspaper man to reach out longingly for an occasional whiff of the blue smoke. The reporter picked up a book which was lying upon a table and found it to be a volume of Mr. Wilde's poems. The edges were rough and uncut, and the poems were scattered through the volume without regard to order or neatness. It was unnecessary to look at the title-page to tell that the book came from an English press.

'That,' said Mr. Wilde, 'is an English volume of my poems.'

'Is it finished?' asked the reporter, gazing doubtfully at the rough edges.

'Certainly.'

'I shouldn't think such a volume would appeal to the beautiful. It wouldn't do in America?'

'The American editions of my poems look frightful. That is the way a book should be gotten up. The contents and not the covers of a book are what we look for.'[2]

Here a colored gentleman entered the room, deposited a few whispered words in the great esthete's left ear, and Oscar said, 'Not this evening. I dine out, and I want a carriage at a quarter of 7,' and the liveried lackey salaamed Mr. Wilde, went out, and slammed the door.

'I must say goodbye to you,' said Mr. Wilde to the newspaper man. 'I am glad to have met you, and hope that you will endeavor to infuse a new life into American journalism. You can tell people more interesting things than what sort of a necktie I wear. By the way, how it is that all American journalists aspire to be humorists?'

'Humorists are born in this country, not made,' volunteered the reporter. 'Men who are running country papers often attract attention by their witty sayings, their humorous remarks are copied, and they acquire a reputation as a humorist. Then they write a book, go on a lecturing tour, and give out.'

'Well,' laughed Mr. Wilde. 'I hope you won't give out'; and he retired to dress for dinner.

1   Wilde had told his Chicago audience that their city's water-tower was 'a castellated monstrosity with pepper-boxes stuck all over it'. The remark elicited a laugh.
2   In fact, Wilde had strong opinions about how his published works should appear. He involved himself in all aspects of their design.

'Come and Gone', *The Cleveland Herald* (Cleveland, OH), 20 Feb. 1882, 8

'Oscar Wilde and servant, of England, Room 55.'

That was the legend which a *Herald* reporter read upon the register of the Forest City House Saturday afternoon about 5 o'clock. A card asking the courtesy of an interview, and assuring the notorious stranger that the writer would be both brief and unaggressive, soon found its way up to the room of the aesthete; and by return porter an answer was sent granting the privilege asked, but craving ten minutes time in which to finish a midday repast. In precisely two minutes the reporter stood at the door of room 55, and rapped with gentle timidity.

Mr. Wilde did not answer the summons in person. His colored valet opened the door and ushered the caller into the presence of the far-famed apostle of the lily and the sunflower.

Oscar was lolling on an elegant sofa, and did not rise until his visitor had crossed the room. He then arose slowly, extended his hand reluctantly and pointed the reporter to a chair beside his own luxurious divan.

In the center of the room was a small, unaesthetic-looking table, at which the languid poet had just dined. The viands which remained unconsumed were just such as would be looked for in the menu of the aesthete—jellies, custards, pastry, etc., all served on decorated china. The sofa upon which the poet languished had offended his fastidious taste, and he had accordingly caused to be spread over it an afghan and a silk shawl of an old gold tint.

Mr. Wilde himself was attired in a velvet coat and vest of brown, and substantial looking pair of ordinary pantaloons. In personal appearance he is exactly what the prevailing photographs represent him to be, save that a pair of rather obtrusive front teeth are displayed in conversation, which have failed to appear in any of the representations of the poet. His face is even more smooth and girlish than would appear in the photographs, and caused to flit though the scribe's mind the horrible suspicion that Oscar has never yet had occasion to shave. Between his thumb and fore finger he held a dainty cigarette, which, from time to time, he thrust between his rubicund lips, puffing the fragrant smoke above his head in circling clouds that delighted his yearning soul.

'Mr. Wilde,' began the inquisitor, kindly but firmly, 'may I inquire what first resolved you of your mission, and inspired you to champion this modern aesthetical movement?'

'Well, my passion for art was greatly encouraged, if not created, by a visit to Italy when I was a boy.[1] Then subsequently at Oxford I was greatly influenced by Ruskin. I was also much pained and saddened by seeing how unkindly all of England's great men were received, especially her literary men; how Byron, Shelley, Keats, Wordsworth, and all the rest were ridiculed![2] This, I now conceive to be the fate of all prominent men who depart from the common place in any degree, and I am no longer disturbed by it.'

'Then you are able to take philosophically all the sarcasm and good-natured fun which has been directed at you since you came to America?'

'Philosophically? Why, I don't mind it in the least. At the very worst, it can only amount to a *personal inconvenience*, as though some one sought to throw mud at you while you were crossing the street. Why, all innovators must be indestructible. In crusading against the popular stupidity and stagnation, I expect to hear ridicule; but I am absolutely impervious to it—it doesn't interfere with my serenity or my fixedness of purpose at all. It is not done from malice, and what is the use, then, in being troubled by it? It is done by a world which cannot understand; that has not been educated up to the aesthetical movement.'

'How would you have the world changed?'

'I would create an artistic temperament. I would surround men with elevating environments that their lives might be beautiful. This is the secret of all joyousness in life, and the keynote of all civilization—this artistic temperament; and it cannot be produced in any other way than by giving the people an opportunity to grow up in an atmosphere of noble and beautiful things. I think that every year in a great country, in America as much as in England, a certain amount of artistic intelligence and power is produced, and that the aim of any rational civilization is to seek out those men and women who have this power of design, this nobility of imagination, this love of the beautiful, and by means of a school of design in each city to give men an opportunity of producing beautiful art. You in America don't want that we should look upon you as a mere collection of money-making merchants. You would like to influence the civilization of Europe. You are ambitious and should be so; but the only way you can influence us is by producing noble art and a noble civilization. Believe me, that we value your American poets much more than your American millionaires; and that we estimate you by the amount of great men you have produced, not by your hoarded wealth.'

'That's a rather severe implication, Mr. Wilde. Evidently you place a rather low estimate upon American art and civilization, when comparing them with English art and civilization?'

'Why, my dear young man,' said Mr. Wilde, springing to his feet with a show of real enthusiasm, and addressing his visitor earnestly, 'do you really think that American progress in these departments can be compared with that of England?'

The abashed reporter hung his head in mortification, and the poet went on:

'Can you seriously compare your art with ours? I have just been in Chicago, and while there I saw millions and millions of dollars sunk in public buildings, but I failed to find one single architectural triumph. Your poets are not to be compared with ours.'

'Of course you have been misrepresented in the papers, Mr. Wilde. Would you care to disclaim, at this time, some of the things which have been identified with your aesthetical movement?'

'My dear sir,' responded the aesthete, 'when I read all this trash in the newspapers about some one whom the editors are wont to call Oscar Wilde, I really wonder what the young man is like after all, and wish that I might see him myself. If it really mattered in the least what the newspapers say, I might take pains to refute some things; but it won't pay.'

'Then you don't have a very high idea of American journalism?'

'You know well enough how artificial and meaningless it is, if you have been in the business at all. The press is comic, without being amusing or fair. Nothing which I read by way of criticism gives me pain; nothing by way of commendation gives me pleasure. Who are the editors, anyway? Most frequently they are from the number of escaped convicts and other depraved characters.'

The reporter only weighs 125 pounds, so he smothered his desire for revenge, and did not annihilate the six foot sunflower on the spot. Besides that, he did not care to mar the furniture or gore up the carpet. He left, and the aesthete still lives to roam through America.

1   Wilde was twenty when he first visited Italy, and appears to have wished it thought that he had taken the trip earlier. See also p. 161, n6.

2   Lord Byron (1788–1824) was an English Romantic poet. William Wordsworth (1770–1850) was Poet Laureate of the United Kingdom from 1843 until his death.

'With Mr. Oscar Wilde', *Cincinnati Daily Gazette* (Cincinnati, OH), 21 Feb. 1882, 10

Mr. Oscar Wilde arrived in this city yesterday morning from Cleveland, en route to Louisville, where he is to lecture this evening. He remained over a day, wishing to have a preliminary glance at certain objects of interest here before his return on Thursday for his lecture on 'The English Renaissance' at the grand Opera House on the afternoon of that day.

A *Gazette* representative having early information of the arrival of the great apostle of aestheticism, called upon him at the Burnet and was duly requested to follow his card to parlor No. 62, where Mr. Wilde was bestowed. The poet and aesthete was found rather languidly reclining upon a couch, over which was thrown, in careless grace, a rich fur-lined railway traveling rug, smoking a cigarette in a thoughtful mood. There was a litter of letters upon the table, in the midst of which was a magnificent basket of roses, pink and red, which Mr. Wilde explained were a rest and comfort to his soul after the horrors of a railway journey. Against the side of the room stands a battered, but substantial English leather 'box,' which the *Gazette* representative gazed at reverently in the pauses of the conversation, knowing that it was the casket that contained the silken raiment which has excited the rage of the heathen in two continents.

Mr. Wilde was curiously like, but yet utterly unlike, the Maudle of the organ of the Philistines, *Punch*, and the fact reminds one of the proverb that a lie is never so dangerous as when it has in it a modicum of truth. The large, long face, framed in thick locks of brown hair, parted in the center and falling on either side of the cheeks almost to the shoulders, which gives to it a certain womanly air, is Du Maurier's, but in place of the vacant stare is a bright smile, and a perpetually changing expression, clear gray eyes, a tall and manly figure, a carriage the perfection of good form, and a bearing that bespeaks him a thorough man of the world. He wore a morning suit of light mastic colored tweed; the coat of velvet, a little pronounced in the matter of braid; a pale red silk handkerchief drooped from the breast pocket, and matched in color the ample neckerchief knotted in sailor fashion beneath his low turned shirt collar. He was faultlessly shod in patent leather, with gray gaiters, and wore no jewelry but a very large seal ring—a fine antique intaglio of Mercury cut in amethyst. With this he seals his billet doux and those other 'winged messengers' which have roused the dull British Philistine from his vulgar lethargy—or anyhow have showed him the true path out of the mire.

Mr. Wilde was most cordial. Would the *Gazette* act as cicerone, and show the stranger Rookwood, the School of Design, the Art Museum?[1]

Why, certainly; if the *Gazette* desires one good thing more than another, it is to stimulate the zeal and devotion of the people, and make room for what is purely true and precious in art. Meanwhile, what does Mr. Wilde think of America?

'I am pleased with it. It has great possibilities; each city in the years to come will be the center of a school of art, as is Venice, Florence, Rome. It is folly to talk of a national art: there is no such thing. Each city has its center of inspiration. In Florence the inspiration was of a religious type, God and the angels; in Venice it was the noble men and women of the republic; in Rome, traditions and noble deeds.

'I am especially delighted with the West, it is so new and fresh, and the people are so generous and free from prejudice. The older cities in the East,' Mr. Wilde said, musingly blowing little rings of smoke from his lips—'The people are enveloped in a perfect mist of prejudice, quite unlimited; they have imported so many old-world ideas, absurdities, and affectations that they have lost all sincerity and naturalness.' (The Boston Philistines made the aesthete have a thoroughly 'bad time' evidently.) 'You have no architecture, no scenery, but individuals are doing beautiful work, and you have great art possibilities.'

'In what direction?'

'America is the country for a great school of sculpture, because it is dependent upon the sunlight which you have, and is an art which depends absolutely upon present and active conditions of life, and not

The Young Sophocles Leading the Chorus of Victory after the Battle of Salamis (1885; cast 1911) by John Donoghue.

upon remembrance or tradition. I met in Chicago,' Mr. Wilde said reflectively, 'a young sculptor whom we would love and be so proud of if he were in Europe—a Mr. Donoghue. He reminded me of the old Italian stories of the struggle of genius. Born of poor people, he felt a desire to create beauty. Seeing some workmen modeling a cornice one day, be begged some clay of them, and went home and began to model. A man who saw what was in him gave him money for a year in Paris. He went, and has come back. The way I found him was, he sent to me a little bas relief of a seated girl, illustrating a verse of my poem, 'Requiescat.' I went and saw him; found him in a bare little room at the top of a great building, and in the center was a statuette of the young Sophocles leading the dance and the song after the battle of Salamis, a piece of the highest artistic beauty and perfect workmanship, waiting there in the clay, to be cast into bronze. It was by far the best piece of sculpture I have seen in America.[2]

'Meanwhile the artist starves upon a radish and a crust, the stoic's fare. Perhaps, but he will win in the end, and trouble is light if one is an artist. A man is not successful,' said Mr. Wilde, sententiously, but truly, 'because the world praises him, but because his work is good.'

'What have you seen commendable in a decorative way in your visit?'

'Many good houses in Philadelphia, Boston, and Washington, and I have seen a Daisy Miller. I cannot tell you where (this in response to eager questionings), because I am to go back there, and I should never be forgiven, but the sight of her has increased my admiration for Henry James a thousand fold.[3]

'Col. John Hay, of Cleveland, with whom I lunched yesterday, had a charming house.[4] But the room which has most impressed me was a little bare white-washed room in Camden Town, where I met Walt Whitman, whom I admire intensely. There was a big chair for him and a little stool for me, a pine table on which was a copy of Shakespeare, a translation of Dante,[5] and a cruse of water. Sunlight filled the room, and over the roofs of the houses opposite were the masts of the ships that lay in the river. But then the poet needs no rose to blossom on his walls for him, because he carries nature always in his heart. This room contains all the simple conditions for art—sunlight, good air, pure water, a sight of ships, and the poet's works.

'I saw another of your great poets in his beautiful home.' Mr. Wilde looked out of the window into the smoke and mist and sighed. It was a day to make the children of light to sigh and the heathen to mock and rage.

'This kind of weather,' he continued, consoling himself with a fresh cigarette, 'always gives me a sense of failure. I am always on the side of extremes—in winter I would always be sleighing, in summer always in a summer garden of flowers. I went to see Longfellow in a snow storm and returned in a hurricane, quite the right conditions for a visit to a poet. When I remember Boston, I think only of this lovely old man, who is himself a poem, and the bright party of men I met at Dr. Holmes's.'[6]

At 1 o'clock Mr. Wilde donned his green overcoat, trimmed with otter, adjusted a bon silene rosebud in his coat lapel, drew on a pair of pale tan colored gloves, and with an ivory stick in his hand and a brown stiff felt hat on his head, was driven first to Robert Clarke & Co.'s, where he selected various books, among them the works of Howells, James, Miss McLaughlin, and others, and thence to Rookwood, the School of Design, the Art Museum, whose doors were inhospitably closed, and a half hour was delightfully spent at the delightful home of

Mrs. Col. Nichols, on the Grandin road.[7] By request of Mr. Wilde, his impressions of the art industries of the city are not made public. He will embody them in his lecture on Thursday afternoon.[8] Mr. Wilde has a keen and quiet wit that enlivens his conversation upon worldly subjects delightfully.

When shown the School of Design, with its forlorn corridors and dark rooms, his eye lighted on the legend 'No Smoking,' painted in the window. 'Great heaven, they speak of smoking as if it were a crime. I wonder they do not caution the students not to murder each other on the landings. Such a place is enough to incite a man to the commission of any crime,' and then, 'most unkindest cut of all,'[9] 'I wonder no criminal has ever pleaded the ugliness of your city as an excuse for his crimes!'

The suburbs Mr. Wilde kindly approved. Seen through the rain and mist, the stately villas of Grandin road were quite English with their green sweep of turf and crowding chimneys.

Of all men Mr. Wilde least loves a critic. 'Let the poet sing,' he cries, 'and let the artist paint, and let the people look and listen—and so they would, and learn, too—but the critic, a kind of middleman, comes between them, and, like the bird in Shelley's song, shuts his eyes and declares it is night. Sometimes the critic himself, lured on by a hope of fame, paints, or writes, or sings, and then a great and sacred joy fills the soul of all artists, and his fate overtakes him.' The real critic should be a poet, Mr. Wilde thinks, and in proof cites Coleridge, Keats, Goethe, Matthew Arnold, the greatest of living English critics, all poets,[10] and quotes with glee Theophile Gautier's reproof of a critic who lectured him on the iniquity of his ways. 'It is of great advantage to a man never to have done anything, but he must not abuse it.'[11]

'I forgive everything, the critics' ignorance, even. I applaud Bunthorne languidly from my opera box. I greet Du Maurier blandly at the club; but the unpardonable sin is to say I am impractical. That is to stick a dagger in me. This aesthetic movement is the first of any practical value in art in England. It has changed the whole character of English decorative art. It has given to every handicraftsman in England beautiful designs, which are at the foundation of all good art. We have relieved the whole English people from the incubus of the upholsterer. He now exists only in the museums as a warning.'

Mr. Wilde looked in at the opera last night to see the diva and the audience, and was in the manager's box for half an hour.[12] He leaves this morning for Louisville, and returns, as before stated, for a matinee on Thursday at the Grand.

1   'Rookwood' is the Rookwood Pottery Company, founded in 1880.
2   *The Young Sophocles Leading the Chorus of Victory after the Battle of Salamis* was not cast in bronze until 1911, eight years after Donoghue's death.
3   Daisy Miller is the eponymous character in an 1879 story by American author Henry James (1843–1916). She is a young American woman whose flirtatiousness is frowned upon when she visits Europe.
4   John Milton Hay (1838–1905) was an American politician.
5   Dante Alighieri (c. 1265–1321) was a Italian poet. His works include *Divina Commedia* (*The Divine Comedy*) and *La Vita Nuova* (*The New Life*).
6   Oliver Wendell Holmes Sr (1809–1894) was an American physician and poet.
7   William Dean Howells (1837–1920) was an American novelist. Mary Louise McLaughlin (1847–1939) was a potter and ceramic painter who worked in Cincinnati. Maria Longworth Nichols née Storer (1849–1932) was the founder of Rookwood Pottery.
8   Despite this request, Wilde did make brief comments to another interviewer that day (see p. 68). In his first lecture in Cincinnati he criticised much of what he had seen at Rookwood, but managed to keep his audience on side.
9   The reporter quotes Antony in Shakespeare's *Julius Caesar* (3.2.171).
10   Samuel Taylor Coleridge (1772–1834) was an English poet, critic, and philosopher. Best known for his long poem *The Rime of the Ancient Mariner* (1798), he also lectured on various topics, including education, Shakespeare, and the English poets. Matthew Arnold (1822–1888) was an English poet, critic, and inspector of schools. Wilde listed him among the 'very few masters' of English prose.
11   Théophile Gautier (1811–1872) was a French poet and critic.
12   The diva referred to is the Italian soprano Adelina Patti (1843–1919).

'Oscar Wilde', *The Cincinnati Enquirer* (Cincinnati, OH), 21 Feb. 1882, 4

Oscar Wilde, the aesthete, arrived in the city yesterday, and took up his quarters in Burnet House, where a representative of the *Enquirer* met him late yesterday afternoon. The original of 'Bunthorne' was reclining on a fauteuil when our ambassador entered his apartments. He arose rather more quickly than poetic grace demanded, and with a pleasant smile extended his right hand and gave him a cordial greeting. In person he is very tall, with broad shoulders and a plethora of arms and legs—that is, he has the usual complement of limbs, but they appear longer and more loosely jointed than perfect accord with manly beauty requires. His face is long and narrow, and appears narrower than it really is on account of the length of his hair, which is light brown in color, is parted in the middle, and touches the shoulders like a dark flaxen mane. His eyes are large and light blue in color. Their outside corners are lower than the inside like a Chinaman's, though they are far from being almond-shaped. His nose is long, large and aquiline, and his mouth betrays his Hibernian origin, his lips being thick and the upper one so shut that his speech partakes somewhat of the character of a lisp. His teeth, especially the upper ones, are long, large and irregular. His chin is protuberant, and he has very high cheek-bones. His sack-coat and natty vest were of cobwebby grey velvet hue, with a cold gravy bloom;[1] his trousers were light in color and loose and limp in make. His shoes were of patent leather, with buff gaiters, and his low-cut Byronic collar was encircled by a silk cravat that was tied in a sailor knot, and was between a Dunducketty grey and a dull pink in color.[2] In the left lapel of his coat was a beautiful rosebud, and he held another in his left hand, whose delicate exhalations he ever and anon inhaled with evident rapture. Within easy reach stood a marble-topped table, on which was a vase containing four splendid calla lilies, whose faint perfume almost drowned the senses with olfactory delight. As soon as the greetings were over and our guileless youth took the chair which was proffered him by Mr. Wilde, he began operations by remarking: 'Mr. Wilde, I presume by this time you are sufficiently acquainted with the customs of this country to know that you are face to face with the ubiquitous interviewer?'

'Oh, yes,' smilingly replied the aesthetic apostle, 'and I am glad of it, for some of the brightest hours I have passed in this country have been with the gentlemen of the press who have interviewed me, and I have found them among the most intelligent men I have met here.'

'Taffy,' mentally ejaculated our reporter,[3] and then said: 'How long will you remain in this city?'

'Only until morning. I am on my way to Louisville, where I will lecture tomorrow evening; then I go to Indianapolis, and on Thursday I return to this city and lecture here. Today I drove to the Rookwood pottery, with Mrs. George Ward Nichols, and inspected its work very closely.'

'How did you like it?'

'Some of it was very good, and much of it indifferent. On the whole I was very much pleased, as it showed what can be done for art even by one person, as in the case of Mrs. Nichols. There is one young man named Bowen at Rookwood whom I am sure has true poetic art and fervor. His productions are wonderful, and he should be encouraged.'[4]

'I am going to tell you something that I fear will shock you,' said our scribe.

'Shock me?' interrupted Oscar.

'Yes,' was the reply. 'Several years ago one of our promising young artists was employed by a number of our merchants to make a series of pictures for the Vienna Exposition. He executed the commission, his pictures attracted great attention, and, I believe, received a medal. What do you think was their theme?'

'Indeed, I can't tell.'

'Hog killing!'

'Well I don't know but even that could be treated in an artistic manner. You see there is no such thing as a poetic subject no more than that there is a natural school of painting. You hear people speak of the Italian school of painting, when no such thing exists. The Venetian style differs from the Florentine as it differs from that of other Italian cities. Each locality has its own school as distinct and separate as the towns themselves. The so-called Dutch school is remarkable for its warmth of color, and yet its subjects are mostly commonplace. All through Holland you will see pictures mostly of brawls and quarrels in drinking-rooms. Yet every once in a while you will see in one of them a gleam of light streaming through a window and tinting the glasses on the table with all the glories of the prism. Another will display a bit of coloring as warm and as sweet as the kiss of love. The men who painted these pictures poetized the subjects until the ordinariness of their character is forgotten. This shows that they were earnest and sincere, and that their heart was in their work. I have little faith in a young man who chooses what are called heroic subjects for his early efforts. It looks as though he was depending on his subject, and not on his own powers, for success. The lowliest subject, treated with loving earnestness and sincerity, will, if the artist is competent, give the best results, just as the plainest words are the most effective in the mouth of an actor.'

'I understand that you will give us a new lecture here,' inquired our representative. 'What will be its subject?'

'Decorative art,' was the answer.

'Will it contain any local allusions?'

'Yes, I think it will. I think I will speak of what I have seen at Rookwood. Wherever I go I try to see what there is of decorative art in it, and I speak of what I see in my lectures. I think it will be judicious to do so here.'

1   In *Patience*, the aesthete Lady Jane dislikes the soldiers' red and yellow uniforms ('Primary colours!') and suggests they wear 'a cobwebby grey velvet, with a tender bloom like cold gravy'.
2   Dunducketty is a dull colour, as of mud.
3   Taffy: American slang for flattery.
4   'Bowen' is Henry Joseph Breuer (c. 1854–1932). His name was frequently misspelt. He and Wilde socialised in New York later in the year.

'English Renaissance', *Louisville Commercial* (Louisville, KY), 22 Feb. 1882

'I find nothing unique in America,' said Mr. Oscar Wilde, the distinguished English poet and apostle of art-culture to a *Commercialist*, who spent a short time in parlor 101 at the Louisville Hotel yesterday. 'To a stranger like myself it appears monotonous.' Mr. Wilde was reclining easily upon a sofa, over which was spread a dark skin and a soft olive cloth of some kind. He leaned easily on his right arm and his left was thrown behind his head, except when he removed his cigarette and puffed little pale-blue circlets of smoke above the marble-topped table which stood directly in front of him, and upon which was a vase containing some lilies and roses and a slowly settling glass of champagne that had apparently been just touched. The room was darkened a little, and the shutters of the window just behind his head were partially closed, throwing him, as a picture, into a soft but not indistinct light. It was a fine and graceful figure upon the sofa. Six feet of manly outline were displayed. He wore a dark olive smoking doublet, lined with rose-colored stuff, and profusely ornamented with cord and lace. This was turned back from the throat, encircled by a low-cut Byron collar, at which a dark necktie was negligently knotted. His pantaloons were light and loose and limp, the patent leather shoes pointed and topped with lavender gaiters. In all these details there was only the suggestion of the tastes and appearance of other men of leisure in their smoking parlors. The head and face, however, were remarkable, and disappointing to one who had become familiar with his photographs which, to say the least, 'flatter' him. The face is very long, sallow and oval, the cheek-bones high, the chin prominent, the nose long and aquiline. His eyes, almond-shaped, full and dark, are unusually fine and intelligent, imbedded in the face as if upon cream cushions. His mouth is a poor feature. The upper lip is heavy but short, the front teeth long and protruding, and there is a slight suggestion of lisp in his enunciation. The forehead is not remarkable, but, on the contrary, his head is small at the crown and on either side falls a long, straight and ungainly mass of dark flaxen hair, which is not parted and is totally devoid of any beauty. It gives him an uncertain 'womanish' appearance.

'I find nothing unique in America,' Mr. Wilde said in answer to a question whether the peculiar bustle and rush of so representative a western city as Chicago had nothing unique in it. 'Chicago is not unique. It is bare looking and monotonous. The architecture is so poor that it amounts to none at all. That is true of all American cities. And yet you must depend on the individual cities for your architecture as for all art. There is no National school of art. In Europe each city has its own school. This is more noticeably true of architecture, because when architectural monuments are raised they stand there forever, impressing a character upon the locality which cannot be removed. The same is true of painting. When you see Italian pictures it is not enough to know they were painted in Italy. You must know whether they were executed in Venice, or Florence, or Naples. These cities form schools of their own, and do not all form a National school. It is not so with music to as great an extent. A piece of music, when composed, goes out to all the world, and its influence is felt universally. Still there is a local coloring in

Wilde photographed by Sarony wearing his smoking jacket (1882; detail). The jacket was olive-green and had red lapels and cuffs.

the composition, and there are local schools. Buildings and art galleries remain where they are erected and formed, and are exclusively the result of local development. American architecture is cold and bare. It amounts to nothing as art.'

'What do you think of the American himself?'

'I am exceedingly pleased with their kindness to me and the intelligence and appreciation everywhere to be met.'

'In this respect how does the West compare with the East?'

'Oh, I have only lectured once in the West—in Chicago. The people there were very cultivated and intelligent, and received me with every indication of attention. On the whole, I believe I think better of the West than the East. In the East you know there is much folly flying. It comes from European association and influence. In the West you are working out your own civilization by yourselves, and there is more readiness to hear thoughtful suggestions and opinions.'

'You have not been annoyed in the West by the impertinences you met with in the East?'

Mr. Wilde had spoken before with an easy earnestness. His face was serious and there was none of the drawl which has been attributed to him, more than any man would display under the irksomeness of newspaper interviewing long continued. At this question, however, a furtive and half amused smile crossed his face.

'Oh,' said he, 'I met with some annoyances in two provincial towns, but I do not think the less of the Eastern people, because of the impertinence and ill-behavior of a few school boys. I assure you my reception has been too cordial for such incidents to weigh against.

'I notice,' he continued after a moment, 'that your river is swollen and high.'

It was hoped by the interviewer that he who had been disappointed in the Atlantic Ocean, and stood unmoved by Niagara, would express himself upon the waste that engulfed Shippingsport and the coal yards as in a maelstrom. Vain hope. He added:

'The worst of this is that it gives you very bad water.'

'The people of the great rushing West,' responded the reporter, 'have not the time to object to a few ounces of mud more or less to the gallon of water.'

'Haven't the time?' inquired the great aesthetic with mild surprise; 'why pure water is as necessary as pure air. Every drop of the water for your city should be filtered until it is pure.'

The reporter paused and contemplated the suggested millenium when the Water Company would furnish more water than mud, and President Long and Councilman Feely would lie down together. The idea was so overpowering that he needed fresh air to recover in. Mr. Wilde said he would leave this afternoon for Indianapolis, where he lectures tonight, and bidding the reporter farewell, bowed him with evident relief out of the room.

'Utterly Utter', *St. Louis Post-Dispatch* (St. Louis, MO), 25 Feb. 1882, 4

An unusual bustle was visible about the corridors of the Southern this morning, which puzzled the guests as they entered. Knots of young men generally known in society stood around the pillars in attempted attitudes and seemed to be waiting intently. The clerks were more chipper than usual, and appeared to be expecting something. Many of the ladies who were down town shopping extended their promenade to Walnut street, a thing very unusual, and as they passed the hotel, craned their pretty necks in an attempt to gaze inside. Each carriage that stopped was watched curiously, and the appearances all indicated that something was going to happen. Every time a tall, slender young man with hair longer than usual advanced towards the register, the aforesaid young men would form ranks and follow him. As he registered 'Fritz Hoffszleuttle, Omaha,' or something equally astounding, the followers would turn, somebody would say, 'Pshaw, that's not he,' and back they went to the waiting place. The cause of the commotion was the coming of Oscar Wilde. He was expected on the morning train and the loiterers were on hand to see what he looked like. At 10 o'clock he had not come, and the watch was nearly given up. A half hour later Oscar alighted from a hack at the ladies' entrance, accompanied by his agent, stepped into the elevator and went to his room. He was clad in a large, heavy all-fur overcoat, with a slouched hat, such as Texans affect. His arrival soon became noised about, and the great question was what did he look like. A *Post-Dispatch* reporter sent his card to parlor 70, where the aesthetic apostle had been domiciled, and was immediately invited to walk up. The tap at the door was answered by a musical 'Come in,' and the entrance was followed by disappointment. Anybody who imagines Wilde to be long, lank and angular is badly deceived. At the side of the room a sofa was placed, over one corner of which had been thrown a large and heavy drapery of old gold with tassels. The back was covered with a robe of long fur which hung down from the seat to the floor. Carelessly seated in the middle of the robe, and leaning back in a graceful pose, sat Oscar, with a tiny cigarette between his fingers.

As he rose to greet the visitor he looked as unlike the usual description of him as could well be imagined. He is a stout, rather heavily-built young man, possibly 5 feet 10 inches in height. His hair, which is of dark brown, is his distinguishing feature. It reaches his shoulders, is thick and heavy, not parted at all, but combed straight back in front, and he has a feminine way of tossing back stray locks which occasionally attempt to hang over the sides of his face. He wore a sack coat and high-buttoned vest of gray velvet, trimmed with wide braid of a like shade. His pantaloons were of a rough gray material, cut loose, and he wore shoes of patent leather and yellow morocco. His smooth face is large and pronounced and suggests at once the features of Henry Ward

Beecher.[1] The eyes are big, brown and almond shaped, the nose slightly aquiline, the lips rather thick, and the chin pronounced and heavy. Oscar's worst features are his teeth, the upper ones being large, projecting and uneven. He wore a dark pea-green scarf, under a turn-down collar, which concealed the shirt front. A handkerchief of the same shade appeared from his side pocket. He wore no jewelry save a large seal ring on his left hand, a pair of wide flapped cuffs at his wrists being fastened with plain pearled buttons. He looks like a stout, well-fed, active young Englishman, and his long hair gives him a poetical aspect. The reporter gazed anxiously over the room, but Wilde understood the glances and with a smile seemed to say:

'No, there are no sunflowers and lilies, no flowers of any kind. I suppose you thought I could not travel without them. Well, I can. You see I did.'

'You must be fatigued after your journey?' ventured the reporter, not knowing how to begin an aesthetic interview, and, therefore, dropping to every-day subjects.

'Oh no,' said Wilde with a smile, in which the English accent was very noticeable. 'I do not think I would have been able to endure it, however, but for one of your delightful novelists, W. D. Howells. I have read all his books since I came here, and he is a most charming writer.' A pause occurred here while Oscar hunted under his yellow dog-skin gloves on the table. A little box was found, out of which a small cigarette was fished out and lit, and the aesthete was himself again.

'I was much disappointed in this way,' continued he. 'We in England have no idea of the distances in your country. The impression seems to be that all the large cities are located in the suburbs of New York, then come the Rocky Mountains, next the Indians, and then San Francisco and the ocean. We do not half understand that large cities like Chicago and Cincinnati are located in the heart of the country.'

'How are you pleased with your visit so far?'

'Oh, your country is so large. It is a world. But it looks so barren and rugged in winter time. To one accustomed to a little place like England, which has been tilled for centuries, this change is remarkable.'

'What do you think of your treatment by the newspapers?'

'I do not mind that,' said Wilde, with a smile. 'It does not cause me any annoyance.'

'Do you read what is said about you?'

'Oh, yes, every line. When I come in at night, tired and weary, the reading of a good vigorous attack acts like a dish of caviar. Of course, some of it is not what I have been used to, as the English papers still have a sort of old fashioned regard for truth. They are not so much given to imagination as the journals here. Then the attacks come from such curious sources. I remember I was dressing at Washington for a dinner party, when a card was brought to me. The name was a curious one, and the card detailed for how many Western papers the owner was correspondent. I think there were eleven in all. I was slightly flurried, you may suppose. I said, "Now, here is the man who moulds the thoughts of the West; I must be on my best behavior." I requested the gentleman to come up, when in walked a boy, positively not more than 16. "Is this your card?" I asked. "Oh, yes," said he. The scene was too ridiculous.

'"Have you been to school much?" I asked.

'The juvenile interviewer said he had.

'"Have you learned French?"

'No, he had not. I told him that if he wished to be a journalist he ought to study French, gave him a big orange and dismissed him. What he did with the orange afterwards I don't know, but he seemed very much pleased to get it. Now I have had this experience several times. Boys have been my critics. What do I care about the expressions of a man who does not know anything in regard to my writings. It does not affect me any more than if the writer should say I had written a good sonnet or a bad sonnet. He does not know and I do not care.'

'But there have been more bitter attacks?'

'Oh yes. Before I came to Baltimore, the *American* there published a most uncalled for attack upon me. It stated that I had accepted an invitation to attend a club reception there, and at the last moment had sent word that my terms were $500 for such services, that the club had very properly declined the offer, and that I would therefore not be present.[2] I had never heard of the club at that time, had never received any invitation, and the fact is that when I came to Baltimore they tendered me a reception. But the story was printed and was believed. There is no use denying such things, and I did not do so.[3] When I went to Baltimore, however, I found out the man who wrote the article and sent for him. He came. He was a young man about my own age. I simply asked him what he was paid for writing the article. He said, "Six dollars." "Well," said I, "the rate for lying is not very high in America. That is all I wanted to ascertain. Good day."'

'It must have annoyed you considerably?'

'No. I mind nothing about their attacks but the effect they have on the public. I am not injured at all, but the public is deceived. After all, there is so much to do in life that there is not time to be troubled about such matters. Our duty is to admire and worship the beautiful and the good. Everything else, including the annoyances, is mere failures, simply shadows.'

'What are your impressions of the people as you have met them?'

'Ah, there is a wide difference between your papers and your men and women. From the latter I have always met with the kindest treatment. You have a great country, and the things that are said about me I am willing to bear. Of course the treatment is not fair. Some of our best lecturers would not come here, Ruskin, for instance, on account of the newspapers. When I declared I was coming they all wondered. "Why," said Mr. Ruskin, "everything will be said about you. They will spare nothing." But I said I would come, and I came. The feeling there is almost fear of your papers, but I do not mind it. The ludicrous things are said in good part, and as for the rest I let it pass me by.'

1   Henry Ward Beecher (1813–1887) was an American clergyman.
2   The *Baltimore American* had reported that Wilde demanded $300.
3   In fact, Wilde repeatedly denied the story.

'A Home Ruler', *St. Louis Daily Globe-Democrat* (St. Louis, MO), 27 Feb. 1882, 6

'What are your feelings with regard to the Land League?' queried a *Globe-Democrat* reporter of Oscar Wilde last evening.[1]

The 'aesthete' was sipping a glass of Appolinaris and smoking a cigarette. He promptly replied:

'As regards the general principle, that the only basis of legislation should be the general welfare of the people—and that is the only test by which the right of any citizen to hold property or possess any privileges should be tested—I am entirely at one with the position held by the Land League,' replied Mr. Wilde. He continued: 'The land of Ireland, like the land of England, is perfectly unfairly divided, and the peasantry of Ireland have never had the proper conditions necessary for any real civilization at all. They have lived in the most impoverished way, in a certain state of life in which the only opening for any improvement was for them to leave their own country.'

'In this connection,' interrupted the reporter, 'I will ask you, do you believe in the wholesale emigration of the Irish from their native land?'

The question was scarcely asked when Mr. Wilde replied, 'I shall always hope that there shall be some people left in Ireland.' After thinking a while he said: 'With regard to emigration from Ireland, it has a great deal of influence in one way—in the way of reaction from America, not merely in people returning from America, a people bringing with them money to an impoverished country, but in a reaction of American thought on Irish politics. This modern public spirit with Irish politics is an entirely new departure in the history of Ireland. It is due entirely to the reflex influence of American thought.'

The aesthete here lit a cigarette, and continued:

'With regard to the land bill, the mistake which I think the English Government are making is in thinking that they can permanently benefit one class in a community by permanently impoverishing the other. Up to this the gentry of Ireland have been rich and the peasant poor. They have merely transferred the burden from the peasant to the educated classes. They have not really alleviated the poverty of Ireland. They have merely removed its position and in one single act of legislation have swept away a great deal of the best civilization in Ireland. What I should wish to see would be the Government purchasing the land of Ireland from the landlords at a fair rate, giving them compensation as they gave the members of the Irish Church, and distributing that land amongst the people, issuing State bonds on which the people would pay an interest. This was the method adopted in Prussia, and it has there been in the highest degree beneficial.'

'What do you think of the "no-rent manifesto?"' asked the reporter.

'It is the one foolish thing that the Land League have done,' replied Mr. Wilde.

Charles Stewart Parnell, an Irish nationalist politician who served as a leader of the Home Rule League from 1880 to 1882.

'Why so?'

'Because,' replied he, 'it strikes at the root of all civilization, of all fair dealing and of all common sense.'

The 'no-rent manifesto' having been explained to Mr. Wilde, the latter replied:

'You must remember that a manifesto of that kind, besides the mere words of it, there is always a latent spirit in it which is always understood to mean more than it expresses. In Ireland it was understood to be absolutely "No rent," which, however, I have no doubt that the most thoughtful amongst the Land League would not approve of.'

'You know Parnell, Sullivan, McCarthy and other members of the Land League?'[2]

'I do,' he replied.

'Do you think that they would advocate anything unreasonable or nonsensical?'

'It is no compliment to generalize about a man,' answered Mr. Wilde. 'With regard to any agitation of this kind it is entirely a question of result. The means of every revolution are justified only by one thing—by the success of that revolution. A compulsory sale and a fair compensation clause seems to me to be the remedy for the present evil system of land tenure in Ireland.

'It is easy,' he added, 'for one to point out in revolutions great excesses, even great crimes. No measure probably in the world ever produced so much immediate suffering and immediate crime as the French revolution, and no measure was ever productive of such permanent good afterward. It is very easy to object to the means of a revolution, to lay one's finger on certain excesses; the only way to judge of an agitation is by the success. In a political party it is not a question of whether they were wise or fair; the only way we can tell whether they are wise is by their success.'

'Their measures are unwise if they do not succeed?'

'Certainly. Politics is a practical science. An unsuccessful revolution is merely treason; a successful one is a great era in the history of a country.'

'Are you in favour of the total separation of Ireland from the United Kingdom?'

'There is another folly,' replied Mr. Wilde. 'It is only a question of whether a country is able to assert its independence. At present, I think it would be unwise in Ireland to claim total separation, because I do not think she would be able to preserve it, and to attempt anything that one cannot do is the only crime in politics. The first step to do should be a local Parliament, which I sincerely hope they will get, and it is an issue which my father was one of the first men in Ireland to advocate.'

'Then,' said the reporter, as he took his leave, 'I may put you down as a Home Ruler?'

'You may,' he emphatically replied.

1   The Irish National Land League was seeking to transfer ownership of Irish agricultural land from landlords to tenant farmers. In 1881 they issued the No Rent Manifesto. Wilde's family owned land in Ireland and their tenants were among those who withheld rent.
2   Charles Stewart Parnell (1846–1891) was elected president of the Land League upon its formation in 1879, and became leader of the Irish Parliamentary Party in May 1882. 'Sullivan' may be Timothy Daniel Sullivan (1827–1914) or his brother Alexander Martin Sullivan (1829–1884), both of whom were affiliated with the Land League. 'McCarthy' is Justin McCarthy (1830–1912), an Irish nationalist and novelist.

'Oscar Back Again', *The Daily Inter Ocean* (Chicago, IL), 1 Mar. 1882, 8

Oscar Wilde is in the city for a short rest from his lecturing tour, and has rooms at the Grand Pacific. A reporter for *The Inter Ocean* called yesterday afternoon about 2:30 o'clock and sent up his card. The bell-boy returned in due time and said:

'Mr. Wilde is asleep, sah.'

'Did he tell you so himself?' asked the reporter.

'No, sah,' said the bell boy with dignity. 'His servant told me so, sah.'

The question then resolved itself into two points: should the reporter wait for Mr. Wilde to finish his nap, or should he 'rattle him up,' anyway, and remind him of his duty to society? After some mental debate the latter course was decided upon, and he climbed the stairs and stood in front of No. 11. All was still. A good solid rap on the door had the effect of producing a smothered sound from within, but whether it was an invitation to come in or go to… somewhere else, the reporter was not sure. He gave Mr. Wilde the benefit of the doubt, and rapped again. This time there was no mistake about it. 'Come in' was hurled at the door as if it was a boot-jack. The reporter entered. The room at first glance seemed empty, but it was pervaded by an unseen presence that seemed to fill it to the transom. But where was the aesthete? There was no couch in the room. The reporter even glanced under the sofa, although he well knew it was useless. Upon a chair were Mr. Wilde's sacred breeches: at a little distance a pair of exquisitely all-but gaiters, and near them a pair of ecstatic socks. Various other articles of *lingerie* were scattered around in graceful if somewhat careless forms, but the reporter had no time to take an inventory.

A voice came from the alcove which the reporter now saw for the first time, and which was concealed by a closely drawn lace curtain, saying:

'Where is my servant?'

'I don't know,' said the reporter, wishing he was at home, but taking off his hat to the pantaloons, gaiters, et al.

'Well, what do you want?'

'I am a representative of the press—'

Just then the missing servant came in out of breath, and brushing some cracker crumbs off his coat collar. Plainly, he didn't drink lemon-ade.

'I have been traveling night and day, and wanted some rest,' said the gentleman behind the curtains, while the servant looked as if he would like to receive an order to bounce the intruder. 'Ah, couldn't you come up again in an hour?'

'Certainly, I can,' said the reporter, thanking heaven for the escape: and he went down to the office and matched pennies with Sam Parker.[1]

When the appointed time had expired, the reporter rapped again at the door of No. 11, and upon entering was much relieved to see that the gaiters, etc., were no longer on the chairs, but were on the graceful form of Mr. Wilde. He was as cordial as ever, and seated the caller with great politeness. His dress was a black velvet smoking jacket, light brown pantaloons, or perhaps a wood color, socks of the same grade, and patent-leather shoes finished at the top with cloth off the same piece as the pantaloons. The room was arranged with an eye to picturesque effect. The chairs were draped with skins of beasts, and Mr. Wilde's own chair was ornamented with a silk shawl. A bright fire blazed in the grate, and the table was heaped with books, letters, and papers of all kinds.

'What were your impressions of St. Louis?' asked the reporter.

'In St. Louis,' he said, 'they have the best arranged museum of art that I have seen in America. The collections are not extensive, but all is most excellent and beautiful. It has the first quality of a good museum—nothing in it that could possibly lead a young art student astray. Of all things in it—oil paintings, plaster casts, or statuary—there is nothing but good.'

'That is high praise from such a source, Mr. Wilde,' said the reporter.

He swallowed the taffy without winking, and continued: 'But I think in America you are a little too exclusive—a great deal too exclusive—in your admiration for the French school. The examples of English art that I have seen in America all belong to the period of Benjamin West and Haydon, but of the modern school of English painters I have seen no examples.[2] I have not, for instance, seen in any of your public museums or private galleries any of John Millais' work.[3] He is one of the greatest painters that England has ever produced. He will be remembered with Gainsborough and Sir Joshua Reynolds as one of our greatest portrait

Christ in the House of His Parents (1849–1850) by John Everett Millais.

painters,[4] and no man now living in England, or, indeed, in the whole history of English painting, has done such a splendid amount of artistic work in style so entirely different. When he was a young man he belonged to the Pre-Raphaelite brotherhood, and was their greatest painter. His early pictures are full of the most beautiful imagination and most wonderful technical power, and his picture of *Christ in the Carpenter Shop* is the only beautiful religious picture, with the exception of Rossetti's *Annunciation*, that I have ever seen.[5]

'From the earliest poetical sentiment of his pictures, when he chose his subjects from Florentine legend and sacred story, he passed with an increased realism of technical power to nature drawn from the life of our day. *The Highland Woman Delivering the Order of Release to the Jailer for Her Imprisoned Husband*; the *Girl Bidding Good By to Her Sweetheart who is Going to the Wars*, are great witnesses of how much splendid imaginative work can be got out of modern life. Millais then passed to landscape, in which he is a really great master. His picture of *Chill October* is one of the most pathetic and beautiful landscapes I have ever seen; and lately his fame rests upon his powers as a portrait painter, in which he will rank with Sir Joshua Reynolds and Gainsborough. No one has painted children with such delicacy and love of the beauty of childhood and perfection of treatment as he since Reynolds painted

Penelope Boothby. No one has painted great men with such dignity and strength. His picture of Mr. Gladstone is one of the great pictures of this century, and he was painting one of Lord Beaconsfield at the time when that wonderful genius died. Any museum or gallery is quite incomplete without a specimen of his work.'[6]

'What do you think of the Mississippi River?' asked the reporter, getting ready to write 'grand,' 'majestic,' etc. He was surprised to hear Mr. Wilde say, quietly, and without a gleam of fun:

'I don't think a well-behaved river should run over that way, don't you know?'

The reporter thought it was rather reprehensible conduct.

'The want of pure water,' he continued, 'in each city, caused by the overflow, and the dreadful condition of the streets in nearly all the cities I have visited, seem to show a curious want of provision against what I suppose a not extraordinary test. It is quite impossible to have any art unless you have good air, good water, and clean cities.'

'You have visited a number of Western cities, have you not?'

'Yes; I have lectured at Cincinnati, St. Louis, Detroit, Cleveland, Indianapolis, Fort Wayne, Springfield, Ill., and some other cities.'

'How did you like Cincinnati?'

'In Cincinnati I was particularly pleased. There is not merely a great love of art, but of fine collections. Of course, all schools of art which are young and inexperienced will commit many faults; but still their work is very good, a great deal of it, and they are going to work in the right way.'

'You like the West better than the East, I believe?'

'The Western cities seem to be more distinctively American, and as such are objects of great interest to all Englishmen. In the West seems to be the civilization you have created by yourselves and for yourselves. So much in the East is a mere repetition of European thought, and so much that is a mere misunderstanding of it.'

'What do you think of the London press?'

The two best written papers in London are the *World* and *Truth*. You have already heard Mr. Edmund Yates, the editor of the *World*, when on his lecture tour.[7] He is a very brilliant lecturer. I understand Mr. Labouchère, editor of *Truth*, is to make a lecturing tour in America. I am sure you will be interested to hear him.'[8]

Henry Irving and Ellen Terry.

'Are not the poor people of England all "Radicals?"'

'There is no connection between poverty and radicalism, but there is between handicraft and republicanism. To work at any handicraft induces that sense of independence which is the key-note of all republicanism. In the great cities of England there is a constant spirit of discussion and certain clash of ideas which make men think for themselves, so that the political thought of England progresses always in the manufacturing towns, and never in the agricultural places. An agricultural laborer's view of politics is founded entirely on the weather.'

'Would you please talk a little about dramatic art?'

'Oh, yes: I love to do so. Henry Irving is our greatest tragedian. He stands at the head of our Shakespearean actors. He is a man of most curious and wonderful personality, with an interesting realism in his acting which was for us in London an entirely new departure from the new found school of Macready. He is certainly as great an artist as Charles Kean. If he comes to America he will bring with him our most beautiful and fascinating actress, Miss Ellen Terry.'[9]

'Do you not have a dramatic censor in London?'

'Yes. He would not allow Sarah Bernhardt to play *La Dame aux Camelias* for a long time, and has recently decided that the most moral system of British morality would be undermined if the Paris Royal Com-

Joseph Jefferson and Edwin Booth.

pany played *Divorçons*.[10] If there was a censor to prevent bad acting we would all support the office with all the means in our power, but, unfortunately, there is no law to prevent any man or woman from murdering any great part in public.'

'That kind of a censor would be popular in Chicago,' said the reporter. 'Do you think Mrs. Langtry will come to America?'

'She will probably come. She is one of the most beautiful women in the world. Her figure is molded like a Greek statue. She is not petite, and I wouldn't say she is tall. She is a perfect artistic height. She has a most beautiful voice. On the stage she has a joyousness of manner which is the beauty of all good comedy acting, and when she has studied her art she will be able to act Shakespeare's Rosalind in a way in which most of us have never seen the part.'[11]

'Better than Neilson?'[12]

'You can't compare artists, but you can easily compare mediocrity. I have not the slightest doubt of her dramatic genius. She is one of the most remarkable women of this age in England.'

How do you like Jefferson?'[13]

'I saw him in *Rip Van Winkle*. He is one of the greatest artists I have ever seen. His acting in London was, for all of us who loved and studied acting, one of the greatest we had ever seen in that play.'

'How do you like Booth?'

'Booth is a very, very great artist. He speaks English much better than almost any of our own actors. His perfect enunciation, perfect ideas of blank verse and knowledge of emphasis, and consciousness that when he is speaking Shakespeare he is speaking music is a source of the greatest delight to all of us in London. His acting of King Lear I consider to rank along with Salvini's Othello, Henry Irving's Shylock, or the greatest thing in acting I have ever seen.'[14]

'Do you like McCullough?'

'I saw him the other night in *Spartacus*. He is very strong, exceedingly powerful, and is a master of stage effects.'[15]

'You have seen Clara Morris?'

'Yes; she interested me wondrously. Sarah Bernhardt told me that there were only two things in America worth seeing, one was Clara Morris, and the other some dreadful way you have of killing hogs in the Chicago stock yards. I have seen Miss Morris; the other visit I have postponed indefinitely.'

'You lecture here again, I believe, Mr. Wilde?'

'Yes, at Central Music Hall, on Saturday evening, March 11, on "Interior and Exterior House Decoration."'

'Would you mind giving me a few points on the lecture?'

'No. I can't do that,' he said, good naturedly. 'But I will begin with the door-knob and end with the attic. Beyond that there only remains heaven, which subject I leave to the church.'

1   Match pennies is a game in which two players each secretly turn a penny to heads or tails. They then simultaneously reveal the pennies, with one player receiving both pennies if they match and the other player receiving them if they do not.

2   Benjamin West (1738–1820) was a painter of historical and religious subjects who was born in Pennsylvania and settled in London. Benjamin Robert Haydon (1786–1846) was an English painter who also specialised in historical paintings.

3   John Everett Millais (1829–1896) was an English painter and one of the founders of the Pre-Raphaelite Brotherhood.

4   Thomas Gainsborough (1727–1788) was an English portrait and landscape painter. Sir Joshua Reynolds (1723–1792) was an English portrait painter and the first president of the Royal Academy of Arts.

5   'Christ in the Carpenter Shop' is better known as *Christ in the House of His Parents* (1849-1850); Rossetti's 'Annunciation', as *Ecce Ancilla Domini* (1850).

6   The picture Wilde refers to as 'The Highland Woman Delivering the Order of Release' is better known as *The Order of Release, 1746* (1853). 'Girl Bidding Good By' is *The Black Brunswicker* (1860). *Chill October* was painted in 1870. Reynolds painted *Penelope Boothby* in 1788. Millais's portraits of children include *Cherry Ripe* (1879); his best known is *A Child's World* (1886). Millais painted William Ewart Gladstone, Prime Minister of the United Kingdom, in 1879, and his rival, Benjamin Disraeli, Earl of Beaconsfield (1804-1881), in 1881.

7   Edmund Hodgson Yates (1831-1894) was a British journalist, novelist, and dramatist. He toured America in the early 1870s.

8   Henry Du Pré Labouchère (1831-1912) was an English politician and journalist. He is best known for drafting the law criminalising all sexual activity between men under which Wilde was convicted in 1895.

9   Henry Irving (1838-1905) was an English actor. William Charles Macready (1793-1873) was an English actor who performed in several Shakespearian tragedies and histories. Charles Kean (1811-1868) was an Irish-born English actor. Ellen Terry was an English actress (1847-1928) who starred alongside Irving for twenty-four years. Irving and Terry embarked on their first American tour in October 1883.

10   *La Dame aux Camélias* is a tragedy about a courtesan that was adapted for the stage in 1852 by Alexandre Dumas fils (1824-1895) from his own 1848 novel. It was the play for which Sarah Bernhardt was most famous. She successfully toured North America with it in 1880-1881, and was permitted by the Lord Chamberlain to stage it in London in 1881. *Divorçons* (1880) was written by Victorien Sardou (1831-1908) and Émile de Najac (1828-1889). It treats of a young woman who decides to divorce her husband so she can marry an attractive scoundrel.

11   Langtry made her London stage debut in December 1881. Her visit to the US was confirmed in July 1882; she arrived in October and appeared in several roles, including Rosalind in Shakespeare's *As You Like It*.

12   Lilian Adelaide Neilson (1848-1880) was an English actress who toured America during the 1870s. In the years after her death she was often invoked as the standard against which new actresses should be measured.

13   Joseph Jefferson (1829-1905) was an American actor, most famous for his portrayal of Rip Van Winkle, a character he played for forty years.

14   Booth played Lear in London between February and March 1881. The Italian actor Tommaso Salvini (1829-1915) was by consensus the era's greatest Othello.

15   Wilde had seen the Irish-born American actor John McCullough (1832-1885) as Spartacus in *The Gladiator* on 19 February 1882.

'Professor Swing and Oscar', *The Daily Inter Ocean* (Chicago, IL), 6 Mar. 1882, 8

Professor David Swing's criticism of Oscar Wilde, published in the *Alliance* recently, seems to have been read by the latter and to cause him some annoyance.[1] Mr. Wilde was interviewed by a representative of *The Inter Ocean* on Saturday at the Grand Pacific Hotel in response to a written request from the apostle of the lily and kneebreech. He said: 'I lectured in Rockford, Ill., lately, and there learned that Mr. Swing's article had induced the lady principal of a seminary who had purchased a couple of tickets to my lecture to return them to the box office. The audience was small. I felt that an attack that could so influence a whole city must be at least remarkable, and I looked forward to reading it with pleasurable emotions. I usually pay no attention to newspaper ridicule or criticism, and have long ago learned to entirely disregard it. But next to having a staunch friend is the pleasure of having a brilliant enemy. There is nothing so depressing as to be attacked by a fool, for you cannot answer or fight him with his own weapons.'

'You have read the article, then?' said the reporter.

'Yes; but I confess to having been greatly disappointed at Professor Swing's article. If a man attacks one for the clothes that one likes to wear, he should go for his answer to the tailor who made them; and if he assails me for a preference in flowers, he should argue the matter with a gardener. As for his sneer at me for receiving a fee for lecturing, I can assure him that he is not the first clergyman who has thus condemned me. But this shaft loses its sting when I consider that it comes from a body of men, most of whom preach for a salary.

'I can only conclude,' continued Mr. Wilde, 'that Professor Swing did not attend my lecture. If he had done so he would have seen that I divided it into two parts, in the first of which I dwelt upon the necessity of teaching the handicraftsman to work not only with his hands, like a machine, but with his heart and with his head. If he does not do so his work will be nothing more than commonplace and have no beauty of art in it at all. I dwelt on the moral education that working in every art would give a man the two things upon which all good art is founded—truth and honesty. In the world of business it is possible for the liar and cheat to escape detection all their lives—not so in art. A workman who

The Chicago preacher David Swing, who attacked Wilde in the press.

creates a sham or does dishonest work in his art, such as painting wood to represent marble, or staining paper to represent stone, or pretending that a thing is solid when it is merely a hollow sham, knows that in consequence of it his work is worthless and will not last. In the second part of my lecture I treated of those who only look at art and do not create, the ordinary man or woman of life, and showed of what nature the refining influence of noble and beautiful art would be to them from their childhood to their manhood. I spoke of what influence the arts would have in producing between all countries a common, intellectual spirit, for no truth of history is clearer than this, that national hatreds are always strongest when civilization is lowest. I acknowledge that I am surprised to find that anyone with the name of David should be found fighting in the ranks of the Philistines. He ought to take a pebble from the banks of the Chicago River and hurl it at that monstrous Goliath of Chicago architecture, the water-tower, instead of praising it as being, as he calls it, calm and rational. Those two epithets are very unfortunate in this connection. Perhaps I am wrong in taking the Professor seriously, for, from what I have seen of American literature, I have found that the sermon of the divine is always humorous, and the writing of the humorous always depressing. I hope in my next lecture to dwell at length on the relations between art and morality, which have been so much misunderstood.'

'When will you lecture here again?'

'Next Saturday evening, in Central Music Hall, on "Interior and Exterior House Decorations."'

'Did you ever lecture in England?'

'No; I made my debut as a lecturer in New York City.'

1   David Swing (1830–1894) was a popular Chicago-based preacher. His critique of Wilde, published in the 21 February number of his magazine, *The Alliance*, was titled 'Oscar the Small'.

'Oscar Wilde', *The Omaha Daily Herald* (Omaha, NE), 22 Mar. 1882, 8

Mr. Wilde and his servant and Mr Vale, his business manager, arrived in Omaha yesterday from Sioux City and ensconced themselves at the Withnell house. The day without the four walls of the hotel was blustering and the wind swept occasional eddies of dust along the streets, rendering it very disagreeable for anyone not habituated to the climate who should venture out.

Consequently when *The Herald* ambassador was admitted to Mr. Wilde's presence toward evening after sending up his card, he found that gentleman not prepared to speak advisedly upon the architecture or other salient points of Omaha and the conversation was rather general in its scope. *En passant*, it may be remarked for the edification of those who desire to know how Mr. Wilde exemplifies his ideas of dress in private life, that his negligee consists of a black velvet jacket, dark trousers, leather gaiters faced with yellow cloth, and that a maroon silk scarf is tied at his throat and a handkerchief of like color and material peeps from the breast pocket of his jacket.

One of the first questions put by the *Herald* representative was:

'How do you find our western cities?'

'You have not the lower orders of the eastern cities,' replied Mr. Wilde. 'I find less prejudice and more simple and sane people.' He added, however, 'The west part of America is really the part of the country that interests us in England less, because it seems to us that it has a civilization that you are making for yourselves and by yourselves—not the complementary echo of British thought.'[1]

'You have pronounced ideas upon our architecture.'

'I find in all the eastern cities these general characteristics: the fault in American architecture is in an entire want of any definite conception of what style is suitable for your cities. The architecture should be as universal as the country and as easily understood. Most of the buildings are mere constructions of incongruous anachronisms.'

'You have plans for future work, I presume?'

'For my life, do you mean?' and Mr. Wilde laughed merrily and lighted a cigarette as he threw himself back in his chair. 'Well, I'm a very ambitious young man. I want to do everything in the world. I cannot conceive of anything that I do not want to do. I want to write a great deal more poetry. I want to study painting more than I've been able to. I want to write a great many more plays, and I want to make this artistic movement the basis for a new civilization.'

'That is the highest and greatest of all your ambitions, I take it,' said the interviewer. 'But do you consider that there is an organized aesthetic school?'

Mr. Wilde replied: 'There is a definite school of criticism and of attitude toward art. Up to this in England we have always had great artists, great portrait painters—for instance, in the last century; and the great landscape painters at the beginning of this age. But there has been an entire want of any concentration of artistic power. The great men stood, as it were, in a sort of sublime isolation, and their work was not understood by the common people and so not loved by them; and so both sides suffered, the artists missing the sympathy to which all artists are so sensitive; and the people not understanding their work. We, on the other hand, are concentrating all the stylistic genius of England, so that each art will gain and learn so much from its brother arts that the people will understand and love art more; for the decorative arts will indeed become part of their daily life. It will make beautiful the common vessels of the house, and it will become so natural to beautify their surroundings that even if the people wish to escape from it they will not be able.

'We also are making our artisans artists by giving them beautiful designs and noble models,—for all the decorative arts of England have been gradually falling into disuse and nothing that was made for the ordinary service of the house was either honestly made or beautiful. We look to this as the real strength of our movement. It is indeed to become a part of the people's life. It must begin not in the scholar's study—not even in the studio of the great artist, but with the handicraftsmen always. And by handicraftsmen I mean a man who works with his hands; and not with his hands merely, but with his head and his heart. The evil that machinery is doing is not merely in the consequences of its work but in the fact that it makes men themselves machines also. Whereas, we wish them to be artists, that is to say men. Now you see what we want.

'How do your audiences in the west impress you?' asked the interviewer.

'I should never wish—and no man could—to have a better audience, more simple, more understanding, more quick in their appreciation than the audiences I had in Chicago, Cincinnati and many of the western cities.'

Mr. Wilde remarked that he had seen many men of marvelous physique and many beautiful women in the west and this elicited his opinion that 'Physical beauty is really, absolutely the basis of all great and strong art.' He believes, too, that all true art work must be wrought by healthy and happy men and women.

1   The reporter almost certainly misheard Wilde. Elsewhere Wilde consistently expressed the opposite opinion: that he was more interested in the west than the east of America.

[J. A. Woodson], 'Oscar Arrives', *The Daily Record-Union* (Sacramento, CA), 27 Mar. 1882, 3

As a fitting introduction to the apostle of modern estheticism, a *Record Union* representative yesterday morning met Oscar Wilde at the depot with a bouquet of the choicest flowers that could be culled from Sacramento's floral wealth, and being received by that gentleman with cordiality, the twain sat down to breakfast and had a chat, which, being unconcluded when train time was up, the apostle and the news-gatherer, having found themselves upon pleasantly-debatable ground, continued the conversation in the cars as they went Bayward.

Mr. Wilde is one of the best talked about men of the day. This cultured young English poet is, his friends claim, the most misrepresented of foreigners that ever visited the country. The Oxonian, who is a genial companion and an admirable conversationalist, showed no disinclination to unbosom himself, and the determination being announced to give him for once a perfectly 'fair show' in a representative American newspaper, responded to the questions propounded to him with ready fluency and sincere earnestness. He is scarcely 26 years of age, very tall and quite slender. This 'build' gives him the appearance of slightly stooping in the shoulders when he addresses men of ordinary stature. He dresses plainly, to severity, indulges in a broad turn-down collar, a simple knotted scarf without jewelry, and wears a broad-brimmed white sombrero decidedly Spanish in style. His clean-shaven face is long, broadest at the lower jaw, with a full, round and over-sized chin; a large and well-developed nose, a broad mouth, with full lips opening over large, prominent teeth, the upper lip a shade too short, and eyes very full, large and handsome and an apology between gray and blue, are arched by delicately lined eyebrows. His forehead is high, narrows as it ascends, and on either side his straight brown hair, which from a middle parting falls to a level with his chin in unstudied negligence, and shades a neck rather long and with a tendency to crane forward.

The expression of his countenance is very amiable, and a constant smile of perfect content rests upon his over-full features, which are almost effeminate in apparent lack of vigor and force, but which in that respect belie the man, whose conversation proves him to be shrewd, perfectly self-possessed, and entirely able to take care of himself in this world. With a Chesterfieldian bow, he returned his thanks for a button-hole bouquet a Sacramento lady sent by the news-man for 'the lover of the beautiful,' and the esthete settled himself in the cushions of a palace car, and signified his readiness to be put upon the categorical rack.

The news-gleaner opened the ball: 'Are we to correctly understand you, Mr. Wilde, that your belief is that a true love for art for its own sake, and in its highest development, marks the best forms and systems of civilization most easily attainable?'

The Esthete—'Yes. Life without industry is barbarism; industry without art is barren. We should first teach the people to use their hands in the work of art. All that is artistic must begin in handicraft.'

'You have been quoted as pronouncing the devotion to beauty and the production of the beautiful as making a man's life immortal. Would you be understood as erecting that into a creed of a religion of culture?'

The Esthete—'The best service of God is found in the worship of all that is beautiful. Such a worshiper can do no wrong wilfully. We should remember that all things worthy should be satisfying. The religions of the world too often tell us to love the Creator without keeping in view the created things. How starved is such a belief—it sees the Creator and is blind to His work; it teaches of Him, but makes no effort to teach of His work's beauty and grandeur.'

'In one of your addresses, Mr. Wilde, you speak of the necessity of every household possessing the things that give pleasure to the user and were a pleasure to the maker. Do I understand from you by that, that if we surround ourselves and children by beautiful things, and keep both within, as you put it, "the atmosphere of fair things," that we will soonest bring the race to the purest state, and to despise and utterly forsake the vulgar and coarse and wicked?"[1]

The Poet—'Yes, indeed. The man who lives in such an atmosphere must be a better man, a better workman, a better citizen; and there will follow such a better civilization. The mistake in our educational systems has been that we have sought to teach truth abstractly. Great special truth must grow up in us. Truth comes to the child through the atmosphere of his surroundings. Purify that, and you purify him. Surround him by the beautiful, the useful and the good, and what must result? The theory of beautiful surroundings that finds expression in Europe is true of nations. The life of every nation is influenced by its surroundings. Taine, in the history of literature, is constantly turning to the hills and the valleys—to the scenery of England.[2] He could not resist it, nor dissociate them from his theme. Formerly the products of the man's mind were treated abstractly—the man was treated abstractly, and not as to his surroundings. The first thing to teach the boy is to use his eyes, his ears and his hands. But we are always trying to educate his mind before we give him a mind, for mind is creative. The child is endowed with intellectual faculties, but the mind is the result of growth;

and I need not say to what extent we control that. To a child the teaching of abstract truth is folly.'

'You conclude one of your lectures with the words: "The secret of life is in art."[3] Would you add a word, and tell us how the masses can best attain a knowledge and love of art?'

Mr. Wilde—'I hope that the masses will come to be the creators in art. That is what I mean—that art will some time cease to be simply the accomplishment and luxury of the rich; but the possession, as it is the rightful heritage, of all, poor and rich alike. The difficulty I have felt and met in America is, not that there is a lack of interest in art; not that they do not love it; not that they are not receptive—no, they have a great love for the beautiful—but the difficulty is that they do not hold the handicrafts in greater honor and respect. I would dignify labor by stripping it of its degradation, and that by developing all that is beautiful in the laborer's surroundings and opening his eyes to it. Ah! I would speak to the hard-working people, whom I wish I could reach through the prejudice that shuts them and me away from each other. Why, it is to the mechanics and workers of your country that I look for the triumph that must come. Why, back here in the West I met a railroad-repairer—a man working out on the line at a hard, laborious task. It was his daily business. He talked with me, wanted to know what we are trying to do. Why that man quoted Pope to me,[4] analyzed his method, discussed my positions with me, understood me, and where he doubted gave his reasons in homely phrases, but unmistakeably and clearly. He took an interest in the best of life; was keen, kindly, receptive and pugnacious in need, withal—altogether a charming fellow. Now, in England, in men of his class such a conversation would be simply impossible. Here I learn that a man is fairly representative of a myriad.'

'Mr. Wilde, the decorative art rage, as it is called, is thought by many to be indulged in to the extreme. Do you think there is a danger to the true art culture in the rush and push in the former line, or is it one of the signs of our renaissance?'

The Poet—'Oh, of course; for the people have not had the opportunity, in all respects, as yet to get on well, so they are constantly going wrong. Still the desire to go at all is something, and much has been and is being accomplished. But if this desire is to culminate in anything great, it must be by the affectionate study of art and beautiful things.

The truth about decorative art, like all in art, is to be revealed to those who are receptive of the beautiful. The present revelation is the cause of the revival in decorative art.'

'There is one question I much desire to ask you, whether you think the drama most popular now, the spectacular and the class that appeals more to the fancy and the eye and the emotions than to the intellect and the reason—whether it is not a stumbling block in the path to higher art culture?'

Mr. Wilde—'No, no. So far from that being the case, the fault I find with the modern stage is the departure from the true spirit that intended it for the pageant. In this modern life, where we have given up so much of color, so much of the beautiful, let us leave on the stage all we can in beauty of dress, in richness of scenery, in graceful groupings. The trouble is the controllers of the stage belittle these spectacular effects by sensational scenes of the most improbable kind, and work up all sorts of morbid situations, with flying trains and sinking steamers, and all that. The stage is art in action. See how much we have fallen away from that ideal. On the stage we should see all we can of rich color, beautiful drapery and grouping, and all things that will cultivate a taste among the people for beautiful and chaste things. When they thus see how beautiful things can be made by their surroundings, they will look to their own, and discover possibilities before unknown to them.'

'In your first address in America you spoke of the hope of perfection in your movement that you felt there was in America, because we are "young." Do you mean by that that the absence of the influence of the architecture, the art schools and culture of Europe, etc., is no drawback to our people in art advancement?'[5]

Mr. Wilde—'No art is better than bad art. I'd sooner the people studied no art than some of the bad art of Europe—they would be more receptive of the true when it does come to them. Why, sir, architecture in England is deteriorating. The handicrafts are falling into disrepute. Against this it is to be said that England has had great examples and eminent exemplars; but they have isolated ones, like Turner. They were surrounded by masses that did not appreciate them. They had admirers, votaries, supporters, but not in the masses. Against this non-appreciative spirit we are fighting. So I say that a new people, not under the dead weight of crowded Europe, give hope for quicker appreciation of the true and the beautiful. As I have said, "the very absence of tradition with you is the source of your freedom and strength."'[6]

'You have been much caricatured, and your theories much satirized. How has that affected your judgment of the American people?'

Mr. Wilde—'I rarely think of it; when I do, I think nothing of it. It does not in the slightest degree represent to me the strength or the sanity of a great modern nation. One must always remember that wisdom does not brawl upon the street. The voice of folly is always shrill and very loud, but it passes away. Of one thing I am convinced, and that is, the fool has no influence; he may for the moment—that is all.'

'*Harper's Monthly* criticises you in a little dash this month, and dislikes your extravagance and eccentricities.'[7]

Mr. Wilde—'Do you call that a little dash? I call it as cruel as it is unjust. Suppose it is true—admitting it for argument sake only—that people come to hear me out of curiosity? Well, I get a hearing, and still hope to do some good in my day. But it isn't true. I've found in America truly appreciative audiences. True, caricature and misrepresentation have excited curiosity. Why in Chicago I had an audience of 3,000 people, and spoke for an hour and twenty minutes. And only one man left the room before the close, and he came to apologize for the necessity requiring it. That speaks of appreciation, at least for respectful hearing. I think the West is very fair to those who address it.'

'So you do not fear ridicule?'

Mr. Wilde—'Indeed, no. I want what I have to advance to stand on its merit. I ask no quarter. I have not the remotest doubt as to which side will win. I think the school I am in will win, because it represents great principles, and they are working for us, no matter what I may do.'

'But has the press given you a fair show?'

Mr. Wilde—'Oh, the papers! They run in grooves a good deal. They might just as well take the other side. The praise of the man who can't understand me is quite as injurious as the abuse of any enemy can be. There is no limit to the nonsense some men will write if it raises the circulation of the paper from one to two.'

'What do you think of this country so far as you have had opportunity to observe? Does it come up to or fall below your preconceived ideas?'

Mr. Wilde (with a merry twinkle of the eye)—'My dear sir, I was sensible enough (pardon me) not to have any preconceived ideas about it. I came to see and learn. Well, thus far I find far more independence of thought here than in Europe.'

'You are reported as saying that the commercial spirit in England is killing nobility and purity.[8] Coupling this with your expression of hope for art culture in America, are we to infer that you think this nation of traders less sordid than your people?'

Mr. Wilde—'I mean the spirit of commerce is misunderstood. Some of the most beautiful cities have been built by commercial men, as Genoa, Florence, Venice. But in England men have been made machines, quite as soulless and ignoble as the whirling wheels of machinery. I don't speak now of the flood of bad patterns and ugly designs as resulting; but I speak of the injury to the workmen themselves, so deep that they cannot realize the nobility of life. In America I don't think it goes to that extent. I don't think the American workman will submit to such a position.'

'I have read in Emerson's essay on "The Poet" these words: "The beautiful rests on the foundations of the necessary." Do you agree with that sentiment, Mr. Wilde?'

The Esthete—'The moment art becomes a luxury it loses, for it must arise out of necessity. All art is the expression of the noble and joyous in life. Luxury gives us the gaudy, the vulgar, the transient. It may help but it never creates art. For instance, luxury gives great prices for French landscapes of the modern school. Now, while I admire French landscapes, the indulgence by luxury in them does not dignify American handicraft at all, or help home effort.'

'But, Mr. Wilde, if surroundings have so great an influence, does not the architecture, the great models, the atmosphere of art in Europe, account for the preference?'

Mr. Wilde—'Familiarity with the beautiful in architecture does not belittle it with him who appreciates it. It grows on you. Italy is the loveliest country of Europe, but Italy gives you no landscapes from her studios. You speak of the broad field for the study of the lofty and the beautiful and awe-inspiring in California. Well, it is not necessary to have great natural wonders at home to develop art. It is in the eye and the heart of the artist that we find the secret of success. The landscapes of Italy are all-satisfying, and so the Italian artist does not reproduce them. You must go to the cloudy, the misty lands, for great landscape painters—the blue and the golden light of Italy is unapproachable.'

'An American woman, Mr. Wilde, has written of beauty in lines with which you will accord, I presume: Mrs. Sarah J. Hale.[9] Never heard the lines? They are:

Beauty was lent to nature as the type
Of Heaven's unspeakable and holy joy,
Where all perfection makes the sum of bliss.

Mr. Wilde—'Yes, certainly.'

'By the way, Mr. Wilde, what do you in England think of the international copyright question?'

The Poet—'That a country gets small good from a literature it steals.'

'But you are retaliating now?'

Mr. Wilde—'Very little. It don't change the principle. Why, in all your cars I find newsmen selling my poems—stolen! I never can resist the impulse to read out a lesson on the heinousness of the offence.'[10]

'But there is a genuine American edition?'

Mr. Wilde—'Oh, yes! by a Boston house.'

'I heard you were getting out a work in America.'

Mr. Wilde—'That is a volume of poems by a friend, Rennell Rodd, an English officer. It will appear in Philadelphia.'

'Why not issue it in your own country?'

Mr. Wilde—'I desire to introduce the author to the American public. I think it will appreciate him. It will have an introduction that I have written. In that I point out the strong quality of this young man's work, and show how the artist can best use the life around him. Young workers in art are apt to go too blindly in. They perceive too often without rule or principle, and don't cultivate our sense of beauty. They are slow to perceive how all art is a desire for perfection.'

The conversation was continued at much length. What has been given exemplifies its tone and character.

Wilde has an apparently affected drawl in his speech, but it is evidently his normal style of delivery. Divest him of his flowing locks, add crispness to his enunciation and vigor to his tone, and there would be nothing about him to give ground for ridicule, except, perhaps, his expressive and languidly poetic eyes, the almost boyish fullness and effeminacy of his face, and the full lips that speak of the possible voluptuary. His friends on the train complained bitterly of the rudeness of the crowds at small stations on the road beyond the Sierras—especially of the attempt at Corinne, Utah, of a grotesquely-accoutered crowd, with a band, that sought to invade the car.

Some of the crowds will probably be chagrined to now learn that the Oscar Wilde many of them saw was not *the* Oscar Wilde, but was that inimitable comedian John Howson, of the Comley-Barton Opera Troupe, who, being on the train, several times put on his 'Bunthorne' wig, contorted his features into an admirable resemblance of the ever-dwelling smile on Oscar's countenance, and showed himself at times to save his friend and to have a bit of fun on his own account.[11]

At Sacramento there was no embarrassing staring at Wilde, and no crowd gathered about him. He was not subjected either to any vulgar inquisitiveness by the great crowd on the Oakland ferry-boat. The people hunted him out, glanced at him and passed on without offensive staring.

Mr. Wilde expressed often his warm admiration for what he had seen of America and its people. In all his conversation many will be disappointed to learn he never used the words 'superlatively beautiful,' 'ravishingly beautiful,' 'too utterly utter,' 'too too,' or any phraseology to which ridicule and satire have given point as to esthetes.

The poet, esthete and romantic philosopher, will remain on the coast three weeks, and will put in one day at Sacramento, when all the curious can for themselves see the present lion of curiosity.

These things impressed the press representative yesterday after a long conversation with Mr. Wilde, and after observing him in a great crowd of representative people and making note of their expressions. He is scholarly, studiedly polite, a gentleman, shrewd, fearless, observant, self-possessed and of poetic temperament. He has been considerably misrepresented and unduly ridiculed. He is apparently sincere and earnest. He is, however, ludicrously odd to the American eye in personal appearance; is eccentric (or affected) in this regard, and lacks the manifestations of manliness in his countenance, and frequently in his manner. If he was more an object of curiosity than respect to Californians yesterday it was due to the latter causes, to the ridicule showered on him at the East, and in part to the present public conception of the tendency of his teachings.

1   The reporter refers to Wilde's lecture, 'The English Renaissance': 'So, in years to come there will be nothing in any man's house which has not given delight to its maker and does not give delight to its user. The children, like the children of Plato's perfect city, will grow up "in a simple atmosphere of all fair things"'.

2   Hyppolyte Adolphe Taine (1828–1893) was a French critic and historian. His *History of English Literature* was published in five volumes in 1863.

3   'The English Renaissance' ends: 'We spend our days, each one of us, in looking for the secret of life. Well, the secret of life is in art.'

4   Alexander Pope (1688–1744) was an English poet.

5   'The English Renaissance': 'It is rather, perhaps, to you [America] that we [the English] should turn to complete and perfect this great movement of ours [....] For you, at least, are young; "no hungry generations tread you down," and the past does not weary you with the intolerable burden of its memories nor mock you with the ruins of a beauty, the secret of whose creation you have lost.'

6   'The English Renaissance': 'That very absence of tradition, which Mr. Ruskin thought would rob your rivers of their laughter and your flowers of their light, may be rather the source of your freedom and your strength.'

7   The *Harper's* article argues that Wilde's audiences go to see him chiefly because of his 'oddities of apparel', and that his complaints about America are unjustified as he would have been treated in much the same manner if he had toured in knee-breeches in England.

8   'The English Renaissance': 'For there can be no great sculpture without a beautiful national life, and the commercial spirit of England has killed that; no great drama without a noble national life, and the commercial spirit of England has killed that too.'

9   Sarah Josepha Hale née Buell (1788–1879) was an American writer and editor.

10   In 'Personal Impressions of America' Wilde would describe his encounter with newsboys who sold pirated copies of his *Poems*: 'Calling these boys on one side I told them that though poets like to be popular they desire to be paid, and selling editions of my poems without giving me a profit is dealing a blow at literature which must have a disastrous effect on poetical aspirants. The invariable reply that they made was that they themselves made a profit out of the transaction and that was all they cared about.'

11   John Jerome Howson (1842–1887) was an Australian comic actor. The Comley-Barton Opera Company's production of *Patience* was authorised by Carte.

'Oscar Wilde', *The Daily Examiner* (San Francisco, CA), 27 Mar. 1882, 2

Oscar Wilde arrived in this city at noon yesterday by the overland train. The news that he was on the train induced hundreds of curious persons to go over to the Oakland depot in order to catch a first glimpse of this new lion. To these persons a cursory inspection revealed a tall, well-built, clean-shaven, eccentrically-dressed young man with remarkable features, a somber, melancholy face, lighted up at intervals in the conversation going on around him and directed entirely at him, by a frank, pleased smile that came readily and passed away quickly, leaving the face in repose, as before. Wherever he moved the crowd, guided by a large, wide-brimmed, white slouch hat he wore, followed, not obtrusively, but quietly and respectfully. Mr. Wilde was dressed in a style that would attract general attention anywhere outside of an artist's studio or chambers, and there was no need for anyone to point in order to identify him. From beneath his large white hat fell long light-brown hair, reaching in somewhat straggling masses to the shoulders, half hiding a face inclined to sallowness. A close-fitting black velvet frock coat showed off strong, square shoulders, manly waist and hips. Pants dun brown, highly polished pointed shoes, a velvet waistcoat, low, wide collar, puce-colored tie folded wide, yellow gloves completed the appearance in dress of the outward man. A boutonniere, somewhat withered, made up of heliotropes, a brightly-foliated daisy and a tuberose, decorated his coat front. A dark olive-green summer overcoat was carried carelessly over his left arm, and the right hand, when not resting lightly against the chin as if aiding the poet in thought, grasped a thick ivory cane. Thus the object of curiosity appeared to those who yesterday saw him crossing the bay to this city.

A quiet conversation with Oscar Wilde would have disclosed nobler material than dress anomalistic of the man. Unfortunately this converse could not be had yesterday in the rush of car and boat, each bend in their rapid onward flight cityward, revealing to the ardent lover of nature scenes of picturesque beauty, silencing ordinary speech and thought; a changing panorama of soft murky outlines and hazy tints of color, the center always the sea-green bay, spangled with grassy Yerba

Buena, and the gold of Alcatraz, which sparkled like brilliant splotches against indistinct backgrounds of black and indigo, coloring the far-off, woody mountain summits and curving shore-lines; the Golden Gate lost in a sunlit mist beyond;[1] San Francisco's hills, roadways, houses, dimly seen; at its feet a mist from which rose the tall, straight masts of merchant ships, tapering above the mist that hung over the wharves. Not alone the poet, but everyone ending the weary journey here were impressed by what to nearly all was the first view of the 'uttermost Occident.' Mr. Wilde was met at Port Costa by several persons, who, for one reason or another laid a claim to his attention, among them an *Examiner* representative. All were met with the quiet, dignified courtesy of a gentlemen and a man of the world. In speaking Mr. Wilde preserves a cold but polite and attentive air, and it is only when some favorite subject is touched upon that the face lights up and the gray–green eyes seek those of the person who has aroused his deeper attention, and smiles encouragement or appreciation. The long, rather thin face, the pointed chin and well-shaped nose seem to feel the influence of the smile, and an otherwise homely face appears momentarily handsome. A second later, the spurt of enthusiasm or interest having passed, the face becomes again immobile, the eyelids lower, the eyes grow dull with a far-away glance, or seek the ground as the tall body bends slightly to come to a nearer level with its companion.

Talking, Mr. Wilde speaks in a low, melodious tone, the broad English pronunciation being harmonized almost to rhythm. He gesticulates very little, and from constant practice has a habit of brushing loose hairs back behind his ears.

After apologizing for the intrusion, the reporter asked Mr. Wilde if the trip overland was a pleasant one?

'Partly,' he replied, 'but excessively long and tedious.'

'Does the mountain scenery meet your expectations?'

'Hardly; I saw it at an unfavorable time, I suppose. The view from the top of the Sierra Nevadas, however, was beautiful.'

'Do you like our country, Mr. Wilde, or are you disappointed with America and Americans?'

'There is very much here to like and admire. The further West one comes the more there is to like. The Western people are much more genial than those of the East, and I fancy that I shall be greatly pleased with California.' Mr. Wilde merely smiled when told that California audiences would never think of showing him disrespect, and the only thing that might appear annoying to him will be the curiosity of all classes to see the man who has lately been so much read and talked about. 'I like your country and its people,' he said, as though apologizing for the latter.

'There is something quickening in the young life of a powerful nation. There is a wonderful opportunity for the growth and expansion of art in a country where a national life is unfolding. But there are too many amateurs here. Amateur art is worse than no art.'

Reporter—'Mr. Wilde, do your admirers believe that you have created a new school of poetry?'

Oscar Wilde—'They certainly should not—that is if I have any admirers. The Pre-Raphaelite school, to which I belong, owes its origin to Keats more than to anyone else. He was the forerunner of the school, as was Phidias of Grecian art,[2] Dante of the intensity, passion and color of Italian painting. Later, Burne-Jones in painting and Morris, Rossetti and Swinburne in poetry, represent the fruit of which Keats was the blossom.'

The turn which the conversation had taken had evidently aroused Mr. Wilde from apathy, for his face and manner showed that he was thoroughly interested in the theme. The reporter improved the occasion to remark: 'Judging from the tenor of your own poems, I fancy that "Charmides" (pronouncing the name with the soft accent) is your favourite poem, Mr. Wilde?'

'Char—Charmides,' he replied correcting; 'yes, that is my favourite poem. I think it my best. It is the most finished and perfect. The people of America have taken very kindly to my "Ave Imperatrix," however.'

'Perhaps a feeling of nationality prompts this choice.'

Mr. Wilde—'Probably so.'

Reporter—'Does the "Sonnet to Liberty" voice your political creed?'

Oscar Wilde—'You mean the sonnet beginning:

"Not that I love thy children, whose dull eyes
See nothing save their own unlovely woe,
Whose minds know nothing, nothing care to know" ——

'No, that is not my political creed. I wrote that when I was younger. (Mr. Wilde is 26 now.)[3] Perhaps something of the fire of youth prompted it.'

Mr. Wilde's recital of the lines was surprisingly impressive and pleasing, a perfect modulation and an earnest, almost pathetic tone giving the recital deep interest.

'If you would like to know my political creed,' he said, after a short pause, 'read the "Libertatis Sacra Fames"—I think it is the seventh sonnet.'

The sonnet referred to is as follows:

Albeit nurtured in democracy,
    And liking best that state republican
    Where every man is kinglike, and no man
Is crowned above his fellows, yet I see,
Spite of this modern fret for Liberty,
    Better the rule of One whom all obey
    Than to let clamorous demagogues betray
Our freedom with the kiss of anarchy.
Wherefore I love them not whose hands profane
    Plant the red flag upon the piled-up street
    For no right causes, beneath whose ignorant reign
Arts, Culture, Reverence, Honor—all things fade,
    Save Treason and the dagger of her trade,
    And Murder, with his silent, bloody feet.

'Mr. Wilde, one of your critics has denounced your poetry as impure and immoral.'[4]

'A poem,' replied Mr. Wilde, 'is well written or badly written.[5] In art there should be no reference to a standard of good or evil. The presence of such a reference implies incompleteness of vision. The Greeks understood this principle, and with perfect serenity enjoyed works of art that, I suppose, some of my critics would never allow their families to look at. The enjoyment of poetry does not come from the subject, but from the language and rhythm. Art must be loved for its own sake, and not criticised by a standard of morality.'

The conversation turning somewhat upon his life, Mr. Wilde said that he felt proud of his Irish birth and parentage. 'I live in London for its artistic life and opportunities,' he said. 'There is no lack of culture in Ireland, but it is nearly all absorbed in politics. Had I remained there my career would have been a political one.'

'When do you expect to return to London, Mr. Wilde?'

'If lecturing does not kill me, very soon.'

'Then you do not like lecturing?'

'Yes, I do,' he responded quickly. 'I like lecturing because it brings me face to face with those I desire should hear me. In England this is impossible.'

By this time the train had run into the new depot on Long Wharf, and the passengers filed into the waiting-room. Here the conspicuous figure of the coming lecturer attracted general attention. Even the shaggy fur overcoat, made famous by Du Maurier's sketches in *Punch*, caused a crowd to gather where the porter laid it with a valise in the corner.

On the ferryboat Mr. Wilde placed himself so that his back was turned to the crowd. The sights on the bay interested him greatly, and he asked many questions about the city, whose streetways, appearing like huge bleached ribs of a gigantic skeleton with the head pointing oceanward, were distinctly visible.

He asked many questions about the Chinese, and had the Chinese quarters pointed out to him. Speaking of Chinese art, he said that it possesses no element of beauty, the horrible and grotesque appearing to be standards of perfection. 'Their art and music,' he said, 'are extraordinary developments of national life. I have seen much that is admirable in Japanese art but nothing of excellence in Chinese art.[6] When I was a lad I heard a Chinese fiddle, or so it was called, at the Paris Exposition, but I could discern no music in it. When the Shah of Persia was in London the only music he cared for was the violin.' In answer to a question as to whether the harbor is fortified, Alcatraz and Fort Point were pointed out.

Mr. Wilde impressed all those with whom he came in contact as being 'a veray parfit gentil knight.'[7] His manner is courteous, deferential and self-possessed, his language clear and forcible, without ever descending to those excesses commonly attributed to him as daily talk. Nothing in his manner would attract unusual attention, and certainly not ridicule.

The Market-street slip reached, Mr. Wilde and his agent, Mr. Vale, took a carriage for their hotel.

1   Yerba Buena and Alcatraz are islands in San Francisco Bay. The Golden
     Gate is the strait that connects the bay to the Pacific Ocean (the Golden
     Gate Bridge spanning the strait was built in 1937).
2   Phidias (c. 180–430 BCE) was a Greek sculptor and architect. His works
     include the lost massive chryselephantine sculptures of Zeus for the
     Temple of Zeus at Olympia and of Athena for the Parthenon.
3   Wilde was 27.
4   This is presumably a reference to Thomas Wentworth Higginson (1823–
     1911), an American minister and author. In February he had published an
     article in which he questioned Wilde's masculinity and the morality of
     his poems.
5   Wilde would later write in the preface to his only novel, *The Picture of
     Dorian Gray*: 'There is no such thing as a moral or an immoral book.
     Books are well written, or badly written. That is all.'
6   Wilde would revise his opinion of Chinese art after visiting San Fran-
     cisco's Chinatown.
7   The reference is to Geoffrey Chaucer's *The Canterbury Tales*.

Mary Watson, 'Oscar Wilde at Home', *The Daily Examiner* (San Francisco, CA), 9 Apr. 1882, 1

The English language is popularly supposed to be a vehicle of expression
that was perfected long ago. It is intended not to conceal but to express
thought, and only persons who labor after originality, like Robert Browning,[1] for instance, give themselves the trouble to twist its words into
new meanings. Yet, strange to say, there are two words in the English
language which of late are employed as frequently as any other two that
could be named, if we make due exception of 'charming' and 'awful,'
and they are 'aesthetic' and 'utter,' about the signification of which
there seem to be no general agreement; yet all concede that they apply
to an unknown quantity in artistic niceness, and at once the more complex form of intensified aestheticism in the shape of 'utter' presents
itself. The most agreeable and perhaps the most effective solution of
the much-used word outside of dictionarial definition would be to get
the meaning from the fountain head, that is, from the apostoletic source
of Aestheticism, Oscar Wilde himself. I saw the lion in his lair, saw
him stirred up, poetically speaking, and an interesting process it was. It
took place at the Palace Hotel, where the young poet resided during

his stay here. Without further preliminaries I will endeavor to picture Oscar Wilde's at-home manner and how he exists in so unaesthetic a caravansary as the Palace Hotel. Fortunately, there was plenty of time to get a good look at the room and peer about without transgressing any social rules, for when I arrived, as per appointment, there was no one but his servant at home, and the opportunity was afforded to get an uninterrupted few moments and jot down whatever there was remarkable. Between the fear of not seeing everything and of his sudden arrival, I could only get cursory glimpses of all the peculiarities the room offered, and had little time to think of what I was to ask him when he did make his appearance. At any rate, all the questions that I had in my mind in reference to Mr. Wilde flew from me when he entered a few moments after I did.

And my hard effort to explain in a depressed sort of way, occasioned by my feeling of strangeness, soon made matters rather one-sided. He talked, and talked well, and soon I regained my ordinary frame of mind, but with still a misgiving as to how to broach my subject; but his action in throwing off his circular cloak, the quick and well-rehearsed movement of the servant, who reached the center of the room just at the right moment to catch the outside wraps of the poet, and his subsequent position on the sofa, partaking rather of an easy posture, half reclining, half sitting, set me quite at ease; and the poet, whom I had expected to lead me in the empyrean ways of poetic fancy, for which I was half prepared, made me believe so utterly in the mere commonplace that I felt a sense of disappointment, for it is so awful to believe in a man's superiority and then find him out. The rooms were of the usual hotel order, with the walls as innocent of cheerfulness as the sunless light which filtered in from the window. It suggested a question and I haphazarded it.

'How do you manage to live in these rooms without any surrounding signs of the beautiful?'

Quoth he, with an accompaniment of a rather comfortable shudder, 'Don't mention it.'

Since the request of not mentioning it was so vigorously put to me, I dropped the question of the beautiful in art, or whatever else was in my mind pertaining to the subject, and naturally did what ninety-nine people out of every hundred, when a lack of material for conversation occurred, would do. I spoke of myself.

'Is not this something new for you, Mr. Wilde. You have never met a lady reporter?'

'No,' replied he, smilingly; 'I have not. We do not have them in our country.'

I looked toward the bay-window, wherein was placed a table, and on it a vase with a large bouquet of white flowers, beautifully arranged, and, to give it effect, a silk handkerchief had been thrown carelessly across the two lower branches, and the air coming from the window swayed the ends in graceful movements. Glancing from the top of the table to the floor, the pile of newspapers met my gaze, and naturally suggested the next question:

'Are you pleased at the newspaper reports of yourself and the reporters' interviews?'

Evidently this had struck a rich vein, for he looked up with a peculiar and hearty smile; but, evidently remembering that his questioner was of the same genus as the subject spoken about, he seemed to restrain himself; but replied, with a laugh:

'Frankly, then, I read them all, and not only here but all over America I have been quite amused at the struggle each of the gentlemen have had to write what I did not say; but I have the most sympathy with the writers of the articles which strive to be what is called here in the United States "funny." Their hard work has been so apparent.'

From this on the conversation was quite easy, and Mr. Wilde displayed a fund of shrewd common sense hardly to be expected from an art enthusiast and a poet. The conversation on his part which followed gave me full opportunity to memorize the disposition of every article in the room, and that a certain eccentric individuality of the man was displayed in every phase of the furniture could not be gainsaid. There were three tables in the room, the one mentioned in the embrasure of the bay-window, one inside the room and one about the center, and all in a row. The sofa on which the poet was reclining was on the left hand and the mantel on the right. On the table where the striking posy of white flowers was placed were also strewn in confusion scraps of paper, letters, books, etc., and at the foot the newspapers, which fortunately suggested the opening of a conversation which by this time was flowing along smoothly enough. On the table in the center of the room were also a lot of papers and cards from various business houses, evidently intended to convey to the much advertised aesthete the pleasure every merchant would have in showing him his wares, to be used in the future as an advertisement no doubt. On the table near the window and about four feet from the other was a large silver fruit-dish, filled with oranges, two plates and a knife, and placed there innocently enough as a living example of an effective and suggestive picture of still life. On the sofa was carelessly thrown a dark brown rug with a pillow, over which was thrown a crepe shawl of the same color, with long fringe to match. During our conversation several cards were handed in, and among other things the servant brought in an autographic album with some one's compliments and a request for Mr. Wilde's little contribution to the general collection. He arose, seated himself at the table with the open book before him, and in a posture which excellently expressed 'thought,' he tried to evolve something for the inevitable autograph-hunter and great American nuisance. The inspirational mood was not on him then. He arose, gracefully spread his arm over an almost impossible distance, and, with an admirable breadth of reach, got hold of a copy of his own poems, sat down again and said to me:

'One sometimes forgets one's own lines.'

The struggle was short and had to be given up, so he bade the servant—

'Tell the messenger to leave the album, as I am too much engaged just now.' This with a glance at me.

A few moments later, another autograph album was sent in and the message repeated—without the glance, however. He then wheeled the sofa in front of me and threw himself upon it—not, of course, lying down, but in a careless posture, with his arm thrown careless over the pillow. I got a good glance at his necktie, and I noticed that the handkerchief in his coat pocket and the scarf were of exactly the same tint of satin—a peculiar shade of olive bronze.

Among the other questions, and they were a legion, I asked him:

'At what hour of the day do you find it most convenient to write?'

'At no particular hour. In writing a verse I sometimes wait for the exact mood, and it takes weeks at times before I get the right word to express my thought in the completion of a sentence or a line. Sometimes a subject is presented to me when I least expect it, perhaps in a company of friends, perhaps traveling, or in a crowded street.'

The manuscript of John Keats's untitled poem on blue, given to Wilde in America by the poet's niece.

In an animated conversation, and especially about himself, Mr. Wilde, in a youthful sort of way, becomes quite enthusiastic. From the conversation which followed I gathered that he was born at No. 1 Merrion Square, Dublin,[2] and that his mother, of whom he seems very proud, inspired him with a desire to become a poet. He showed me her picture, and, from her portrait, she seems to be a handsome woman of about 47,[3] with a clear sunny expression of face, and not at all like a woman who is given to writing poetry. Mr. Wilde does not resemble his mother a particle, although there seems to be a deep bond of sympathy between them. He assured me that until the age of 18 he never thought of writing a line; and in proof that others have the same enthusiasm, and entertain the same views of poetry, art and literature as himself, he pointed out the fact that a young classmate of his has written a volume on the same subject and dedicated it to Mr. Wilde himself. Mr. Wilde is now having it published and it will be out shortly.[4] He showed me a bit of manuscript which he declared he appreciated, and valued above anything which had ever been given him. It was the original manuscript of 'An Ode to Blue,' written by Keats in a handwriting peculiarly dainty and small. The manuscript, old and yellow, was presented to Mr. Wilde on his recent visit to Louisville. While there, he received a note from a young lady asking him to call, signed simply Miss Keats. It was from this lady, to whom the poet was a relative, that the young disciple received his treasured ode.[5] That Mr. Wilde is not sure of his ground, nor has he a fixed idea, is best illustrated by his reply to a question relative to his new book. He said: 'My other book may be a perfect contradiction of the first;' and, on being asked about his return to England, he said: 'I don't know. I never make plans, but go whither my feelings prompt. I wish, however, to be back in time for the salons.'

Mr. Wilde regrets exceedingly that he entered into a contract with Sarony, the New York photographer, not to have anyone else take his pictures while in this country.[6] He admires the pictures produced by some of our local photographers, and, in an art sense, apparently believes in the superiority of San Francisco workmanship to that of New York. He had some fine specimens from the principal photographers of the city. On being asked as to the age expressed in the last words of his poem, which interests all women —

'I have made my choice, have lived my poems,
   and though youth is gone in wasted days,
I have found the lover's crown of myrtle better
   than the poet's crown of bays!'[7]

He replied: 'Sometimes one feels older at 20 than he will at 40.'

During his conversation about his poems he certainly evidenced a belief in them and gave way to his enthusiasm by frequent gestures. His voice, in ordinary conversation, does not partake of the same tone as that used on the rostrum, nor are the same unpleasant monotones employed with all their faulty intonations. Youthful fervor carries with it a sense of truth, and if the word 'utter,' as expressed by this aesthete, means ardor, coupled with a sense of art and what is beautiful in the world, it is a good word and ought to be a welcome one in our vocabulary, which, after all, is not replete with adjectives expressive of things that are beautiful, as a lady reporter can testify.

1   Robert Browning (1812–1889) was an English poet and playwright.
2   Wilde was born at 21 Westland Row; the family moved the short distance to 1 Merrion Square when Oscar was aged one.
3   Lady Wilde had recently turned sixty, but perhaps the picture that Wilde carried was not recent.
4   Rennell Rodd's *Rose Leaf and Apple Leaf*.

5   Emma Speed née Keats (1823–1883) was the daughter of George Keats, the poet's younger brother. She wrote to Wilde on 12 March, enclosing the manuscript of an untitled poem on blue. Wilde later displayed the manuscript in his study (see p. 214); it was sold in the 1895 auction of his household effects.

6   Napoleon Sarony (1821–1896) was an American photographer with studios in New York's Union Square. He specialised in celebrity portraits.

7   The closing lines of 'ΓΛΥΚΥΠΙΚΡΟΣ ΕΡΩΣ'.

'Oscar Wilde', *Rocky Mountain News* (Denver, CO), 13 Apr. 1882, 8

The esthete has come. The man whose life and talents are devoted to the study and cultivation of the beautiful, and the business of making money, has arrived in this prosaic city, where dollars and cents rank high, and where beauty is valued only for its money value.

Last evening's train over the Cheyenne division was delayed about half an hour, and seated in the drawing room car of that train was the much talked of Oscar Wilde, who manifested some regret and annoyance at the unexpected delay. The esthete is not handsome, and yet he is remarkably fine-looking. About his person there is an air of refinement, culture and grace that makes a striking contrast to the typical American man. Oscar wilde is tall and elegantly proportioned. His head is not large, and yet it is good-sized. His hair, a dark brown, is parted nearly in the middle and is worn long, giving him a somewhat peculiar appearance. His face is long and oval in shape. He wears no beard or mustache, his mouth is rather large and the lips are full and as bright colored as a girl's. His teeth are large and not particularly handsome, his forehead is low. His eyes are extremely beautiful; they are blue and very large. His nose is long and thin, and if breeding and blood are indicated by the nose, Mr. Wilde can lay claim to a large quantity of the genuine 'blue.' His complexion is so clear and beautiful that the maidens may well grow green with envy, for no balm or powder can give to their cheeks the peculiar beauty of the esthete's complexion. His hands are well-shaped, his fingers long and tapering as if made to handle beautiful objects or wield the pen while the poetic mind dictates words of fire. His feet are large and well proportioned to his body. Taken all in all, Mr. Wilde can be truly called an elegant looking gentleman.

His looks would indicate that he was the descendant of a well-bred, fine, old English family, and his conversation marks him as a man of sense, strength and sympathy. During repose his face might be called plain, but when conversing his eyes grow bright, the color rises to his cheeks, his gestures are free and easy, and he is the picture of animation.

On the train last evening he wore a pair of dark brown trousers, well cut and neat fitting, and a black velvet coat, rather after the fashion of a sacque. It was cut high in the neck, leaving visible only the necktie, which was a cream colored silk scarf tied in a large bow. His collar was of fine white linen, and was not noticeably large. He wore a long heavy overcoat of *gen d'arme* blue cloth, lined throughout with fur, a broad fur collar and deep cuffs finishing the outside, of this handsome garment. Around his neck, a gold-colored embroidered scarf hung untied. The ends were fringed. Upon leaving the car, the scarf was carelessly drawn close about the neck under the overcoat. Upon his head Mr. Wilde wore a large black, or deep blue, slouch hat. Upon the third finger of his right hand he wore a large handsomely carved intaglio ring which was his only ornament.

After shaking hands with *The News* representative Mr. Wilde at once entered into conversation with an ease that is not ordinary even among public speakers. His voice is pleasant to listen to and gives one the impression of much power, yet he always talks in a monotone which must grow tedious. He talks rapidly, uses beautiful language and pronounces his words in a way which Americans will be very apt to call affected. His gestures during conversation are graceful and yet very emphatic.

Sinking back into the seat and assuming a comfortable position, Mr. Wilde said:

'Yes I am very sorry about this delay. I fear I shall be obliged to keep the audience waiting.'

Upon being asked how he was impressed with the country through which he had recently passed, he said:

'Oh everything looks so brown, bare and disconsolate. You know I have just come from California, which is a garden of beauty. Oh, it is so lovely! The cities of the Atlantic coast look bare and dreary at this time of the year. You know, at home, in England, it is always green. We have only the little island and it is well-tilled, every inch of it. It is always beautiful. For five months I have been longing for that garden spot, and California was such a delight to me. The green was such a rest to my weary eyes. It is the most restful of all colors. The California people are delightful; I disliked to leave San Francisco and should love to visit it again.

Mr. Wilde then asked a question which is only natural, considering what the ride from Denver to Cheyenne is. He inquired:

'What is there beautiful in Colorado?'

Being desirous of obtaining the esthete's views of the cities he had visited, the reporter said:

'Mr. Wilde, if it is not impertinent to ask, which city of those you have visited have you found the most esthetic?'

Mr. Wilde, smiling a little sarcastically, replied: 'You cannot ask an impertinent question of me. But really I cannot specify any one city. New York being so near Europe has many of the characteristics of a foreign city. Boston and Philadelphia both are paying considerable attention to art. But what especially pleased and interested me were the cities further removed from the Atlantic coast. Cincinnati has an art school and a good one, a school of wood-carving. Chicago people are very enthusiastic over art. I had large audiences in that city. I talked to about 3,300 people, who listened with the closest attention to all I had to say. St. Louis, too, is full of people who are interested in art, and San Francisco—'

Here Mr. Wilde was interrupted, but it is safe to infer all he had to say was in hearty praise of the esthetic movement among the dwellers in the city of the golden gate.

'You would bring art into the humblest houses, would you not? You would have art among the multitude? Is that your doctrine?' queried the reporter.

'It is. Art, but not poor amateur art.'

Here Mr. Wilde shook his head in a disgusted manner and said:

'We had better have no art than bad art. We can live without art but we cannot live with bad art. Let our architects build good, substantial houses and let them be beautiful if they can. Let our chairs and tables be made first for use and second for beauty. Estheticism should begin with the handicraftsmen and when it does we will have more beautiful homes than we have at present.'

'What about estheticism in dress?'

'Women's dress at present is too sombre, more bright colors should be worn. In England these ideas are being adopted rapidly. The milliner is being done away with, and the draper is taking her place. What is prettier than drapery, stately folds for the matron and becoming curves for the maiden? The milliner does away with graceful folds and gives us awkward bows instead.'

Speaking of places of amusement, he said:

'There should only be two things consulted in building a theatre—first the audience, then the actor. The trouble with too many theatres is, we have blue skies, red seats, green hangings, a great display of gilding, and then what is the actor to do? His costumes fall flat. Instead of this the house, the scenery and the stage should be only a setting. Let the woods used be dark and rich-looking. Let the hangings be of oriental materials, for they are the best example of correct tone in coloring. I was delighted with the Chinese quarters in San Francisco. Their theatre was plain and the stage was devoid of ornamentation. Those Chinese quarters fascinated me. I wish those people had a quarter in London. I should take pleasure in visiting it often.

'Common things should be made beautiful. When I was in San Francisco, at the hotel I was obliged to drink my chocolate or coffee out of a cup an inch thick, and I enjoyed going down into the Chinese quarters and sitting in a pretty latticed balcony and drinking my tea out of a cup so dainty and delicate that a lady would handle it with care. Yet this was not an expensive place for wealthy people to go to. It was for the common people. The laborers on the railroad came here, with pick and shovel, and drank their refreshing beverage out of a pretty cup of the two beautiful colors blue and white, while I was thought unworthy of anything better than a cup so thick that it suggested the idea that it was intended as a weapon, to be hurled at the heads of those seated at the next table. Beautiful things for everyday use are what we want. The child is not taught by books and lessons alone. We know how we used to throw our books aside and rush out into the air and sunshine. The child must be taught by constant association with beautiful things. Beauty should be as free as the air and water, and then it cannot fail to leave its impress on all minds.'

Talking of beauty in men's dress, Mr. Wilde said:

'We dress without the slightest regard to beauty or even comfort. When a man is going to walk, or row or perform feats which require a display of strength and muscle, the trousers are done away with and knee-breeches are worn. Then again black broadcloth is chosen for dress suits, and no material can be more devoid of beauty than broadcloth. Velvet should be chosen instead, for it is a material which is always becoming.'

Mr. Wilde believes that there will be a complete revolution in gentlemen's wearing apparel within the next few years; but for the sake of those gentlemen who are not of stately build it is to be hoped that knee-breeches will not become fashionable.

Mr. Wilde, speaking of the press, said: 'When I read the papers and see what they say about me, it gives me a peculiar sensation. I feel as it I was traveling about in a country of barbarians.'

The esthete spoke enthusiastically of the cordial way in which he had been received. Being asked how long he would remain in America, he shrugged his shoulders and said: 'If I survive, I shall remain until June.' So it is evident that Mr. Wilde has not fallen desperately in love with America.

Of American women he said: 'In this country I see any quantity of beautiful young girls, girls whose faces are charming with the flush of youth, whose eyes are radiant and whose forms are full of beauty. But there are few handsome matrons in this country.'

Speaking of his first appearance in this country, Mr. Wilde said: 'With the exception of speaking at an occasional wine supper at Oxford, I had never spoken in public until I lectured in New York. I then found out what a difficult task I had undertaken. Americans are natural orators. I never heard a spontaneous burst of oratory until I came to America and listened to an American.'

'Art and Aesthetics', *Denver Tribune* (Denver, CO), 13 Apr. 1882, 8

The train which brought Oscar Wilde over the Denver Pacific railroad last night was thirty minutes late, on account of a delayed connection at Cheyenne, and for this reason alone he was exactly thirty minutes behind the usual time for raising the curtain at Tabor Grand Opera house. He arrived in the midst of a spell of weather that is not specially palatable to aesthetic taste, and for that reason only there was not an overflowing audience, but the parquet and dress circle were filled.

The train arrived just five minutes ahead of the time announced by telegraph, and baffled the designs of a large crowd of unaesthetics whose curiosity caused them to gather about the platforms, or take refuge from the snow storm in the sitting rooms of the Union depot. Even the enterprising advance agent, Mr. Locke, was thrown off his guard by the premature movement of the train and was two minutes late, while Mr. J. S. Vale, the manager of the athletic looking aesthetic, was out prowling around in unknown places for the agent.

A reporter for *The Tribune* had taken precaution against the uncertainties of telegraphic reports or railroad time, and having waited beside the track for half an hour, boarded the train the instant it landed. While the passengers of the palace car were hurrying to and fro with their baggage in the usual unaccountable haste of the railroad passenger to be the first out of the narrow door, the reporter was elbowing his way through, eagerly scanning the face of every man for a recognition of Oscar Wilde. At the rear end of the little smoking room the distinguished poet was found all alone, standing and waiting for somebody to receive him. The reporter, feeling that this duty devolved upon him in behalf of the city, introduced himself to Mr. Wilde, welcomed him to Denver, and relieved his uneasiness by the information that his carriage was waiting at the front of the depot. Mr. Wilde was dressed for the evening's entertainment, but covered with a pair of loose trousers and a large, heavy overcoat with a broad fur collar. A muffler was wrapped about his neck and he wore a broad brimmed felt hat. He was conspicuous for his splendid physique, his long hair and singular cast of features, which in repose would be that half of man and half of woman. In every movement of the man it was easy to detect a something which gave an effeminate shade to his masculinity, bearing a striking resemblance to the *Scribner* portrait of George Eliot. But behind and beyond all that was, unusual or eccentric, to a man of observation, the strength of manhood and the character of genius.

Wilde photographed by Sarony wearing the broad-brimmed hat and cape he adopted during his time in the American West (1882; detail).

When the reporter introduced himself Mr. Wilde received him cordially and began to say a great many pleasant things, which he ended by declaring that his trip had been very tiresome. Just then Mr. Vale and Mr. Locke entered the car and conducted the poet to the carriage which was waiting for the party. A large crowd had gathered on the platform, and there were many young men who have not the slightest conception of the poetry that lives in the sunflower or the beauties that grow in the lily, followed in the footsteps and almost trod upon the heels of the aesthetic apostle. In still greater numbers they blockaded his way and surrounded his carriage, till the pressure of the crowd became disagreeable and even an annoyance. Some of them said such things as:

'Hello, Oscar!'

'Let us see you, Oscar, old boy!'

'Put your head out the window, Oscar, for we know you're in there!'

And this they continued till the carriage drove away. One fellow was so anxious to see the famous poet that he pressed his nose against the glass window till he got the full benefit of a peep into the carriage.

'I suppose this scene is familiar to you, Mr. Wilde,' remarked *The Tribune* reporter, as the horses were turned and started off in a brisk toward the opera house.

'Yes; it is so everywhere,' answered the poet artist, with a happy smile, which at once revealed a happy, philosophic disposition and a handsomely-formed and well-kept but somewhat irregular set of teeth. In such a smile there is less of the spiritual in the eye and a gentility of expression which makes the nose and the mouth a part of the index to a brain that is as practical as it is sentimental.

'Yes, such scenes *are* familiar,' said Mr. Wilde. 'This is simply curiosity, you know. It is the evidence of an unfinished civilization.'

'But do you not find such curiosity universal?'

'Oh, yes, curiosity I find a universal characteristic; but in Europe the people are less curious about public characters, and they are not rude.'

Mr. Wilde was evidently pained by the familiarity of the young men who called Oscar.

'Did you have many such experiences on your California trip?'

'Oh! my!' ejaculated the young man as he threw up his hands with a half languishing smile. 'In daytime, at almost every station, they crowded the platforms, besieged the car windows and would become actually angry if I did not make an appearance. But,' said Mr. Wilde, 'this was only a manifestation of idle curiosity.'

He mentioned a few exceptions among those he met enroute. One was that of an old gentleman who wrote him one of the most delightful letters he had ever read and then met him on the train. There were some evidences among the men he met, of deserved culture among the people of the west, but he had not had the time to cultivate them.

The carriage stopped at the stage entrance of the Opera house at 10 minutes after 8 o'clock. His audience had already gathered. He was ushered into the private dressing-room, where especial preparations had been made for his reception. While making his toilet he ordered a small bottle of Piper Heidsieck, which he touched quite temperately, leaving fully one-half till after the lecture.

At the close of his lecture Mr. Wilde, accompanied by *The Tribune* reporter, walked into his dressing room, remarking as he came off the stage, 'Well, this is somewhat jolly; to travel in the close atmosphere of those coaches six hundred miles on a stretch and then give a lecture before resting.'

'I suppose it must be very tiresome.'

'O, no; not the lecture, but the miserable travel,' and Mr. Wilde emptied the remaining half bottle of Piper Heidsieck into a goblet. After refreshing himself, he talked away to the reporter about art and poetry, art schools in Europe, and the lack of them in America, and said many pleasant things as chiruppy as though he had just awakened from a refreshing sleep upon a bed of posies.

Then the carriage was ready, and Mr. Wilde and his attendants were whirled off to the Windsor hotel, where all things were prepared for his quiet reception. Taking the elevator to the second floor, he was escorted straightway to his room, succeeding in escaping the crowd which had waited all evening to see him. Only three gentlemen and three ladies who were promenading the hall caught a glance of the stalwart aesthete as he passed on to his room. There everything was prepared for his comfort and convenience. First of all was his supper, which was spread upon a small table. It was not by any means an extravagant bill of fare. There was a plate of fish, a dish of potatoes, an omelet, a pair of mutton chops, relishes, bread, butter and a cup of tea. Throwing off his overcoat Mr. Wilde sat down at once to the table.

'Take away this tea and bring me a bottle of this wine,' said he, pointing to the wine list. 'With two glasses,' he added.

The servant quickly returned with a bottle of Grave Bordeaux. Mr. Wilde took one bite of the broiled fish and then ordered the plate removed. Just as he cut the first morsel from a mutton chop (after a glass of wine) and tested the bread and butter very sparingly, there commenced a series of raps on the door. Mr. Wilde abandoned his meal for the time, though he was almost famished, and gave himself to the duty of entertaining. Governor Tabor was among his visitors, and in the course of his interview, among other things, arranged to treat the poet to a visit to the Matchless mine at Leadville after his lecture tonight.[1]

Mr. Wilde expressed himself delighted, for he said of all things, that which he desired most was to see a mine.

When his visitors had ceased calling Mr. Wilde resumed his meal and *The Tribune* interviewer again unfolded his note book.

'When will your new book of poems appear?' asked the reporter.

'Not until after I return to Europe. I hardly think it practicable to write it here. There are so many things which I had intended which are impracticable, you know.'

Horace Tabor, the Lieutenant Governor of Colorado. He invited Wilde to visit his Leadville silver mine.

Mr. Wilde then related that in leaving Europe he left his preface to the work with a friend.[2] He said he could not write in America. His subjects would form a new departure, and he could not find either the time or the surroundings in America suitable to his themes. Besides, there were so many new experiences crowding upon him in his travels that he could only take notes. 'When I return to Venice,' said he, 'I will begin to write, and whatever I have seen to impress me in America, whether of the beauties of nature or of men and women, I will write, and give America credit for it.'

As to his drama, which has been prepared for two years past, he had little to say, except that it would soon be produced upon the stage.[3]

'How were you impressed by your trip to California?'

'How can I tell you? I could talk to you all night about it. California is a very Italy without its art. There are subjects for the artist, but it is universally true that the only scenery which inspires utterance is that which man feels himself the master of. The mountains of California are so gigantic that they are not favorable to art or poetry. The scenery for definite utterance is that which man is lord of. There are good poets in England, but none in Switzerland. There the mountains are too high. Art cannot add to nature. There is no imitative art.'

Mr. Wilde continued to illustrate by showing that the only landscape schools of art in the world were situated in countries where the scenery was less attractive and vice versa where the beauties and grandeurs of nature existed the schools were devoted to faces and figures.

'What class of people do you think are the most susceptible to the impressions that inspire poetry and art?'

'That depends upon the nationality. All classes of the Celtic race are the most susceptible to these finer touches of nature. With these people it matters little about their station in life. They are naturally sympathetic and their impressions are manifest in art and poetry.'

Here Mr. Wilde finished one mutton chop and the omelet, pushed the dishes aside and took another glass of wine.

The conversation was just beginning to assume a delightful form and Mr. Wilde, though weary, had become enthused with his favorite theme, and his words were pouring forth in a fluent stream of poetic beauties when he was abruptly arrested by a question as to the Mormons of Salt Lake and his impression of them.

'Oh, I could tell you a great many things. I was entertained by the president, Mr. Taylor.[4] I found him a courteous, kindly and charming gentleman. The house had a good deal of feeling in it in the way of pleasing works of art and good furniture. But the Tabernacle has the shape of a soup kettle and the decorations are suitable to a jail. It was the most purely dreadful building I ever saw. There was not even the honesty to tell the truth, because they painted sham pillars. There are no pillars in the building. In the house of God, I think, no lies should be told. The city interested me because it was the first city that ever gave a chance to ugly women, and so with feelings of philanthropy I looked with kindly eye upon it; it is a city of execrable architecture, and yet I felt that it also robbed life of a great deal of its romance; for the romance of life is that one can love so many people and only marry one. The people, as a body of humanity, have the most ignoble forms I ever saw, and the women are commonplace in every sense of the word.'

Mr. Wilde was asked what he thought of the American people in comparison with the Europeans. He answered:

'I came with only one idea about this country, and that was that it was free from prejudice. To us in Europe, America is looked upon as a nation simple and grand, and I thought that the moment they heard what I had to say they would understand me and realize what I meant by life and art. I find that I was wrong.'

Mr. Wilde spoke further of the prejudices of those who criticised from ignorant views of the position he maintained, but he always felt that in every audience there were some intelligent listeners. He had found audiences in the West which listened with more simplicity, more real interest and desire to know what he had to say than in many audiences of the Eastern cities, showing that the West has kept itself free and independent, while the East has caught and spoiled itself with many of the flirting follies of Europe.

Mr. Wilde at the conclusion of the interview referred to the many foolish and unjust things which have been said of him by the newspapers, and then turned himself to a great pile of letters, which he glanced over, and many of them he threw away, saying, 'If only I should read all of these I would not rest much tonight.'

'And if you were to read all the letters you receive you would become pretty well acquainted with the people in America?'

'Well—,' and Mr. Wilde significantly shrugged his shoulders for a reply, when the reporter extended his hand and bade the gifted young gentleman an affectionate adieu.

1   Horace Austin Warner Tabor (1830–1899) was an American prospector, businessman, and politician. In 1878 a huge lode of silver was discovered at a mine in which he was a partner. He was elected as Lieutenant Governor of Colorado later that year. He bought the Matchless Mine, which Wilde visited on the evening of 13 April after his lecture in Leadville.
2   No such preface survives. The reporter may have misunderstood Wilde's reference to the preface he had written for Rennell Rodd's *Rose Leaf and Apple Leaf*.
3   Plans had not yet been made for the production of *Vera; or, The Nihilists*.
4   John Taylor (1808–1887) was born in England. He became the President of the Church of Latter Day Saints in 1880.

'Oscar's Oddities', *The Pueblo Daily Chieftain* (Pueblo, CO), 15 Apr. 1882, 3

The noon train from Leadville yesterday carried through our city the far-famed aesthetic apostle, Mr. Oscar Wilde, who was returning from a lecturing visit to the great carbonate camp,[1] and en route to Colorado

Springs, where he entertained the curious of that city with the delivery of one of his intellectual dissertations last evening. Mr. Wilde alighted from the train, and was met by the *Chieftain* apostle, who accompanied him to a room in the depot hotel. He expressed himself as being somewhat wearied by the tedium of travel, and was burdened with a hopeful feeling that a slight ablutionary indulgence would remove, to a telling degree, the provoking lassitude, and restore his temperament to its usual equipoise. After the wash-act was neatly and tastily performed, Mr. Wilde freed himself of a deep sigh of relief, and the reporter knew that tranquility reigned supreme within his bosom.

During the time occupied by Mr. Wilde in refreshing himself, the reporter noted the many peculiar and unique characteristics of the aesthete's dress and style, which have made him renowned in the two hemispheres. He is tall, and were it not for a preponderance of native grace, would incline to a slight awkwardness. He is extremely youthful in appearance, and his large intellectual face is as smooth and fair as a woman's; his hair does not know the touch of cold steel, and is profuse, and reaches below his collar. He wore a large black felt hat; brown velveteen coat, fastened before with embroidered clasps and silken cords; light pantaloons, gaiters of patent-leather and light colored cloth tops; thrown over his entire body, from his shoulders to his feet, he wore a black and richly trimmed mantle, that greatly added to his singular and attractive appearance. After noting his personal perfections and defections, the Faberonian fiend then applied the interviewing pump, and drew forth the following flow:

'Yes, I have been to Leadville and was favorably impressed with that wonderful city; just think of it! that great, large city, was built up within the lapse of time necessarily required for the erection of one house in England. I lectured to a splendid audience last night, who listened to me with rapt attention, and I have none but pleasant recollections of Leadville and its people. At the conclusion of my labor I visited the 'Matchless' mine, as I had promised Mr. Tabor I would, while in Denver recently, and passed several hours under ground, being most deeply interested by the intricate and skillful work found there. I am extremely sorry that a limitation of time compels me to hurry through the mountains and canyons of Colorado as I would, I know, be much profited both in beholding their grandeur and noting the comparisons with mountains abroad. From the few and hurried glimpses I have had of your rugged peaks and deep canyons, however, I am free to say that they are so sublimely grand that the brush of the artist cannot do them justice.'

With these few kindly and well delivered remarks Mr. Wilde was spared by the reporter while a repast in the dining room was partaken of. The young foreigner was the cynosure of all eyes while he ate his dinner—to which was added a bottle of Piper Heidsieck.

After dinner Mr. Wilde returned to his seat in the coach and re-engaged in a pleasant conversation with the reporter. He seemed slightly perturbed by the staring of the crowd that had by this time gathered about the car, and mildly requested the porter to draw the curtains at the windows. Two ladies, more bold than the rest, entered the coach and begged the favor of an autograph from Mr. Wilde, who graciously and most happily complied.

About this time a be-hooded woman with her arms full of books and her face full of seductive smiles, elbowed her way through the aisle, and sidling up to Mr. Wilde, exclaimed: 'Why, don't you know me? I am the lady whom the state press says should be the one to take the nonsense out of you. I am Mrs. Churchill, editress of the *Antelope*.' Mr. Wilde lost none of his complacency, but quietly replied: 'You have, then, a prodigious task before you, madam; indeed, one that would take you until the end of the century to accomplish.'[2]

The train beginning to move caused the reporter to withdraw, after bidding Mr. Wilde a hearty goodbye.

Mr. Wilde impressed the reporter as having more than the usual culture, and his conversation, carried on in a low monotone, showed that he is the possessor of a rich musical voice—not at all effeminate, as might be supposed from his face. The massive head and graceful contour of his features are partially hidden by his long hair, which, to a certain degree, conceals his forehead. His hands, from their appearance, receive much attention at the toilet, but are large, though as white as any lady's.

There is nothing aesthetic or beautiful about his autograph—indeed, as a chirographist, he is not a success. His name, in large scrawl, resembles a rail fence after an encounter with an enraged bull, more than anything else within the imagination of the reporter.

Altogether, Mr. Wilde is a pleasing gentleman to meet, and always commands respect from those with whom he converses. He is accompanied by Mr. Locke, his business manager, who is, without a doubt, reaping a harvest from the lectures given by his latest novelty. Mr. Wilde will not lecture in Pueblo, as has been reported on the streets.

1   A nickname of Leadville.
2   Caroline Nichols Churchill (1833–1926) was a Canadian-born travel writer and the editor of *The Colorado Antelope*, a newspaper that advocated for women's political equality.

'Oscar Wilde', *Kansas City Daily Journal* (Kansas City, MO), 18 Apr. 1882, 2

'Oscar Wilde and servant, of Ireland,' was the entry in the Coates house register which attracted the attention of a *Journal* representative yesterday afternoon. His card was at once sent up to 'parlor 3,' and presently the pleasing intelligence was returned that 'Mr. Wilde would receive the gentleman; would he please step up to the room.' He would, and following the attendant the timid youth was ushered into the presence of the great apostle of the beautiful, who arose from a reclining position upon a divan to greet his visitor. After shaking hands with the worshipper of decorative art, the reporter was invited to take a seat. The poet presents a great contrast to the descriptions which have been published of him.

In fact, he is anything but the consumptive being which has been caricatured in the East. Upon the reporter's entrance he closed a volume of Warder's poems, sent him during the day, which he spoke of being charming.[1]

'How do you like our Western country, Mr. Wilde?' asked the reporter, after the first greeting.

'Oh, I am delighted with its beauties and find something every day to interest me,' said the poet, speaking rapidly with rather broad accent. 'Everything is new, the people, their ways and the country, all possess interesting characteristics for study. California, with its beautiful scenery, was especially delightful, and I had charming audiences, so large and appreciative, and continued so throughout the entire four lectures which I delivered in San Francisco. I like the West—the people seem to be simpler and more readily understand than in the East. Now this state presents landscape so much more attractive than the sandy stretch of country between here, and Denver.[2] I had a splendid reception, there, too. The audience was so cultured and refined and gave such close attention. My audiences have been delightful.'

'What will be the subject of your lecture here?'

'My lecture will be more particularly on the subject of "Decorative Art," although all my lectures are upon the general subject of "English Renaissance," and where I only lecture once, I always give my attention especially to the decorative arts—the art of beautifying home. This is all that needs encouragement. Painting and poetry need no encouragement, people love them by nature, and adore them as naturally as the bird sings. America's grand poets, Edgar Allan Poe, Longfellow, Bryant and Hawthorne, will live always, and people do not need to be asked to love them.[3] No, it is the neglected arts of decorating that must be encouraged. By bringing the subject of the beautiful before the people we raise to a higher plane the handicraft of the mechanic and the worker in fabrics, stones and metals. We would make the texture finer and the figures more beautiful in the first; the lines more graceful and flowing in the second; and in the last a greater artistic finish, and so in everything, calling for the same culture in their production as in the higher branches of art. I give my life to the study and spread of art; there are only three things which interest me deeply, and they are divine; beauty of women, beauty of art, and beauty of nature. I find much that excites my curiosity, but nothing which can surpass the study of the beautiful.'

'What did you think of your reception in Boston?'

'That is a fair question,' exclaimed the poet, as he leaned back upon the divan and laughed heartily. 'I can hardly say, however, that I have had a fair opportunity of judging a Boston audience. You remember the lark of those Harvard students—forty of them, who came in a body with sunflowers and lilies. Well, of course, that excited the audience, and they were eager and impatient to hear how I would receive this demonstration. But it ended in the usual way of the rash man who put his head in the lion's mouth,' and he laughed again. 'I had all the advantage, I could talk and they were compelled to remain silent. I shall lecture there again on my return trip.'

'Have you received much annoyance from visitors or newspapers?'

'Oh, no! If I do not wish to see visitors I don't see them, that's all. I have had a number of callers today, but you are the first one I have admitted. I was very much fatigued and needed rest. I shall leave my card at Maj. Warder's in exchange for his. I feel grateful to him for his charming poem to me.[4] The newspapers, of course, publish annoying burlesques, but they do not worry me. I read them all. It has one effect, and that is, it takes about ten minutes after appearance on the stage to dispel and clear away the mists concerning myself.'

'How soon will you return to England, and will you lecture there?'

'I can't possibly say when I shall return. I have several pressing invitations to spend the summer in this country. Henry Ward Beecher has invited me to spend a few months at his villa upon the Hudson, and Julian Hawthorne has kindly urged me to pay a visit to his home and view the scenes and surroundings amid which his father worked.[5] Both of these invitations I shall accept. As to lecturing, I think I shall most assuredly go upon the platform upon my return to England. But do you know that I lectured in New York the first time I ever appeared as a public speaker? The press have criticised my method almost universally. Now I am not a stump speaker and do not wave my hands and clench my fists at every semi-colon, but I feel that I have something of interest to say and have an intense desire to say it. My experiences have been delightful and I haven't suffered in the least from embarrassment. My first audience was composed of 3,000 people and I felt encouraged to go—if the house had been empty benches the result might have been different. I do not think there is a household in England but what has been influenced by our art, and I believe that in time it will be the same in America.'

In conclusion Mr. Wilde spoke of the rapid growth of Kansas City, and laughing said, that cities were built in this country in the same length of time that it took to build houses in England.

1   George Woodward Warder (1848–1907) was a lawyer and poet. He had published collections of poetry in 1873 and 1878.

2   The Coates House Hotel was on the Missouri side of the Kansas–Mis-

souri border. By 'this state', Wilde must be referring to Kansas, through which he had just travelled on his return from California.

3   William Cullen Bryant (1794–1878) was an American poet and journalist. Wilde would later describe him as someone 'who used to be thought an important poet when America had none'. Nathaniel Hawthorne (1804–1864) was an American novelist.

4   On 16 April 1882 *The Kansas City Sunday Times* printed Warder's poem 'A Greeting to Oscar Wilde'.

5   Julian Hawthorne (1846–1934) was an American novelist and journalist and the son of Nathaniel and Sophia Hawthorne. He and Wilde met in London in 1879.

[Champion Clement Chase], 'The Poet in Lincoln', *The Omaha Daily Herald* (Omaha, NE), 26 Apr. 1882, 2

LINCOLN, April 25, 1882.—On one of the front benches in the university chapel yesterday morning sat none other than Oscar Wilde, dressed as he usually dresses, and the students were so anxious to have him speak that he finally consented, though knowing that his manager would strongly object to any free lectures of that kind. For fifteen minutes he discoursed in a most entertaining manner on topics pertinent to the college and its work. He told the story, which those who have heard his lecture will remember, of Ruskin's humanitarian labors near Oxford, and how great is his influence there.[1] Mr. Wilde said that they in England looked to the universities of America to carry on and support the new art movement, and applying it practically here. He would wish that every one might learn some one of the decorative arts, so great a source of valuable pleasure are they.

Mr. Wilde did not hesitate to criticize the miserably poor architecture of the university building, and hoped that as the students grew up they would strive to improve that, as well as establish a gymnasium, where might be seen models of the old Greek athletes, such splendid examples of physical beauty. He would have all strive to live up to the Greek ideal, 'a sound mind in sound body.' The whole spirit of Mr. Wilde's remarks was to show that it was quite as easy to build beautifully as badly.

Oscar was quite taken with some of the pretty faces on the right side of chapel and expressed surprise, as any Englishman would, at our co-educational system. 'Why, if we fellows at Oxford had young ladies there we—well, we'd never study. Can you study under such attractions?' We assured him that we could, and that the young ladies were excellent students also. In conversation with some of the professors he expressed a regret that he had never studied elocution, and acknowledged that they made a rule *not* to learn extempore speaking. So he was told of our literary societies and how much they had done in this direction. 'And do the ladies make speeches too? Well, well!'

In the afternoon some friends took Mr. Wilde out to see the penitentiary. He had never visited a prison and his horror at the bareness of the place and complete sympathy for the convicts was that of a child.[2] Going out those in the carriage were treated to a perfect flood of poetry; to a dissertation in which one British or American author was taken up after another and criticized in short, brief sentences, which showed perfect familiarity with their writings. 'Longfellow,' said Mr. Wilde, 'was not a great poet; he was a great poem. Oh, a fine old man, a fine old man!' He was rapturous over Walt Whitman but said most stinging things of poor Joaquin Miller.[3] Emerson, he said, had been and was still a master for him; Carlyle had ceased to interest him.[4] He was surprised to learn that Emerson had lost his influence on our youth. Of his own countrymen he seems to be passionately devoted to Keats and quotes from him constantly. In fact, as to quotations Mr. Wilde has an abundant supply.

At the prison Warden Nobes showed the visitors the rogue's gallery, a large collection of convicts' photographs, and it was very amusing to hear Oscar's comments upon each. 'Oh, what a dreadful face, what a dreadful face; and what did he do?' Nobes did not hesitate to tell of the crimes in the most terrible way, calculated to shock sensitive poets. 'Oh, here's a beast, an animal,' exclaimed Wilde over one picture, 'nothing of the man left.' It was a negro's picture, but it had not done the man justice as we saw afterwards.

Mr. Wilde was very anxious to see all the prison had to show and while in the cell room conversed with Ayers of Grand Island, who is under sentence to be hung the 20th of June. 'Do you read, my man?' asked the poet.

'Yes, sir.'

'And what?'

'Novels, part of the time. I am now reading the *Heir of Redclyffe*.'[5]

Wilde said that his heart had been turned by the eyes of the doomed man, but if he read the *Heir of Redclyffe* it was perhaps just as well to let the law take its course. Further on they came to the dark cell where refractory prisoners are placed. At Nobes' invitation Mr. Wilde and one of the professors stepped in, whereupon Nobes slammed the solid door to with a terrible bang and gave them a very distinct impression of what black darkness is. Wilde went into another cell where he had caught sight of two neat rows of books which one of the convicts had arranged; quite a little library. He ran over the titles rapidly, until he struck Dante, when he came out, exclaiming, 'Oh, dear, who would have thought of finding Dante here.'[6]

After the penitentiary had been done, Mr. Wilde was asked if he would like to ride over to the insane asylum. He at first protested against additional horrors, but concluded that he would go as he was 'in for it now.' So over to the hospital they went. The scenes just left were being forgotten in another literary discussion, in which Principal Shairp was rather roughly handled.[7] Dr. Mathewson showed Mr. Wilde around the asylum, the first he had ever visited. The sad scenes here would move any heart, and it is no wonder that the aesthetic poet's was troubled to the extreme. He burst out in indignation against the whitewashed walls and 'sticky' floor, as he called it, saying that citizens would go insane with such surroundings, 'with not even a bench to oneself, and one's neighbor's muttering. I would have the gayest colors possible in those wards, would furnish them with fantastic dresses, music boxes, means of enjoyment. Pooh! how dreary, how dreadful!'

Mr. Wilde seemed glad to get away, and the visits to these two abodes of crime and insanity seemed to affect the rest of his afternoon. 'I have greater respect than ever before for virtue and sanity,' he said. He was thoughtful for a while and then remarked that whenever he had the blues or was disgusted with the world he took up *Endymion* and burying himself in that divine poem, forgot the world and its cares.[8] He said he had always been melancholy when a boy, though surrounded by every pleasure, until he went to Italy and learned the new life.

He expects to return to America some time, merely to lecture to universities of art, giving a fortnight's course at each college and refusing all public engagements. He will go again to California in July, with which place and whose people he is fascinated. His lecture here was well attended, but Lincoln people do not like him and the criticisms upon him have been very severe. But Mr. Wilde is one thing above all, he is a perfect gentleman.

1   Ruskin's road. See p. 13.
2   Wilde had visited the Kansas State Penitentiary at Lansing on 22 April.
3   Cincinnatus Heine 'Joaquin' Miller (1837–1913) was an American poet. He and Wilde had met in January. Wilde had previously praised Miller, so if he did criticise the poet on this occasion he must have thought that his remarks would not be reported.
4   Thomas Carlyle (1795–1881) was a British historian.
5   *The Heir of Redclyffe* (1853), by the English novelist Charlotte Mary Yonge (1823–1901), was one of the most popular novels of the nineteenth-century. The plot reflects Yonge's religious outlook and centres on Guy Morville's clashes with a disreputable cousin, which he overcomes thanks to his Christian faith. In an 1889 article Wilde admitted he had still not read the novel: 'I have the sinful pretension to be amused, whereas all our novelists want to reform us, and to show us what a hideous place this world is'.
6   Wilde would find solace in Dante during his own imprisonment.
7   John Campbell Shairp (1819–1885) was elected Professor of Poetry at Oxford in 1877. In an 1887 article Wilde would write disparagingly of Shairp: 'he was always confusing ethical with aesthetical questions, and never had the slightest idea of how to approach such poets as Shelley and Rossetti whom it was his mission to interpret to young Oxford in his later years; while, considered as a poet, he hardly deserves more than a passing reference.'
8   *Endymion* (1818) is a poem by John Keats.

'Aesthetic', *Dayton Daily Democrat* (Dayton, OH), 3 May 1882, 4

Our fair city was visited yesterday as most of our readers know by perhaps the greatest living art critic—one who at least is among the very highest and still on the ascendancy, while the luster of him, who has ruled supreme in the kingdom of art criticism hitherto, during the present generation, is rapidly waning and losing its power. The ignorant laugh at Oscar Wilde's eccentricities, but that matters naught in view of the fact that he is recognized by artists and connoisseurs of art as a man of almost unequaled taste and aesthetic judgement.

He arrived in this city last Monday night, and at once retired to his rooms at the Beckel House, where he remained during the morning.

A representative of the *Democrat* paid Mr. Wilde a visit, in his room at the Beckel House just after he had finished his dinner yesterday. A more opportune moment for an interview could not have been chosen for the old truth, well known, that a man's sociability and talkativeness are at their best when the inner man has been supplied with all that nature demands or culinary skill can supply, was here amply proven and promptly in answer to the reporter's card sent up from the office, came the invitation to walk in.

There sat the great Oscar Wilde half reclining on a sofa, a small table before him bearing writing materials in the use of which he had evidently been interrupted by the entrance of his visitor. Papers were strewn about his feet in profusion. The remains of his dinner stood on another table beside him, and the whole character of the room presented an air more of comfortable utility rather than orthodox neatness. Mr. Wilde himself was in perfect keeping with these surroundings as he sat there, whiffing a fine cigar. His face is well known to our readers through the thousands of pictures that have been scattered over the country since his arrival upon American soil. He looks exactly like these pictures with his long scraggy brown hair, wiry and oil-less, falling over his ears and neck, about his shoulders, his mild blue-gray eyes, his graceful nose but large lips, his soft effeminate flush, but withal his very large, massive head and graceful form. He is odd and eccentric in his dress and style, but it is an eccentricity which loses its conspicuousness in the charm of his conversation, the depth of thought and brilliancy of expression. Eccentric, it is true, but it is the eccentricity of a great man and not the eccentricity of affectation, or else he could not have won for himself the commendation of the greatest artists and literati of this continent and the old world as he undoubtedly has done ere he had reached the age of three decades.

His dress was peculiar although he did not wear his much talked of knee-breeches. He had on a mouse-colored, corduroy blouse with grey worsted pantaloons. About his neck was tied an old silk tie of a warm green hue while from the left breast pocket of his coat protruded a silk handkerchief of the same color.

'How do America and American institutions impress you, Mr. Wilde?' asked the reporter by way of opening conversation after self introduction and cordial greeting had passed.

'Oh what is the use to generalize? This country is much like other countries, we do not find much difference. I think the West is grand; I was far more interested in that part of America than in the East. The East is much more like the countries of Europe. But in California I was perfectly delighted. Everything is so new and novel and interesting. I was charmed with California and the West. But what a dreadful barrier of desert separates you of the East from the West. It seems as though nature had exhausted her resources on the West and had nothing left for those prairies. Oh it is so dreary, so desolate with those miles and miles of level plain sweeping across the country with not a tree, not a flower, not even an animal.'[1]

'I presume, however, that you do not find as much art in the West as in the East?'

'No; but still there are some good artists out there. We do not want to teach the people how to become great artists. We do not want to take a fine Italian masterpiece and put it in the workman's shanty. He would not appreciate it. He could not be made to appreciate it. It would give him no pleasure. What we want to do is to teach the people that they can have beauty in everything, teach them to open their eyes and look at nature, teach them to see the glorious panorama of color that is going on every day in the skies above their heads, and in all nature about them. We want to get them to quit using these horrid forms of furniture and household utensils, and make them understand that there can be beauty in the meanest vessel. We want to educate them to despise these dreadful combinations in color in their wall papers. Either they are so ignorant and insensible to these outrages to taste or else they are existing in utter misery. Now look at that chair. Can anything be more horrid in form, where it curves in it should curve out and where it curves out it ought to curve in. It will not last either; it is badly put up.

'All over the country, in all the hotels I stop at, they give me cups like this to drink my coffee or chocolate from. See how thick and clumsy it is. It is at least half an inch thick, and so barbaric in form that one would think it was made in a barbarous, savage age and intended to be used to hie at the head of an enemy as a weapon of defense. It disgusts me to drink from it. Such rude things make men rude who use them. We ought to have things of beauty in everything about our house. Let children when quite young be accustomed to see and handle delicate things and they will become refined. I was impressed, while out West, in going among the Chinese, to see these navvies who work hard all day on the railroad, shoveling dirt, go home at night and drink their tea out of cups of fine porcelain as thin and delicate as the petals of a white rose, so delicate, indeed, that our ladies even are afraid to handle them for fear of breaking them. That is what we should have for ourselves here. I would place things of beauty, things of delicacy in the houses of all our mechanics as well as of the wealthy. This is the first hotel that I have been in for two or three weeks where my room did not have that horrid dreadful thing called a stove in it. I think the way people make stoves now is an outrage. If we must have them in our houses with their black iron bodies and ugly coiling pipe, let us have them plain and unornamented. But no, they insist on decorating them, and so they put a garland of roses around the bottom—black, grimy horrid machine made cast iron roses! What a desecration! And then on top they put a something that so much resembles a funeral urn that we think we are living in a cemetery or sepulchre all the time. Why not make them plain? Then they can be accepted simply as a disagreeable necessity.'

'Mr. Wilde, do you think that this present so-called "aesthetic craze"—?'

'O *do* not call it a craze. It is no craze. You Americans have such a way of treating serious things as a joke. And yet you are not a joyous people. In society there is all brilliancy and apparent joyousness, but on the railway trains I do not see happy men and women. Everybody has a troubled anxious look, and everybody is pushing forward in some business project. But the people do not appreciate art and so they call it a craze. But it will live, and spread its influences and be continuing in its good and it is no craze.'

'You have answered just the question I was going to ask. I should rather have used the term, "revival." Do you think the present great

A cartoon by Thomas Nast. Wilde often criticised the cast-iron stoves that he found were ubiquitous in American hotel rooms.

revival of interest in art will pass away after a time or will its benefits be lasting?'

'Art and true beauty can never die. There may be a wave of barbarism sweep over Europe by an Asiatic invasion, but true art will not be lost.'

'Pardon me for asking it, Mr. Wilde, but I have a great curiosity, as many other Americans have, to know why it is you have selected the lily and sunflower as the emblems of beauty. You know it has been only since your arrival in America that these flowers have really been discovered by Americans.'

'I love the lily and the sunflower,' answered the great aesthete, laughing, 'because of their perfectness of form and adaptability for decorative purposes. What is more beautiful than the gracefully flowing outlines of the lily and the symmetry of the sunflower with its large round disk of rich reddish brown surrounded by its beautiful rays of yellow. Then with the lily there is such purity of color and it has so many beautiful legends associated with it. And the sunflower's fidelity to the great source of warmth, and light, and truth. It always looks to the sun, never drooping its head towards the cold shadows of earth. The lily is so beautiful for decorating rooms, but the sunflower is not gorgeous for indoor decoration, unless the room is full of richness and color. The rose is a beautiful piece of color, but it has no beauty of form and is not adapted for decoration.'

'Do you think, Mr. Wilde, that you Pre-Raphaelites of the present day, while tending to wean art away from the old heroic style of Michael Angelo, and introducing more of the realistic and more of nature as it is, are bringing it more within the power of appreciation of the masses than it has been hitherto?'

'Why, what could be more realistic than Michael Angelo? The truth is we are only beginning to appreciate the classic art. The infinite beauty of Greek art is only being discovered. But it is a mistake which the Americans so often make, to confuse me with the Pre-Raphaelite. While I owe much to Mr. Ruskin and to Pre-Raphaelite teaching, I do not class myself with that school, but I belong to a very different school entirely.'

'Whom do you consider the greatest living painter?'

'I think Mr. Whistler is by far the greatest artist living and I am glad to be able to say he is an American, although he lives in England.'[2]

'Have you found any artists in America whom you consider equal to your great painters of England?'

'It is hard to institute comparisons between artists and especially between men of genius, because to be a genius a man must possess certain qualities which are exclusively his own, and the value of these qualities cannot be compared with the value of qualities possessed by another. I think Mr. Duveneck of Boston is the greatest painter in America.[3] He and Mr. Whistler are leaders in this new school which I champion.'

'Are there any other great artists who have become allied with this new school you speak of?'

'No, it is followed now only by the younger class of artists.'

'What are the characteristics of the school?'

'Simplicity of treatment and the rendering of subjects taken from scenes of the present day in preference to the old subjects of history. The Pre-Raphaelites estimate the worth of a picture by the story it tells. We do not consider that. It does not matter so much *what* you paint, as *how* you paint it. Our school lays greatest weight on the importance of color. A picture badly colored is no picture at all. Unless, as you approach a picture from a distance, the eye is pleased with the beautiful scheme of color, it is not a good picture no matter how good a story is told.

'I believe that art has a province of its own without invading the provinces of literature. If we want a poem, let us go to a poet; if we want a story, let us go to a story teller, but if we want a picture, a representation of the wonderful beauties around us, then let us go to the artist. Whistler has adopted this idea of the importance of harmony of color that he paints his pictures and names them, solely with this in view. He paints symphonies in color. You may laugh at the idea of a man painting a symphony, but he does it, and he names his pictures "Symphony in Blue and White," or "Symphony in White."

'Why, the most beautiful picture I ever saw is Whistler's *Symphony in White*. It is so simple and yet so lovely. A grey sky lightly flecked with delicate white clouds, a grey sea dotted with white waves. And in the foreground is a white balcony with all the varying shades of white, from the pearly white marble to the rich yellow-white of ivory. Upon the balcony are three little girls, oh! so beautiful, all dressed in white, and one is reaching over and tearing the petals of white blossoms from a tree, and they are borne away upon gentle zephyrs, like little white snowflakes. Could anything be more exquisitely lovely? What purity! What beauty! and then would you turn from this to some dreadful picture of "Mary, Queen of Scots, about to be beheaded," painted by some artist who ought to have been beheaded himself before he was ever allowed to paint such a picture?[4]

'This is the kind of art that is destined to win the day in the present age. We are tired of these bloody, ugly dreadful pictures we have had so long.'

'What do you think of America, Mr. Wilde, viewed from an artistic standpoint?'

'It will never produce great landscape painters. It will be greater in figure painting than in landscape. But it will be greatest in sculpture. The country is new. People look upon the forests from a commercial point of view and do not appreciate them artistically. Men at hard labor in the mines or at agriculture form excellent subjects for figure painting while men who are confined in large cities become stooped and ungraceful. But no country which has the clear atmosphere and the cloudless skies, that America has or that Switzerland or Italy have, can be good for the landscapist. The great landscape painters of the world have been in Holland, France and England, where the hazy, damp atmosphere lend a charm to the view not seen in clearer air.'

'Well, I must express my thanks to you, Mr. Wilde, for this interview. I presume you have found us newspaper men a great annoyance since you have been in America.'

'O no, not at all. I never allow anything to annoy me. If I don't want to see anybody I tell them so.'

Soon after this, the carriage drove up which had been provided by Professor Isaac Broome,[5] through whose efforts Mr. Wilde was brought to Dayton, and by the courtesy of Mr. Wilde and Professor Broome, representatives of the *Democrat* and *Journal* accompanied these two gentlemen on a trip of sightseeing.

The new Presbyterian Church was first visited. Mr. Wilde admired its arrangement very much, and thought the granite pillars in the interior were beautiful, but would have been better if of different colors. He did not compliment the stained glass windows nor the frescoing, but said they were both barren and in bad taste.

He was struck with the elaborately fine jail exterior and afterwards in expressing his admiration of the general beauty of the city said he did not wonder we have so fine a jail for with a city so beautiful people *could* not be very wicked.

At the Art Pottery of the Ladies Decorative Art Society, he was not sparing in his praise of the works of Professor Broome and of the students.

He was particularly complimentary to the underglaze decoration of some pieces of pottery, the work of Miss May Broome, pronouncing them exquisite and in wonderful taste, and he was delighted when Miss Broome presented him a small piece of pottery which he had admired especially. Miss Broome has a right to feel proud of his praises of her work, for he is not accustomed to praise except when he means what he says.

At the Soldiers' Home a visit was paid to Governor Patrick who assisted by Chaplain Earnshaw, Colonel Thomas, Major Watson and Captain Giddinger, entertained their distinguished visitor to the very best of their ability. He was shown the principal attractions of the

Home, although time was limited, and he freely praised the new theater and particularly the handsome drop curtain. Indeed although he has traveled so much and seen so many sights he still has a keen interest in all he sees.

1   'Personal Impressions of America': 'One had to cross the alkali plains, which were so ridiculously vast that Nature, when it came to decorate them, seemed to have become alarmed and given up in despair. There were no trees or flowers – nothing of any colour – nothing of any shape. With the pitiless steel-grey sky overhead it was an expanse of monotony so vast that the train passing over it seemed immobile.'
2   James McNeill Whistler (1834–1903) was a London-based American artist. At this time he and Wilde were friendly, although they would later fall out when Whistler insisted that Wilde had plagiarised his ideas about art.
3   Frank Duveneck (1848–1919) was an American portrait painter. He was born in Kentucky, found success in Boston, and worked for periods in Germany and Italy.
4   Whistler's *The White Symphony: Three Girls* and *Three Figures: Pink and Grey* both depict three women on a balcony tending a potted cherry tree, but several of the details Wilde describes are absent. His embellishments may have been intentional: he would later tell Whistler that his (Wilde's) descriptions of Whistler's paintings were 'just as good, I often think better' than the paintings themselves.
5   Isaac Broome (1835–1922) was a Canadian-born American ceramicist.

'Oscar Wilde', *The Chicago Sunday Tribune* (Chicago, IL), 7 May 1882, 3

NEW YORK, May 6.—Oscar Wilde was met tonight sauntering down Broadway with a friend.

'What! Thomas Burke assassinated! The friend of my father, and who has often dined at our house! And Lord Cavendish, too![1] I do not see why they wish to assassinate mediocrity, for he was just an easy-going, pleasant, mediocre gentleman whom no one could have a grudge against. Such, too, was Mr. Burke. He had filled many official positions, but none that brought him in contact with the Irish people. The assassinations were undoubtedly the result of intoxication at what the Irish thought a complete victory. They turned liberty into license;

 Selected Interviews with Oscar Wilde

The murder of Lord Frederick Cavendish (top right) and Thomas Henry Burke (bottom) in Dublin's Phoenix Park.

but when liberty comes with hands dabbled in blood it is hard to shake hands with her, eh?'[2]

'Hear! Hear!' said Mr. Wilde's friend.

'But, then, we forget how much England is to blame,' said Mr. Wilde. 'She is merely reaping the fruit of seven centuries of injustice. There must be trouble ahead. I presume martial law will be proclaimed, and the Conservative party must come into power again, though I do not care to see it there. Of course, we must not blame the whole Irish nation for the acts of a few men, but I am very sorry to hear the news, and hope it isn't true.'

1   Lord Frederick Cavendish (1836–1882) and Thomas Henry Burke (1829–1882) were fatally stabbed by revolutionaries in Dublin's Phoenix Park on 6 May 1882. Cavendish had recently been appointed Chief Secretary for Ireland; Burke was the most senior Irish civil servant.

2   Parnell had been imprisoned at Kilmainham gaol since October 1881 for his role in Land League demonstrations. Wilde refers to the release of Parnell on 2 May after Parnell and UK Prime Minister William Gladstone had reached an informal agreement (the so-called Kilmainham Treaty): Parnell would endeavour to quell the violence of his supporters, while

Gladstone would allow Irish tenants to appeal for fair rent before the land courts. Wilde's complaint that the assassins had 'turned liberty into license' is ultimately derived from John Milton (1608–1674) and his Sonnet XII, which derides those 'That bawle for freedome in their senceless mood, [....] Licence they mean when they cry libertie'.

'Oscar Wilde', *The Boston Herald* (Boston, MA), 2 Jun. 1882, Supp. 1

Oscar Wilde arrived at the Vendome from Canada yesterday morning. When a *Herald* representative called upon him later on in the forenoon Mr. Wilde was costumed in a pearl-gray velvet jacket, a flowing green tie, Canada-gray trousers, patent leather pumps and scarlet hose. He was both picturesque and charming. Mr. Wilde had just returned from a lecture tour in Canada, and it was but natural that the conversation should turn upon the Dominion and its people. 'Canada,' said the poet, 'is distinctively a land of noble rivers. Away from the rivers the scenery is pastoral. Its cities are nobly situated. Quebec reminds me of Athens, with its high rock and purple hills. Ottawa, the capital city, is beautifully situated over a great rushing, yellow river. Montreal is on a sheet of water, and water and ships are always graceful. I never saw an ugly ship. I was particularly struck in Canada, as compared with the States, with the want of any real rush of life. The cities are wonderfully quiet. The streets of Quebec reminded me of a little village in Brittany.'

'How did you like the Parliament buildings at Ottawa?'

'In proportion and in design they were extremely beautiful, and most delicately proportioned. Where they fail, and where all the public buildings in Canada fail, is in monotony of color. The only stone they have is a red granite. Now, a building should please one by its color, as do the old buildings at Venice, where lines of colored stone are used decoratively. The University of Toronto is one of the most beautiful buildings in Canada.'

'Has Canada any distinctively national art?'

'I do not think that a country can have a national art until it feels two things—perfect independence and absolute unity. Canada, up to this time, has not yet realized itself. To begin with, there are two nations, the French and the English, in many cases absolutely distinct. Then, they have not developed the west of Canada, and, consequently, there has not come to them as there has to you the rush of fresh life. There has not been experienced that backward wave of newer, fresher life which you have had in America.'

'But Canada must have individual artists of merit?'

'Oh, yes. In Toronto I found a young landscape painter, Mr. Watson, a most remarkable man. He has never been to Europe, but he has wonderful mastery over tone in color. His work in grays is exquisite. They have also a young sculptor, Mr. Dunbar, who has done one or two beautiful things.[1] At Ottawa they have a very good school of art—I call it a good school because they have the absolute essential of a school, which is a life class. Unless a school has that, it will never bring out anything good in a pupil. As long as the pupils draw from casts, there will be the coldness of death in their work. If the Princess Louise had stayed in Canada, she would have had a very remarkable influence on Canadian art; but her stay was too short.[2] But I must say that there is in Canada a great deal of growing feeling in art. I had there most interesting and intellectual audiences, in no city more than in Toronto, where I lectured twice.'

Mr. Wilde then passed on to to pay a charming compliment to Mr. Howells. He said: 'There is one perfect guide book to Canada. I know of nothing which can serve so well for Quebec as Mr. Howells' *Chance Acquaintance.* The whole account of Quebec and Canada is most exquisite.[3] I thought on reading Mr. Howells' book how wrong it is to leave the writing of guide books to commonplace people; most guide books are dreadful.'

'You have been to California since you last visited Boston?'

'Yes, I enjoyed myself greatly there. I think the future of America will lie in great measure with the West. Not merely is the country most noble, California being an Italy without its art, but the physique of the men and women is particularly splendid in California and in Colorado. They are the most courteous people. I lectured at a city which is supposed to be the roughest city in the United States, and that is Leadville, on the top of the Rocky Mountains. My audience was almost entirely composed of miners. I lectured to them on the workers in metal. I told them, as simply as I could, of all the wonderful things men had made out of gold and silver, brass and copper, and the like, and nothing could have been more delightful than their courtesy or more wonderful than their interest. They came around after my lecture and asked me to sup with them in one of their great silver mines, the mine called the Matchless mine. I spent my whole night in the silver mine with them, and I rank it as one of the golden memories of my life. No one could have had more delightful companions. I saw that most of these miners were strong, simple, handsome fellows. In the whole West I had only one stupid audience, and that was at Salt Lake City, and I was not sorry that they were so, because so much depends upon our admiration of physical beauty in others; they had the most ignoble physique. They come, you know, from the ugliest peoples in Europe—the Welsh and the Swedes. The president of the Mormons, Mr. Taylor, was very charming; a man of a great deal of refinement. He came to my lecture, and occupied a stage box with his five wives. But the faces of my audience were heavy, dull and common.'

'You visited Denver?'

'Yes; Denver is a remarkable city. I went through Kansas to Missouri, where I had an opportunity of seeing a certain value placed on art. I was in the city of St. Joe when the effects of that picturesque brigand, Jesse James, were being sold at auction. A dustpan was knocked down to a millionaire, and the chromolithograph that he was in the act of nailing up when he was shot commanded a price which, in London or in Paris, only an authentic Titian could command.'[4]

'And did you go to Chicago?'

'Yes; Chicago interested me very much because I found there a young sculptor who has an artistic power and a sense of beauty which are unequalled by any young sculptor of his age in France or England. His name is Mr. Donoghue. When I arrived at Chicago I found waiting for me at the hotel a package containing a little bas relief in clay of a seated girl, with a verse from my own poems graven on the side and a letter from the artist asking me to accept it. The delicacy of the work was so great, and the whole feeling for beauty so rare, that early next morning I went to find the artist, and, in a little garret in the top of one of the great business blocks of Chicago, I found a young man working away modelling—the artist of this bas relief. He had in his studio a little statuette of a boy dancing, which has more of the real Greek feeling in it than any work I have seen by any young man in Europe. I was so filled with wonder at finding in a great, new, commercial city, this young sculptor whose sense of beauty was so exquisite, as if he were the last of a long line of Italian artists, that I spoke about him in my lecture, and to everybody whom I met in Chicago society, and since that, they are, I am glad to say, taking much more notice of him, giving him commissions which he wanted very badly. On my return from California, he came to dine with me and brought with him a large bronze bas relief of two children which he had done for one of the rich Chicago merchants. Of his splendid future I feel quite assured. At Cincinnati I found in the art school a young designer with a real mastery over design, about whom I was able to speak in my lecture also. At San Francisco there is a whole colony of excellent painters, among them a pupil of Mr. F. Duveneck. Indeed, there was hardly a city of any size that I visited in which there was not at least one young man working finely in art.'

'How does provincial art in England compare with provincial art in the United States?'

'In England, you know, there is no such thing as England; there is London. We concentrate into one city all that is intellectual in men and all that is beautiful in women, and we have changed England into this great city. In America you have spread your artistic power over a whole continent: so, though it fails enormously in concentration, it gains in width.'

Here the conversation turned upon the suppression of Walt Whitman's *Leaves of Grass* by the legal authorities of the state.[5] Mr. Wilde, a warm friend of the good, gray poet, chivalrously defended the persecuted bard. 'I heard of that,' he said, 'through the Canadian papers. I think it will be a lasting stain on America if this thing continues. The man Walt Whitman is one of the noblest and purest men I ever met. I know no man in America who touched me more through the dignity and self-sacrifice of his life and through the simplicity and wisdom of his mind. I cannot believe that anyone who reads the prose preface of his *Leaves of Grass* (Mr. Wilde must have had in mind an earlier edition than the one suppressed in Massachusetts, which had no preface, although earlier editions did have) can fail to reverence and to honor him. For creed of life there is nothing more noble. Besides, it should be remembered that the man is to be read as a whole. You must isolate no line from his context. No great book or no great poem could stand such

Walt Whitman, whom Wilde visited twice in 1882. The poet described Wilde as 'genuine, honest, and manly'.

a method of criticism. One must realize him as a whole and one must really give up the modern habit of trying to measure giants with a foot rule. The public don't see in general how that no artist either desires praise or will accept blame. He merely wishes one thing, and that is merely to be understood. If one understands Walt Whitman one will reverence him. If one does not understand him one should say nothing about him. But in no case should one dare to praise or blame him. In 50 years Walt Whitman will have taken his place as one of the greatest writers that America has ever produced. In a letter which I had lately from Mr. Swinburne, he said, with reference to Walt Whitman, and I think it was a very just criticism: "Whenever he writes on the noblest subjects he writes nobly."'

'Some of Whitman's finest and most modern lines have been inspired by machinery, his description of a locomotive in action, for instance—'

'True. I have never seen any machinery that has not been graceful. The most beautiful machinery I ever saw was at Chicago. I never was so struck by the contrast between the ugliness of bad art and the beauty and utility of strength till I visited the water works at Chicago. They have built an imitation Gothic fortress, stuck over with ridiculous pepper boxes that they call turrets, the most foolish building that I ever saw, a mere architectural monstrosity—one of the many unpunished crimes of that great city. But inside was this noble and wonderful machinery—the stately orbit of the circling wheels, the rhythmic rise and fall of the long rods of polished steel, something to me as beautiful as anything undecorated I ever saw. The line of strength must be the line of beauty. A man hauling a rope, hauls it straight if he does it gracefully; if he does it clumsily, he is hauling it crooked. There was nothing particularly graceful about the politicians at Ottawa, but the raftmen who were bringing wood down the river were some of them as noble as if they had stepped off a frieze on the Parthenon. There was a miner at Leadville who was driving a new gallery, and at any moment this man could have become marble or bronze, and have been noble for eternity.'

After his lecture here this afternoon Mr. Wilde goes to New York, and thence to the South for a lecture tour, to extend through June. He is desirous of visiting New Orleans, where a deceased uncle formerly lived.[6] He anticipates much pleasure from meeting the warm-hearted southrons, and, in reply to the suggestion that, on leaving the United States, he would go home to old England, he said, with a laugh: 'Oh, no; I shall first visit Japan, the most artistic country in the world.'

1   Homer Ransford Watson (1855–1936) was a Canadian landscape painter whom Wilde had declared 'the Canadian Constable'. Frederick A. T. Dunbar (c. 1849 – after 1919) was a Canadian sculptor who attended the Art School of Toronto and studied in Florence. Wilde praised Dunbar to his Toronto audience and afterwards sat for a bust that has since been lost.

2   Princess Louise, Duchess of Argyll (1848–1939) was the sixth child of Queen Victoria. The Duke of Argyll was Governor General of Canada from 1878 to 1884. Louise was a patron of Canadian arts but, after a sleighing accident in February 1880, she spent much time in England.

3   Howells's *A Chance Acquaintance* (1873) is a novel. It includes many descriptions of the scenery and places in Quebec.

4   Jesse James (1847–1882) was assassinated by Robert Ford in St Joseph, Missouri, on 3 April. Wilde lectured there on the 18th.

5   The seventh edition of *Leaves of Grass* was published in October 1881 by James R. Osgood and Company of Boston. A district attorney threatened to prosecute Osgood for selling obscene literature. Whitman refused to exclude the offending poems and Osgood withdrew the book.

6   John Kingsbury Elgee (1812–1864) was the elder brother of Wilde's mother. As a young man he immigrated to Louisiana, where he made his fortune and purchased a sugar cane plantation.

'Oscar Wilde', *The Daily Picayune* (New Orleans, LA), 25 Jun. 1882, 11

'There are in Texas two spots which gave me infinite pleasure. These are Galveston and San Antonio. Galveston, set like a jewel in a crystal sea, was beautiful. Its fine beach, its shady avenues of oleander, and its delightful sea breezes were something to be enjoyed. It was in San Antonio, however, that I found more to please me in the beautiful ruins of the old Spanish mission churches and convents, and in the relics of Spanish manners and customs impressed upon the people and the architecture of the city. America is so full of youthful vigor and vitality that one sees those relics of a past age in the midst of so much that is new with a positive sensation of surprise and pleasure. Those old Spanish churches, with their picturesque remains of tower and dome, and their handsome carved stonework, standing amid the verdure and sunshine of a Texas prairie, gave me a thrill of strange pleasure.'

These were the words of Oscar Wilde as he stood by the window of his parlor in the St. Charles Hotel on Saturday evening on his return from a brief pilgrimage to the Lone Star State. Mr. Wilde was looking fresh and bright, and he expressed the pleasure with which he had viewed the striking and picturesque scenery of the swamps in Louisiana and Texas. The giant cypress trees towering above the dense jungle of undergrowth and tangled vines, while long streamers of gray moss waved in the wind from the great branches which the trees thrust forth from the sky, attracted the poet's attention, while he had much to say of the alligators, which sprawled and yawned in the sunshine on the trunks of fallen trees and on the muddy banks of the bayous and the great morasses.

Nothing in the way of animal life, however, seemed to please the poet and art reformer so much as the young negroes.

'I saw them everywhere,' he said, 'happy and careless, basking in the sunshine or dancing in the shade, their half naked bodies gleaming like bronze and their lithe and active movements reminding one of the lizards that were seen flashing along the banks and trunks of the trees.'

'You were in Texas long enough to acquire a military title. A week is quite sufficient, and I have no doubt I would be justified in addressing you as Col. Wilde,' said the reporter.

'Oh, yes: I am a colonel by all the rules and regulations of a Texas brevet. I was dubbed "Colonel" in Galveston and was fully invested with the title by the time I got to Houston. I shall write home to my friends of this new rank and promotion.'

After some further conversation the reporter spoke of Mr. Wilde's reported intention of visiting Hon. Jefferson Davis, on the way from New Orleans to Mobile.[1] Mr. Wilde said he had an intense admiration for the chief of the Southern Confederacy. He had never seen him, but had followed his career with much attention. 'His fall, after such an able and gallant pleading of his own cause, must necessarily arouse sympathy, no matter what might be the merits of his plea. The head may approve the success of the winners, but the heart is sure to be with the fallen.

'The case of the South in the civil war was to my mind much like that of Ireland today. It was a struggle for autonomy, self-government for a people. I do not wish to see the empire dismembered, but only to see the Irish people free, and Ireland still as a willing and integral part of the British Empire. To dismember a great empire in this age of vast armies and overweening ambition on the part of other nations, is to consign the peoples of the broken country to weak and insignificant places in the panorama of nations; but people must have freedom and autonomy before they are capable of their greatest result in the cause of progress. This is my feeling about the Southern people, as it is about my own people, the Irish. I look forward to much pleasure in visiting Mr. Jefferson Davis.'

The poet had an engagement to go out for the evening, and he shortly took his departure with a party of gentlemen, as it was reported, to witness some mysterious and curious ceremonies of the devotees of voudou, which were to inaugurate the recurrence of St. John's night, June 24.

Mr. Wilde will lecture Monday night at Spanish Fort, on the internal decoration of the home, and on Tuesday will depart for Mobile, stopping at Beauvoir, the residence of Jefferson Davis, to spend a day with him.

---

1   Jefferson Davis (1808–1889) served as the president of the Confederate States from 1861 to 1865.

Wilde looked forward to visiting the former Confederate president Jefferson Davis.

'Oscar Wilde', *The Atlanta Constitution* (Atlanta, GA), 5 Jul. 1882, 8

When Oscar Wilde reached Atlanta yesterday from Macon he disembarked from the train and stalked with measured tread to the Markham, flanked by his valet. When he entered the arcade of the Markham, he advanced to the radiator and came to a halt. There he posed, one hand sought the spot where his heart was supposed to be, and the other hung by his side. His head was thrown back, his long locks fell over his shoulder, and he gazed upon the frescoing in the ceiling apparently oblivious of the curious gazes that were directed toward him. His able secretary advanced, and put his autograph upon the register, and then Mr. Wilde was shown to a room on the second floor facing to the west, kept especially for esthetes. Mr. Wilde had scarcely had time to be dusted by his able valet before a *Constitution* reporter sent up his card. The response was an invitation to the young man to 'come up at once,' and accordingly after a very brief lapse of time *The Constitution* was rapping at the door of the room of the great esthete. A deep voice from the inside called, 'Come in,' and the reporter turned the knob and entered. The room was rather narrow and one end opened by two windows upon

Loyd Street. Almost right under the window the colored people were yelling and shouting in true Fourth of July style. The spectacle that met the astonished gaze of the reporter was one long to be remembered. In the farther end of the room, seated in a large rocking chair, was the great esthete. His appearance was striking in the extreme, so odd he appeared. His hair was long and fell about his shoulders. It was parted near the middle and was rather stiff and in great abundance. His face was large, his lips exceedingly so, and his nose prominent. He would weigh evidently about 180 pounds. His dress was not the court costume which he wears while on the stage, but it deserves especial mention. His coat was a black velvet jacket. He wore a white waistcoat with gray woolen pantaloons. A monster moonlight green tie surrounded his throat. His socks were exquisite silk and his shoes dainty gaiters. On a table near him lay a very fine cloth cloak with silk lining. On a bureau lay a large wide brimmed hat and near it an ivory cane. On a table lay a bouquet of sunflowers. Around the poet lecturer lay scattered several books, novels and books of poetry in French. *The Constitution* was not long in making known its business. Mr. Wilde appeared to be irritated by the yelling outside, and rising said:

'Oh, the patriots, the patriots; let's shut down the window and shut out the noise.'

'This is the first 4th of July you ever saw in America?'

'Yes.'

'What do you think of it as you see it now?'

'I don't think that anything so fine as the declaration of independence should be celebrated at all if it cannot be celebrated in a very noble manner. Amongst the most artistic things that any city can do is to celebrate by pageant any great eras in its history. Why should not the 4th of July pageant in Atlanta be as fine as the mardi gras carnival in New Orleans? Indeed a pageant is the most perfect school of art for a people. It shows them what otherwise they would not have a chance of seeing, noble costumes, beautiful colors and sculpturesque grouping. It would be quite impossible to over-estimate the influence on art that any celebration of the kind would have, for in an age like this, where there is such a growing feeling for what is merely grotesque and consequently ignoble, I think the people need to be reminded of the dignity of pure beauty. Amongst the many signs in Europe of a growing feeling for art, perhaps one of the foremost is the revival in so many cities of the beautiful pageants of the past. But I am afraid that the only pageants that most American cities have a hope of seeing are the glaring processions of their traveling circusses, and I feel that they deserve something very much better.'

'You have been to see Mr. Jefferson Davis lately. Tell me something about your visit to him.'

'He lives in a very beautiful house by the sea, amid lovely trees. He impressed me very much as a man of the keenest intellect, and a man fairly to be a leader of men on account of a personality that is as simple as it is strong, and an enthusiasm that is as fervent as it is faultless.[1] We in Ireland are fighting for the principle of autonomy against empire, for independence against centralization, for the principles for which the south fought. So it was a matter of immense interest and pleasure to me to meet the leader of such a great cause. Because although there may be a failure in fact, in idea there is no failure possible. The principles for which Mr. Davis and the south went to war cannot suffer defeat. I had read Mr. Davis's book, which is a masterpiece, although to us in Europe the elaborate detail of military maneuver is at times a little burdensome. But there are passages in which he dwells on the principles of the southern confederacy that were read by us with the keenest interest and delight. It is impossible not to think nobly of a country that has produced Patrick Henry, Thomas Jefferson, George Washington and Jefferson Davis.[2] Besides its great men I admire in the south the wonderful beauty of its vegetation. I have seen no forests in Europe more wonderful, no flowers more exquisite in perfume or in color. It is worthwhile to come over here merely to see the magnolia in full blossom. It should be—the south—the home of art in America, because it possesses the most perfect surroundings: and now that it is recovering from the hideous ruin of the war I have no doubt that all these beautiful arts, in whose cause, I will spend my youth in pleading, will spring up among you. The south has produced the best poet of America—Edgar Allan Poe:[3] and with all its splendid traditions it would be impossible not to believe that she will continue to perfect what she has begun so nobly. The very physique of the people in the south is far finer than that in the north, and a temperament infinitely more susceptible to the influences of beauty.'

'Tell me something about your sunflower ideas?'

'Oh, yes! I have some here that were sent up to me. The reason that we value the sunflower so much, is because it is so perfectly adapted for decorative art. Many flowers will merely be beautiful in color, without having a definite form, such as the magnolia for instance. But this flower is best suited for decoration, because its form is definite and perfect, and of all flowers, perhaps, the sunflower is the one which art has made noblest use of. It appears constantly in the medalic and tapestry of old Europe and is found all through Eastern art. Besides its beautiful form the imagination of the world has surrounded it with a halo of beautiful legions as golden as the halo of its own golden rays. I have been very pleased to find since I came to America, that the people have come to see and to appreciate its wonderful splendor far more than I think they did before, and indeed that is one of the noblest uses of art. It takes up some flower which people have thought common and shows them how beautiful it is.'

'How do you find art in America?'

'The feeling of art and the admiration of beauty is, I think, more general than I expected. I found a greater appreciation of art in Boston, New York, Cincinnati, St. Louis and Chicago than anywhere else.'

'What do you think after your American tour?'

'With regard to my American tour, I may say that nothing could be more interesting to any young man to have the opportunities that I have had of studying the civilizations in many cases very fine and in many cases very incomplete, of this new world. I have found a greater feeling for art than I expected, but far less knowledge of it, a great feeling for beauty and beautiful things, but a very vague idea about how a nation could acquire them. The real question that I have found in America standing in the way of its right artistic development is that the ordinary handicrafts are not held in their proper honor. So many young men whom I have met in railway cars and elsewhere, young men of a great deal of brightness of intellect being contented to select as a profession the occupation of clerks in stores, and the like, which in many cases means no little more than a form of salaried idleness, and on seeing how much finer it would be for them to select a profession in which they could use their hands and really do useful and good work.'

'When will you return to Europe?'

'I shall not be in Europe for a year. After my tour through the south, I shall go to Canada, where I have to deliver ten more lectures. I will then return to California, a part of America which I admire enormously—will go from there to Japan. In Japan I intend to study the method and the education of their ordinary artisans and to try and understand how it is that every ordinary Japanese workman has got this delicacy of hand, this feeling of beauty and this perfectly masterful power of design which are characteristics of their work. I am a wanderer by nature and I hardly know when I will be in Europe. I will sail for Japan about the 15th of August.

1   Davis's appraisal of Wilde was less favourable. The day after the visit he is supposed to have told his wife 'I did not like that man'.
2   Patrick Henry (1736–1799) was a Founding Father best known for his declaration in 1775: 'Give me liberty, or give me death.' Thomas Jefferson (1743–1826) and George Washington (1732–1799) served as the third and first presidents of the United States, respectively.
3   Edgar Allan Poe (1809–1849) was born in Boston, but, orphaned as an infant, was taken in by a family in Richmond, Virginia.

'Sizing Us Up', *The Sunday Herald* (Boston, MA), 20 Aug. 1882, 12

RICHFIELD SPRINGS, N. Y., Aug. 17, 1882.
I have intercepted the laureate of art and unconventionality here, on his way to New York. He has grown more unconventional and conspicuous in his dress since I first met him, and the crude notions of America which then possessed him have been crystallized into positive opinions. He is some months older, too, and these have been eventful months to him. He says he has enjoyed every day of his lecture tour, and I have no doubt of it, for he has gained five pounds since he landed in January, and now turns the scale at 185. Yesterday it was so cool here that gentlemen wore overcoats and ladies shawls, but the Prophet of Beauty radiated on the piazza of the Spring House in a rather-too-short pair of white duck pantaloons; beside which, his costumes consisted of a gray Scotch cutaway, well worn, a broad, soft brown hat, a long, sailor-knotted, terra-

cotta necktie, over a broken-cornered collar, low shoes, black socks and white kid gloves. Nobody else in town wore any garments like unto one of these; so he was much besieged and bestared at.

'Yes,' he said, responsive to my salutation and inquiries. 'I am raking in the shekels—if that is what you call it in America. I have had large audiences, have made considerable money, have had tremendous experiences of various kinds, and now I am going home. To write a book about it? Yes, certainly. I do not now think of any other Englishman who has seen America so thoroughly as I have. I have seen the splendid South in its glory, and have eaten of its savory hoe cake, have partaken of New England's pie and pancakes, have witnessed the wonderful growth of the North-west, have seen the sun rise and set on your great midland ocean of grass and flowers, have camped with the miners of the Pacific slope and taken pot-luck with the Mormons, and now I am going home. About American women? Certainly. I have not found among them very much of the highest order of beauty. An astonishing amount of prettiness, daintiness, intelligence, vivacity, personal attractiveness—but of classic beauty not a great deal. In Europe there are only two Greek things—the Venus of Milo and Mrs. Langtry, and Mrs. Langtry has the advantage of having arms and movements. Do I think she is the most handsome woman in the world? I hesitate to say so now. I said so once to Ruskin when I first saw her, and he answered, "That utterance is a form of blasphemy. You might as well say of a particular flower that it is the finest flower in the world—and the world so full of flowers supremely beautiful." The beauty of many of the prettiest American women seems to me so perishable. It is the beauty of youth, of life, fading tomorrow; but the highest form of beauty is perennial. I shall write sonnets to Mrs. Langtry when she is 95.

'That is a natural enough question of yours, "How does Mr. Langtry take it?" He takes it philosophically. Perhaps he feels, somehow, that he is an intruder, because—No, little boy, I don't want to buy one of your sunflowers. Run away now and sell them to somebody else. Heavens! the idea of picking that gorgeous flower! The sunflower ought never to be picked. It is splendid on the stem, but preposterous in a vase or a girl's corsage. That is quite like marrying a beautiful woman. I have fallen into the habit of thinking that the husbands of beautiful women belong to the criminal classes.[1] They have committed sacrilege and robbery in attempting to monopolize what belongs to all mankind. They are fit candidates for the penitentiary. What if somebody should lock up the air and sunshine?'

When I had first spoken to Mr. Wilde, he sat alone on the porch reading Tennyson's poems, which he usually carries around under his arm. There was nobody near him, and few seemed to notice him. But now it was noised about that Oscar Wilde had come, that this flashing object on the piazza was he, and already 50 women, girls and children were gathered around as if he were a wild Choctaw or a polar bear, or a man from the moon, and groups of handsomely dressed ladies stood and gazed at him at a distance of six or eight feet, evidently catching all they could of the conversation that was conducted in a low tone.

'The most striking thing I have noticed,' he repeated, dropping his voice another note or two and laughing, 'is the curiosity of your people. They have reduced staring to a fine art. I have seen an exhibition of ill-breeding and impudence that amounts to positive barbarism. I do not let it trouble me, for I cultivate indifference to all such vulgarity. The philosophy of life is never to be annoyed. I am satisfied now that there is no affliction on earth that a man of serene temper cannot get used to in six weeks.

'Oh, yes; of course I have met thousands of refined and well-bred people who would be incapable of any discourtesy, but these are in a great and surprising minority. I cannot help thinking that good breeding is commoner in England. When Gladstone or any other well-known Englishman appears in public, he is kindly let alone—neither stared at nor followed. Even there, though, there was a furor over Mrs. Langtry, and, when I took her to the Grosvenor gallery once, she escaped from the mob with great difficulty. But the people who are thus intrusive and impudent are the lower class of our people, while here they seem to include the middle and nearly the upper class. For instance, in Saratoga, last week, I stopped at the States and Congress Hall—two of the best hotels, which one would suppose would be patronized by cultured people. While talking with Judge Brady there was a great crowd came around us, mostly women, and, finding it a bore to be thus stared at, I moved on into the office.[2] There they came flocking after us. I went to the billiard room, but found no refuge there. The women rushed there—ladies in silks, and crapes, and laces, with diamonds in their ears, bringing their daughters with them! To balk the pursuit utterly, I fled to the bar room. Will you believe me that they came there—in 10 minutes, 50 or 100 of them—filling up the place almost. It seemed to me a most painful and dreadful thing—the bold-faced staring and half-audible comment.[3] It seemed much worse than the conduct of abandoned women. Why didn't I say: "What'll you have, ladies?" Oh, it wouldn't have done any good, and all the country would have said I had insulted the ladies at Saratoga. There they came with a rush, and there, before and among them, were the horse racers and gamblers of Saratoga, smoking, drinking and talking loud. Was it not a horror? I was stupefied, and said to myself: "What land is this I have come to?"

'Yes, as you say, I do not travel under normal conditions. I do not see the same average of people that others see. An atmosphere of curiosity and impertinence seems to be created wherever I walk. Wretched me! I, who plead for gentleness and kindliness and gracious courtesy, am doomed to be the destroyer of courtesy every day and hour. I, who preach the importance of good manners, am the very Attila of good manners!'

A group of children were looking up into his face, saying: 'Here he is! That's Oscar Wilde!' etc. One of them stumbled over his patent leathers, and another, a boy of 8 or 10, came up boldly, put a hand on the white linen thigh of the guest and said in a high, rasping, nasal voice: 'Gimme yer card, if yer please!' 'Not now—I am busy,' said Mr. Wilde; 'by and by, perhaps.'

'There's a specimen American child,' he continued. 'The children here are unrestrained savages. I never saw handsomer children than these little Americans, but they are left uncivilized, to grow up hoydens and blackguards. Such juvenile impudence exists nowhere else in the world. Only occasionally do I see your children pay any respect to their elders, even to their parents. It seems to me dreadful. Their audacity seems to me almost depravity. It cannot help harming the rising generation. Yet I love children. They are living flowers. I think of adopting one or two.

'When I marry that Boston lady?[4] Don't speak of it! She is a charming lady, but no such thing as marriage was ever thought of by either of us. It was unspeakably cruel to set such a story afloat and cable it across the sea as they did. Your newspapers have been reasonably good to me, but I don't like them wholly. They are splendid and wonderful news gatherers, but they overdo it. They invade every home like the Goths, intrude on personal rights and make private reserve impossible. Reverence, I fear, is dead in America. I do not mean religious reverence—that I would care less about; I mean a true respect for personal liberty and dignity.

'Marry? Dear me, no! I never shall marry—till I find the one lady, beautiful in person and soul, who will let me go into raptures over all the other lovely women; who, when I come home and wildly say, "My dear, I have seen the most beautiful and charming creature in the world!" would encourage me and sympathize with my passion, and bring my slippers and tea and say, "Now come and tell me all about this lovely creature, and you must go and see her again right away."[5]

' "Right away?" Oh, yes; I have learned nearly all of your Americanisms now, and have even adopted some of your most expressive slang, for slang is the reservoir and fountain of language. Well, as I was saying, I have been madly in love five times since I have been here—in San Francisco, in New Orleans, in Kalamazoo and twice in New England—and I don't know what would have become of me if my agent hadn't dragged me along.

'Much as I had heard of the progress and rapid growth of this country, it is quite startling to me, and somewhat alarming, too, for it is plain that the amenities of life, and the sweet graces which alone make existence worth having, are being forgotten and despised in the rush for riches. I wonder what this country, especially the West, will be in 20 or 30 years from now.

'Edwin Booth? Oh, yes, I have seen him often, and enjoyed his acting highly, of course. I gave a little breakfast party to him before leaving England. The Prince of Wales was there, and I wondered what he would say to Mr. Booth, as I knew he had not been to see him play, and that, as he is so fond of the drama, the actor felt the seeming neglect. Shortly the prince said: "I would like to know Mr. Booth." So I brought Mr. Booth over and presented him. In the conversation the prince said: "I have not yet been to see you, Mr. Booth, for my friends said your support was very bad, and I felt it would be unfortunate to see you for the first time when you were poorly supported." It seemed to me a most graceful speech.

'How came I to be such a devotee of beauty? I will shorten a long story. Coming into life, and finding myself born into a world where most of the things about me were ugly and uncouth, it seemed a tragedy, and I wept all through boyhood at my wretched lot. When I was 16 my father sent me to Florence.[6] On entering that lovely city my load of misery dropped off. Beauty surrounded me. I recognized in it the land from which I had long been in exile. Then I found that art was the panacea for all ills, and the love of art the secret of happiness. Recalled, I was sent to college at the beautiful city of Oxford, and there I met Ruskin, and in him saw the man I so long sought. He is possessed by the true spirit of art. A coterie of us there surrounded ourselves with beautiful things as far as practicable. A friend was admiring a set of blue china in my room one day, when I playfully remarked that I wished I could live up to the level of it. Next Sunday the dean preached to us on modern heathenism, and quoted my remark, in all seriousness, as a very dreadful utterance. To be the subject of a sermon by the dean made me noted at once, and then *Punch* caricatured me, and Gilbert and Sullivan gave me the finishing touch in their grotesque and funny opera. My present "mission," as you call it, is to urge the introduction of beauty into the things of common life.

'No, I am not going home. I am now going to Japan, where I shall spend the autumn. That is a great and wonderful country—the home of art. The absurdity of our speaking of a people as heathen who can teach us in every form of beauty! I shall return here again on my way to England.'

Mr. Wilde lectured here on Monday night to a large house. He wore his black velvet costume, ruffled shirt front and lace cuffs. Today he has gone to the Catskills—thence to Long Branch, and exit.

1   Wilde would later include a version of this line in his novel *The Picture of Dorian Gray*: '"The husbands of very beautiful women belong to the criminal classes," said Lord Henry, sipping his wine.'
2   Judge John Riker Brady (1822-1891) was a Justice of the New York Supreme Court.
3   One woman is supposed to have remarked: 'Well! I'm glad I've seen a gorilla at last!'
4   Reports were circulating that Wilde was engaged to Maud Howe (1854-1948), the daughter of Julia Ward Howe, whose Newport, Rhode Island, summer house he had stayed at in June.

5   Wilde would make this the inciding incident of his unfinished play 'A
     Wife's Tragedy'. Gerald Lovel, a poet staying in Venice, sees a beautiful
     woman in a gondola. He tells his wife, Ellen, about this woman. Ellen rec-
     ommends that Gerald ask after her address at one of the city's fashionable
     dressmakers.
6   Wilde first visited Florence in the summer of 1875 when he was twenty
     years old. He was not 'sent' by his father.

'Wilde', *The Evening Telegram* (Providence, RI), 26 Sep. 1882, 1

'Would you like to meet Oscar Wilde?' said my friend Moore, his manager, last evening, just after the arrival of the New York team, as I stood
in the lobby of the Narragansett Hotel.

'Why, certainly,' said I.

'Well, come up with me,' and we went up to Room 5, and, knocking,
there was a cordial 'Come in,' and opening the door I was ushered
into the presence of the most ridiculed and caricatured man of the
nineteenth century. The general look of his features was the same that
is so well known by the photographs of Sarony, and also the numerous
pictures in the illustrated newspapers, but the aesthetic costume was
lacking, he being clad in a drab linsey-woolsey suit, like ordinary mortals,
with only some slight differences in style and cut, like any ordinary
Briton.

'Won't you sit down, sir?' said he, 'I am waiting for my trunks from
the depot.'

As he stood up beside me I could see that he was built in a powerful
mould, being over six feet in height and broad-shouldered, and looking
much taller and brawnier as he stood up in the room than when he
affects the 'stained-glass attitudes' in aesthetic togs upon the stage;
but when he sat down upon the sofa he was limp and sort of spread out
in the corner of it, due possibly to the fatigue of a long ride in the cars,
or it was his usual manner.

I suggested to him that the drizzly, foggy evening must remind him
of some of the fogs and nights of his own city, London.

'Ah,' said he, 'we are too severe even ourselves on our climate. Of
course the winters are beastly, but the summers are delightful in London.

It is the smoke of the manufactories that adds to the disagreeableness of our atmosphere.'

'How much longer do you remain in this country, Mr. Wilde?' (I could hardly bring myself to say 'Mister,' it seemed sort of inappropriate, and I almost found myself being overfamiliar by ejaculating 'Oscar' whenever I spoke to him.)

'Well, I can hardly tell. Do you know I find it hard to make up my mind to leave. I have found so much that is interesting to me in your country. I expect, however, to make a tour of the provinces, then go to Australia and Japan.'

'Does the country come up to your anticipations?'

'Oh, far ahead of what I ever realized. Do you know that we seem to think of this country over in England more from the standpoint of the West, of the limitless prairie and wildness of that region, than of the cities of the East, of which there is, comparatively speaking, little known. You see the average Englishman, especially among the nobility or rich commoners, land in New York and start right out West for the hunting, so that they see very little of your cities, which accounts, to a great extent, for the prevailing ignorance concerning your larger places. Now, I like New York so much; it is so cosmopolitan, bright, cheery and full of life; and Boston I was just charmed with, the delightful literary people one meets there; in fact, I think we know Boston better than any other city for the influence of its literary minds. Emerson is as well known and his works as great and known in England as in his own country. And then there are some fine buildings in Boston. There is Phillips Brooks' house and his church, both fine specimens of ornamental architecture.[1] Have you any fine buildings here?'

The question staggered me for a moment, and I thought to myself I only wished we had been coming up the river and I could have sprung the gasometer on him as the dome of some church, after descanting on the beauties of the Hospital. However, our old first Baptist Church is always my stand-by, and I spoke of that with commendable pride as being the work of a countryman of his, Sir Christopher Wren, and the spire as one of the most graceful pieces of church architecture in the country.[2] Then there was the City Hall, Narragansett Hotel, Court House—well, there were quite a number after all when I came to sum them up.

'In Newport,' said he, 'I found the most refined audiences I have lectured before, and the domestic architecture the finest I have ever seen. I enjoyed Newport thoroughly. The cottage life is simply charming. More like my own country, where we care nothing for hotel life. I do not care for hotels.'

'Your peculiar ideas of dress seem to be one of the principal things that have made you so well known and criticised.'

'Not peculiar, exactly, it is common sense and comfort I aim at as well as the artistic look at the dress of men today. It is not comfortable, by any means—hats afford no protection from the elements, tight-fitting coats that are not warm. Just look at a crowd of men in the dress of the period; could anything be more unartistic, or ignoble? Why, the best dressed men I have seen were in Colorado; their outdoor life makes their dress consistent and comfortable, broad-brimmed hats that protect their faces from the rain and sun, and at the same time they are graceful. I saw some fine specimens of manly beauty in the West. One great trouble with modern sculpture is that the artist has nothing to go by. The sculptors of earlier ages saw the lines of their models through the drapery and the resulting statuary is natural, easy and graceful. The artist must see something before him in order to reproduce it. It cannot emanate entirely from his own mind. There will be a change here in dress, and it is even now felt to a great extent in England, especially among the ladies, who are adopting these sensible ideas, and there are today in London the finest dressed ladies in the world.'

'How do you think Mrs. Langtry will succeed over here?'

'Excellently. She is one of the most charming of women. She is very handsome, and the fact that she has had all England at her feet for three years and a half, is sufficient proof of her beauty, and you Americans like beautiful women, so that is half of the battle, and then she is really a fine actress, not anything great, of course, for it would not be art that could be acquired in six months, but she possesses one of the most musical of voices, and is thoroughly fascinating, and there is a magnetism about her that has made her, even the short time she has been upon the stage, unusually successful in her chosen profession. I know of no one upon the stage who has such a musical voice except Bernhardt.'

'You see, Mr. Wilde, we are slightly aesthetic in the tint of the paper of the *Telegram*.'

'Ah, yes, like your namesake of New York. Well that gives the paper a cheerful look, and then again it is pleasant for the eye, not so tiresome as the glaring white. Very nice, I assure you.'

Here the valet of the apostle of aestheticism arrived with the trunks, and as it was nearly time for the lecture, I took my departure and left him getting ready to don his aesthetic costume for the evening.

1   Phillips Brooks (1835–1893) became rector of Trinity Church, Boston in 1869. After the church was burned down in 1872, architect Henry Hobson Richardson (1838–1886) built a new church under Brooks's direction. The church was completed in 1877 and lauded for its architectural innovations and decorations. Four stained glass windows designed by Edward Burne-Jones and executed by William Morris were installed in 1882.

2   The First Baptist Meetinghouse was built in 1774–1775. It was designed by Joseph Brown (1733–1785), an American industrialist, astronomer, and architect. Brown was inspired by illustrations of designs by Sir Christopher Wren (1632–1723), an English architect.

'The Apostle of Beauty in Nova Scotia', *Halifax Morning Herald* (Halifax, NS), 10 Oct. 1882, 2

The afternoon train from St. John on Friday, brought beauty's latest evangel to our province. He came, not surrounded by a halo of blue and purple glory, not in a carved car, nor in a Greek urn. He rode on an engine. He saw the little hills rejoicing merrily. He saw Moncton, and noticed the indecent wonder of the *Transcript* editor.[1] He took in the Pre-Raphaelism of Dorchester. He rejoiced at the preciousness of Westcock, and was enraptured at the gaudy leonine beauty of the Tantramar. Oscar praised the railroad and liked the appointment of the cars. He smoked the cigar of peace and he crossed the Missequash [*sic*] but he took no interest in Fort Cumberland, as the battles fought there were not fought for love of beauty but for love of territory.[2]

At Amherst he shook hands with the engine driver, gaily wished him a good day, gave him a stray cigar, and leaped lightly to the platform, declining the proffered help of a hand kindly outstretched to assist him. The station platform was crowded with citizens, trying to get a glimpse of 'wild Oscar,' as they called him, and these were anxiously watching the door of the car where the Evangelist might be supposed to be, while he was quietly getting into a carriage and getting under way for Lamy's. The first impression on looking at Oscar is that he looks like his pictures. You have seen that picture before and are ready to turn over a leaf.

A *Herald* representative called upon Mr. Wilde in his room at Lamy's. He was received with a polite friendliness that was winning. The Apostle had no lily nor yet a sunflower. He wore a velvet jacket which seemed to be a good jacket. He had an ordinary neck-tie and wore a linen collar about number eighteen on a neck half a dozen sizes smaller. His legs were in trousers such as Greenfield might have made, and his boots were apparently the product of New York art, judging by their pointed toes. He wore a ring with a seal of great size. A consensus of the opinions of Amherst people decides that Oscar's hair is not good. It is the color of straw, slightly leonine, and straight as an Indian's. It is faded and bleached looking, and when not looked after goes climbing all over his features.[3] Mr. Wilde was communicative and genial. He said that he found Canada pleasant. He liked the scenery of New Brunswick, as it lent itself readily to art. There were no towering mountains, and deep gulches such as he had seen in the West. There were no large rivers, but the scenery was always changing as one passed through. Every turn in the road brought a small surprise. The streams wound attractively through the land, and there were innumerable hills and valleys of all conceivable forms.

Had our autumn forests finer colors than those in England?

Well, he would not say that. Our timber was finer, but its beauty was of a different sort.

Mr. Wilde uses the word 'timber' in a sense that he thinks American. He talks about the leaves on our timber, etc.

The conversation turned on newspapers.

'The editor of a paper,' said Oscar, 'has an advantage over all other writers. He never waits for his audience, and he is sure that what he writes will be read.'

(Oscar sighed here, doubtless thinking of his poems.)

'American journals are in many respects better than the English. I think the American newspaper is the journal of the future. It is filled with news. The reader of the large New York papers knows everything that goes on in the world that is worth knowing, and much more. Still there is a want of dignity, and an amount of scurrility in the American newspaper which ones gets in smaller towns that is terrible.'

'Did they not discuss your appearance and your lectures in a somewhat unsatisfactory way?'

Oscar at this stage had brought in to him a cup of tea and having asked your representative to partake with him he laughed quietly and pushed his hair behind his ears, as he replied: 'They talk in an incredibly obtuse manner about my message and my work. I think nothing whatever about the criticisms now. It does not interest me as it did at first. I understand the people who say those things about me and I cannot bring myself to care what they say. I cannot possibly do it. At first it surprised me. I came out here, never having spoken in public, in earnest about my message, strongly feeling what I was saying, and I talked seriously to those people. They heard me and went away and talked about my necktie and the way I wore my hair. I could not understand how people could do such a thing. I thought it inexpressibly stupid.'

This last with a sigh and a look of half wearied pity at the thought of these critics. He said 'stupid' with a strong accentuation on the last syllable.

'The English Journals,' he went on, 'are much more serious and earnest in their tone than yours. But a man who has a name that is valuable will not be an English journalist. English newspaper articles are written anonymously. A good writer can get no credit for good work, and so will not write for an English paper. The proprietor is everything, the writer nothing there. In France, where the writers sign their names, better men become journalists.'

'But as a matter of fact you can tell who writes many articles in England.'

'Yes, in some cases you can. There is George Augustus Sala.[4] (This name was uttered with a weary look as if the physical effort of articulating it was nearly too much and the last syllable of Sala was clearly accented.) You can always tell what Sala writes. No other human being can write such intolerable English.'

Oscar made enquiries about the institutions of Amherst.

'Do you tell me that it has only three thousand inhabitants? Why (lying back luxuriously on his bear skin rug and sipping his tea,) I never spoke in a town so small as that. Mr Townshend has driven me about the village and I consider it a beautiful little place.'[5]

He spoke of our style of Government, of democracies generally, of sociology, of Herbert Spencer, whom he had read and admired greatly. He found nothing in his work or in any other work on evolution which differed from Plato and Aristotle.[6]

'There is nothing in art or philosophy in which we are as wise as the Greeks. Spencer has prosecuted enquiries which have led him to verify the Greek philosopher. No, we should *not go back* to the Greek, we should try to get up to the Greek. All that remains for us anywhere is to corroborate the Greeks in everything. They reached a level, the summit of which we cannot yet see. True, they had simpler problems. Their common people were less stupid. It is a wonder we do not have twice the trouble we do have, with the elements that go to make up the countries we now live in. Our conceptions of beauty may reach the Greek conception some time. There is nothing higher to hope for.

'Yes, I have found America pleasant. Out in the West, delightful. At Denver I met the most interesting people I have ever seen.'

'Rough and ready I suppose?'

'Ready, but not rough. They were polished and refined compared with the people I met in large cities farther East. Yes, I *did* see the common people. I spent a night in a silver mine. I dined with the men down there. They were great, strong, well formed men, of graceful attitude and free motion. Poems every one of them. A complete democracy under ground. I find people less rough and coarse in such places. There is no chance for roughness. The revolver is their book of etiquette. This teaches lessons that are not forgotten. I wish I could have gone to Winnipeg. I like free people without the resources of civilization. They are freer and more artistic in their surroundings because they follow nature.'

'Speaking of ladies (he had spoken of them) do you consider American or European ladies the finest looking?'

'That I cannot answer here. I shall wait till I get in mid-ocean, out of sight of both countries. If I were to answer you I should find it to my advantage to be anything but candid.'

Your reporter intimated that the last remark was a sufficient answer.

Oscar, smiling and drinking more tea, proceeded: 'Your women are pretty. I never saw so many pretty women as I have seen here, especially in the South, but the prettiness is in color and freshness and bloom. A truly beautiful woman never grows old. The most of your pretty ladies will not be pretty in ten years.'

'I believe you discovered Mrs. Langtry?'

A look of rapture came to Oscar's face. He flung his locks from where they clustered around his nose, and with a gesture, the first of the interview, he said:

'I would rather have discovered Mrs. Langtry than have discovered America. Her beauty is in outline perfectly moulded. She will be a beauty at eighty-five.

'Yes, it was for such ladies that Troy was destroyed, and well might Troy be destroyed for such a woman. Perhaps it may be true—they say it is—that the siege of Troy was brought about by a quarrel about a harbor, but they thought they fought for a woman; they had the conception that it was for beauty, and that is the same as if it was. It would be a fine thing if nations went to war with each other now over such questions as to which had the most beautiful women. How much better that than the senseless dispute about getting Egypt and possessing Arabi.[7] Now that we have caught Arabi we do not know what to do with him. When I was young I thought the wars of the roses were to decide whether a red or a white rose was the most beautiful. I learned afterward that it was a vulgar dispute. The right of one or two men to a crown or something of that kind.'

This last was spoken in a tone of injured susceptibility, as though York had thrown soup on Oscar's coat, or Lancaster had smoked a black pipe over Oscar's dinner.

'What do I think of your American Literature? I think you have had a great poet in Poe. He is your greatest poet. His sense of form and exquisitiveness of touch are intense. His gold is not to be gilt and his lilies are unpaintable. Joaquin Miller is also a beautiful poet. 'Arizonian' is a poem of great artistic excellence. Fawcett, a new poet, whom we had not heard of when I left England, has written some of the most perfect poetry which I have seen.[8] Walt Whitman if not a poet is a man who sounds a strong note. He writes neither prose nor poetry but something of his own that is unique. He is one of your greatest men.

'No I do not care for the Commemoration ode of Lowell.[9] It has no harmony in its conception. It is oratory of the strongest kind, and is eloquent but does not meet my idea of poetry. Lowell had written a poem on dedication which is delicate poetry. You must like it. You have poets with you. In New Brunswick a young man, Mr. Roberts, has published a little book.[10] You have heard of it.'

The reporter had read Robert's published poems and was delighted to find that Mr. Wilde met and liked them.

'And Mulvany of Toronto, a countryman of my own, a man once well known at Trinity College.[11] He is a man of taste. Frechette, I believe is however your best poet.[12] Wordsworth was undoubtedly a poet. I do not read the poems he liked best of his. I do not care for his "Idiot Boy," "The Excursion," is nothing to me.'

Your correspondent intimated that the poem was too long for what poetry it contained which reduced the average too low.

Said Mr. Wilde, 'I do not like to hear poems spoken of as too long. "The Excursion" is shorter than the *Iliad*. I would not have one line less in the *Iliad*. But I like Wordsworth's sonnets. That beginning: "Milton thou should'st be living at this hour,"[13] is fine, as is that which commences: "The world is too much with us." '[14]

As your representative rose to go, having declined a cup of tea, which was again politely offered, he was asked about Halifax, the nature of the people and style of the town. Mr. Wilde had met Sir John MacDonald and his lady. 'Sir John, (and Mr. Wilde sighed as he said it,) was a man of the world, but his lady was charming and so was he.'[15]

And your correspondent left. There was other talk about the classics, about the French idea of the Dramatic Unities, about Shakespeare and Wordsworth and Keats and Rossetti, but this was of a nature too confidential to be communicated to everybody. It will be remembered that Mr. Wilde begins one of his sonnets with this line: 'I stood by the unvintageable sea.'[16]

Your correspondent thought of this as he was leaving, and remembering that the Tantramar was very muddy as the aesthete passed over it, he asked, 'Do you consider the Tantramar vintageable to any extent?' The apostle laughed gaily at this proof of the presence of a Philistine, but contented himself with praising other streams of less leonine beauty.

It may be said here that Mr. Bigelow deserves the greatest credit for his enterprise and daring in bringing so high priced a man to a small town like Amherst. Mr. Wilde had never spoken in so small a place before. He had a good house and a good hearing.

1	*Daily Transcript*: a Moncton newspaper. Wilde's train passed through Moncton; he would lecture there on 12 October.
2	Dorchester is a town between Moncton and Amherst. Wilde probably only saw it from his train car. Westcock is a town at the mouth of the Tantramar, a river in New Brunswick near the border with Nova Scotia. Wilde had referred to '[t]he gaudy leonine sunflower' in his poem 'Le Jardin'. In 1776 Fort Cumberland was the site of the Battle of Fort Cumberland, when British forces repelled sympathisers of the American Revolution.
3	Wilde's mother found this interview 'most amusing and clever', but did not like the decription of Wilde's hair: 'You ought to have a friseur every morning to curl it before the interviewers arrive'.
4	George Augustus Sala (1828–1895) was an author and journalist who signed his articles for the *Illustrated London News* as G.A.S.
5	C. J. Townshend was the son of a local clergyman; his wife produced *Patience* in Amherst.
6	Herbert Spencer (1820–1903) was a British scientist and political theorist.
7	Ahmed 'Urabi or Orabi Pasha (1841–1911) was an Egyptian nationalist. On 13 September 1882 a British army defeated 'Urabi's army at the Battle of Tell El Kebir, and 'Urabi surrendered.
8.	Edgar Fawcett (1847–1904) was an American novelist and poet.
9	The American poet James Russell Lowell (1819–1891) recited his 'Commemoration Ode' at Harvard University on 21 July 1865.
10	Charles George Douglas Roberts (1860–1943) was a Canadian poet who at the time of Wilde's visit was working as principal of Fredericton's York Street School.
11	Charles Pelham Mulvany (1835–1885) was an Irish-born clergyman and poet. He immigrated to Canada about 1859. Like Wilde he studied classics at Trinity College, Dublin; like Wilde's mother he wrote poetry for the Irish nationalist newspaper *The Nation*.
12	Louis-Honoré Fréchette (1839–1908) was a Canadian poet, short-story writer, and politician.
13	The sonnet quoted is 'London, 1802'. John Milton (1608–1674) was an English poet, best known for his epic, *Paradise Lost* (1667).
14	The sonnet quoted is 'The World Is Too Much with Us'.
15	Sir John Alexander Macdonald (1815–1891) was the Scottish-born first Prime Minister of Canada. He was returned to office in an election on 6 June. Wilde dined with Macdonald on 16 May, the day before parliament was prorogued.
16	The first line of Wilde's poem 'Vita Nuova'.

'Oscar Wilde Explains', *The Boston Herald* (Boston, MA), 16 Oct. 1882, 2

Oscar Wilde has arrived in Boston from St. John, N. B., and, in an interview Sunday afternoon at the hotel Vendome, he gave an explanation of his recent 'arrest' at Moncton, N. B., as stated in Saturday's *Herald*. He regarded the affair as an ill-advised attempt to extort blackmail on the part of the Young Men's Christian Association of Moncton. 'It seems,' to use his own words, 'that last week they telegraphed to my agent in Canada to ask whether I could lecture in Moncton for them on Friday night. I replied that I was engaged to deliver my second lecture at St. John on Friday, and that Thursday was the only open night I had in the week. At the same time I stated my terms. No reply came for 36 hours, and then another gentleman of that town made application for me to lecture. My agent then telegraphed a second time to the Y.M.C.A. to ask them to reply immediately to the previous message. They took no notice of the telegram, and after 48 hours elapsed, he very properly closed with the gentleman who was not connected with the Christian association. These latter people having ascertained that I was engaged by the other party, telegraphed to my agent to say that they would accept his offer, but the agent replied that the date was already fixed for another lecture. On my arrival at Moncton on Thursday last I was waited upon by a representative of the Y.M.C.A. and a local attorney, who asked me whether, in consideration of the disappointment to the association, I would not contribute something to the funds. I replied that I did not consider that the association had any right to make such a claim, and that I was not sufficiently interested in it to subscribe to it. On my refusal they proceeded to the under sheriff, and presented him with a writ, which they had obtained that morning, and asked him to serve it on me as I was stepping on the platform to lecture. The sheriff, a gentleman of some knowledge of the world, naturally declined to do anything so uncalled for and so impertinent, but called on me at my hotel and explained to me the matter. Two gentlemen of Moncton accompanied him and entered into engagements with the sheriff to prevent my being given any further annoyance. The lecture went off very successfully. After the lecture this local attorney made a definite demand on me for $100, on receipt of which he declared he would with-

The journalist George Augustus Sala, whose prose Wilde disliked.

draw his writ. My agent, by my orders, refused to accede to any such gross attempt at extortion, and the matter will proceed for trial before the local judge. Some gentlemen of the town have kindly promised to see to the matter on my behalf.[1] I am glad to say that great indignation was expressed at the behavior of the association and, before I left, most of the leading citizens had withdrawn their names as members of it. The whole thing shows the illegality of most law and the immorality of most moral institutions. Such associations are usually the refuge of the provincial Joseph Surfaces.[2] True, it afforded me an interesting insight into certainly not a very favorable side of Canadian ordinary life, and for experience one would go through a great deal, even to a sudden visit from a sheriff.'

Mr. Wilde further added that his next lectures would shortly be delivered in Maine and New Hampshire, but dates were not definitely arranged. He thought his departure from America would occur about December next and he proposed going to New Zealand and Australia before he went to Japan. He reluctantly admitted that the rumor that he was writing a book on the United States was not incorrect, but hinted that he was not going to publish it perhaps for some years. Speaking of Sala's latest work, *America Revisited*, extracts from which have appeared in the *Herald*, he said no one ever believed Sala to be in earnest. He was one of those disciples of Dickens who indulged in 'grotesque exaggerations.'[3]

1   Wilde's manager offered to pay $20 of the $100 and, when this was refused, a judge set a bond of $35 which Wilde's local sponsors covered. In Wilde's absence, the writ in the case was set aside by the Kent County Court, and the YMCA repudiated the action of its committee.

2   Joseph Surface is a character in *The School for Scandal*, a 1777 play by Richard Brinsley Sheridan (1751–1816). He is a hypocrite but nevertheless enjoys a reputation as a man of good morals.

3   Sala, Edmund Yates, and others, were known as Dickens's 'young men', and acknowledged the older writer as their inspiration. Sala's *America Revisited: From the Bay of New York to the Gulf of Mexico, and from Lake Michigan to the Pacific* was published in two volumes in 1882.

'Oscar Wilde Prostrated', *The Cincinnati Commercial* (Cincinnati, OH), 26 Nov. 1882, 7

NEW YORK, November 25.—Oscar Wilde is living in furnished rooms at present in West Eleventh street. He has not delivered any lectures recently, and although he may occasionally appear upon the platform again in this country, he does not contemplate giving any further serious attention to the lecture business for the benefit and aesthetic enlightenment of Americans. Since his return from the professional tour of the watering places in the summer, he has been living the life of a man about town. Through the kind offices of 'Sam' Ward and other friends he obtained a visitor's card to the Manhattan Club, and has been for some time a frequent caller there.[1] He still goes into society, although it is not exactly the same social crowd as that which took him upon his arrival here. He dines at well known restaurants about 7 o'clock every evening, and is a prominent figure at the theatres on first nights. He comes out into the lobby between the acts like a very commonplace young man,[2] lights a very small cigarette, and throwing himself into the attitude which a prominent photographer, on the payment of a satisfactory sum of money, was allowed to reproduce for the benefit of the people at large,[3] he furnishes a novel and altogether harmless diversion for the lobby loungers. After the play, and probably an incidental aesthetic agony over some 'dreadful' combination of color in the scenery, he indulges in a little supper and an accompanying cogitation over a few critical paragraphs intended for publication[4]—In fact, it will be seen that Mr. Wilde has been leading a very seedy existence, and he now declares that 'he is thoroughly exhausted, you know, and—ah—suffering from severe nervous prostration.' In the meantime many persons have expressed a fear that Mr. Wilde intended staying here. An English paper printed a report that he intended marrying an American heiress. There have been rumors of his starting a society journal in New York. The story has been circulated that his name had been posted for election at the Manhattan Club, and it has been wildly asserted that he intended producing his play, *Vera, the Nihilist*, in a very short time. It seemed indeed that the life of the poet would for a long while be bound up with the life of the metropolis. A *Tribune* reporter, who called at the house, in West Eleventh street, was shown into Mr. Wilde's sitting-room. It is a commonplace room, with the paper portions of three Japanese parasols blown against one of the walls to denote a presence not in harmony with the remainder of the surroundings. Mr. Wilde presently sauntered in. There was a look of utter weariness on his long, smooth face. He threw back his hair in a manner that was both painful and poetic, and sank slowly, gracefully, but with an appearance of unutterable fatigue into an arm chair.

'Have you made any arrangements to produce your play?' was asked.

'Why do you ask?' said Mr. Wilde, opening his eyes.

'The public might like to know.'

'Oh!' and Mr. Wilde closed his eyes and yielded himself up to thought.

'To persons of no reputation,' he presently began, 'small paragraphs are doubtless an advantage, but really I do not care for them.'

'But the production of your play might be a matter of a big paragraph.'

'Oh,' and Mr. Wilde closed his eyes again. 'Well, I have made no arrangements as yet,' he added.[5]

'Are you going to Australia?'

'As soon as I get thoroughly rested. I am tired out. Really all is hollow, hollow.'

Mr. Wilde here passed his hand across his brow, and his eyes again denoted that life for him was full of fatigue and disappointment.

'I am waiting to go to Australia, because I cannot find anyone to go with. I shall probably stay here until January.'

'And how about Japan?'

'Japan will keep. I shall doubtless go there before I am through.'[6]

1   Samuel Cutler 'Uncle Sam' Ward (1814–1884) was a political lobbyist and gourmet and the brother of Julia Ward Howe.
2   The allusion is to *Patience*. When the aesthetic poet Bunthorne threatens his rival, Grosvenor, with a curse, Grosvenor agrees to become 'A commonplace young man | A matter-of-fact young man | A steady and stolidy, jolly Bank-holiday | Everyday young man!'
3   The reporter here refers to Napoleon Sarony (Wilde was photographed by no one else in America).
4   A reference to Wilde's review of Langtry's New York debut for the *World*.
5   Wilde had met with the American actress Marie Prescott (1853–1893) on 12 November to discuss *Vera*.
6   Wilde never visited Japan.

'Mr. Wilde Undisturbed by Rumors', *New-York Tribune* (New York, NY), 25 Dec. 1882, 5

A rumor which caused considerable consternation and excitement was abroad in the city last night to the effect that Oscar Wilde had been swindled by a 'banco steerer' out of $1,100.[1] The report stated that Mr. Wilde had given the confidence man a check on the Madison Square Bank for the amount, and had afterward given notice to the bank not to pay the check. The report had the color of probability lent to it by the fact that Joseph Sellick, alias 'Paper-Collar Joe,' alias 'Hungry Joe,' etc., had been figuring on the police returns at the central office within two days. A searching investigation by a *Tribune* reporter revealed Mr. Wilde at midnight in Delmonico's cafe, seated at a table smoking, in company with two friends. Mr. Wilde was seemingly cool and imperturbable. He lit a fresh cigarette as the reporter spoke to him and blew a bold cloud of smoke into the air, which enveloped a young man with an immaculate white tie just in front of him.

'Mr. Wilde, is it true that you have lost $1,100 in a banco game?' asked the reporter.

'I have heard the report,' replied the poet. 'I received a note while at dinner today asking me about it, and I sent the person a reply.'

'Then I understand you to deny the story?'

'It does not concern me enough to either deny it or affirm it,' said Mr. Wilde, in a soft, low voice. 'Not,' he added with a smile, after a moment's thought, 'but that I should very much object, indeed, to losing $1,100, but I should not object to having it known if I had done so.'[2]

The guileless smile of Mr. Wilde indicated that 'Paper Collar Joe' would have met a foeman worthy of his steel.

1   Banco or bunko is a dice game, but the term was also applied to card games or to any dishonest gambling game. A banco steerer was a member of a confidence trickster gang whose task was to entrap the victim.
2   Wilde admitted that he had 'fallen into a den of thieves' in a letter to a friend.

'Oscar's Adieu', *St. Louis Post-Dispatch* (St. Louis, MO), 28 Dec. 1882, 1

New York, December 28. Oscar Wilde has sailed for Liverpool on the steamer *Bothnia*. The fact of his going was not generally known, and he escaped the scrutiny of curious people who would have otherwise attended his departure. His friend Mr. Norman Forbes, of Mme. Modjeska's troupe, was the only person at the steamer with him.[1] The early morning was chilly, and Mr. Wilde wore his fur collar buttoned closely about his neck, and beneath was tied a heavy old gold silk scarf. It was bright moonlight when Mr. Forbes and a reporter greeted him.

'You see,' he said, as he raised his hat and allowed his long hair to linger for a moment in the moonlight, 'my going away has been kept quiet. Only a few of my personal friends know of it, and I persuaded them not to get up at so early an hour to see me away.'

'Did you enjoy your visit to this country?' asked the reporter.

'Very much indeed,' he replied. 'I think America is a very progressive country, but it is somewhat behind in art, but that, of course, is to be expected. Nevertheless, I was much delighted with the progress that art has made here. There is much that is good, and, individually, I have met many talented gentlemen with whom I am delighted. Of course I had much to contend against, and had I not been a young man, I probably would have been forced to give up my object. I have been subjected to much ridicule and at the same time have made many friends. I have seen very much to be pleased with and believe that I have learned a great deal. I enjoyed my visit to the Western States and wanted to spend more time there.'

'Were you pleased with your reception here, Mr. Wilde?'

'No, I was not,' he replied smiling. 'No man ever came to this country who had to contend with what I did. I am glad that I am on the bright side of thirty, for I do not think that a man past thirty could have accomplished what I have.'

'What do you think of the Americans as a people?'

'Ah,' he said, as he paused in his walk, 'the Americans had a type fifty years ago but they have lost it. In fifty years hence, however, they may regain it. But I like the Americans.' Mr. Wilde spoke with some hesitancy of Mrs. Langtry and Mrs. Labouchère, and said: 'I am very friendly with both the ladies, and Mrs. Langtry is a particular friend of mine. I attach no importance to their quarrel.[2] Mrs. Langtry has a perfect right to choose her friends, and I think I know that she would do nothing to injure her reputation. I think that Mrs. Langtry has been treated very unjustly here. She came to this country to act and to study. She has been misrepresented. Your people, who are so chivalrous, have not treated her with consideration. The press has been too severe in its criticisms. She is young, and all this is very discouraging. A man, for instance, could contend with this, but you should be more chivalrous to the ladies.'

'What's your opinion of the American press?'

Mr. Wilde did not answer directly. He placed his right foot on the rail, rested his chin on his hand, and gazed meditatively at the waning moon. Finally he said, with a smile:

'Of course the American press is very different from our English press. The English press is made up of facts, while the American press is imagination. But you have many brilliant writers and courteous journalists. But, as I said before, your dramatic critics have been rather hard on Mrs. Langtry. They should be a little more chivalrous.'

'Will you ever return to this country, Mr. Wilde?'

'Oh, yes!' he replied, 'I hope to return some time. I like the country very much, and when I return I hope to find a great improvement in decorative art. It is progressing, and I have great hopes of the future. At present I want rest and peace and would like to go to a country where I am not known—if there is such a country.'

'Your lecture tour has been a financial success has it not, Mr. Wilde?'

'Oh, yes, quite a financial success,' he replied.

It was now time for the steamer to leave, and Mr. Forbes and the reporter went on shore, and a few minutes later the *Bothnia* moved away from the wharf.

1   Norman Forbes-Robertson (1858–1932) was an English actor.
2   There were reports that Langtry and her mentor Henrietta Labouchère (1841–1910) had fallen out over Langtry's relationship with Frederick Gebhard (1860–1910), a wealthy New Yorker Langtry had met shortly after arriving in America.

'Oscar Wilde at Home', *The Times* (Philadelphia, PA), 28 Jan. 1883, 2

London, January 9.

The Troubadour of Aestheticism has returned from American shores and today made his first appearance in streets and clubs. He is sad and depressed. The English people, having been instructed by their American cousins how to 'guy' a public character such as Mr. Wilde, have begun already and 'skits' are being made in the public prints and club sarcasm is rife in every direction. As a consequence Oscar Wilde had already announced his intention to leave England for the south of France, to spend the summer, and Willie Wilde, his brother, proposes to go with him, as he too has been the object of a raillery rather malicious than good-natured.[1] Oscar did not care to talk about his experiences in the United States, but said, with some bitterness, that he had been treated so badly by many people and a part of the newspaper press that he could not refrain from saying that he was much disappointed. Yes, really disappointed. He was not angry, but disappointed.

'When I first came to America I was received with a warmth of welcome that bespoke no end of future pleasure. I was led to be too enthusiastic and hopeful. The better class of people were pleasant, and I found some society the equal of our best society here, but not much. The average American is narrow-minded and ignorant. He is self-assertive. He is more opinionated than his English cousin, whom he resembles in all of the bad points and is equal to in none of the good. The average American I found to be without respect or veneration, consequently he has no desire to acquaint himself with the canons of art. He is the most splendid egotist, and frequently demonstrates qualities as the most magnificent liar the world produces. He regards the size of his country as a personal compliment of nature to himself. Having no respect nor veneration and being accustomed to exaggeration, he sneers at what he does not understand and scorns to learn that which does not immediately return a reward.'

'Mr. Wilde, you appear to have some special cause of complaint.'

'Not so. I have no cause of complaint, and only speak as every gentleman must who visits the States and spends, as I have done, a considerable time there. Let me continue. You have no idea, on the other hand, what intellects are to be found there, what wit, elegance, taste and female beauty in the first grade of society. They have artists in painting and sculpture; they have a good social life, which has nothing of the Republic about it, but yet a quiet American dignity at once charming and befitting. There are picture galleries and churches which are very fair. There is some good architecture in the cities, but as a rule it is crude and new. The city of New York is cosmopolitan in its population, and its dwellings and public places reflect that mixture of nationalities in which, as a rule, the elements were not originally the best.'

'You came away rather unexpectedly, did you not?'

'Yes—no—I was preparing to go when an unexpected call from England accelerated my preparations.'

'The cable brought word that you had met a "bunko" man and that you were his.'

'Ah, that is a very absurd story, which has such a little bit of foundation that I won't deny it or explain it. I may say, however, that I did meet "Mr. Drexel's son," as clever Americans had done before me.[2] If that industrious young man has accomplished all the knavery with which he is so liberally credited, his wealth will soon exceed that of his putative father.'

'Was your lecturing tour a financial success?'

'Yes, quite so. It was very successful. I was somewhat startled by the attitude of the newspapers toward me and they ran amuck with their usual graceful and witless criticism. They attracted the public attention to me.'

'What was your opinion of the newspapers?'

'Full of news, but edited without judgment, written with a minimum amount of brains and good English and put together without regard to truth and decency.'

'Perhaps the newspaper press is responsible for your somewhat obvious ill-will against Americans?'

'Do you think it obvious? It is only in appearance, for I adore America and Americans as I would any other curiosity. I have nothing but the kindliest feelings for the Americans, and the newspapers are full of interest and monstrously enterprising. If they spared themself effort and sought to be polished with the same assiduity they seek to be sensational they would be much improved. What I complain of, to be particular, is the fact that they are written by incompetent men, or rather certain subjects are handled by incompetent pens. The man who excels as a descriptive writer on subjects such as fires and arrests in gaming houses is not the man to write intelligently about a statue from the hand of a great sculptor—at least not always—and how can the man whose musical ear has the training only of street music write fairly or well of Berlioz's *Damnation of Faust?* As for art, the ordinary newspaper writer in America gained his knowledge of it by studying art through the glass panes of a print shop and his knowledge of architecture in enforced contemplation of the walls of jails.'

Here somebody said that the newspapers in America had credited Mr. Wilde with having created a sensation in the Lotos Club when he made that remark before.[3] Mr. Wilde said: 'I did say so before and it is none the less true in that I have repeated it.'

Then he went on: 'What impresses itself upon the unprejudiced observer is that the newspapers are stamped with incompetency. They do lots of great big things, but nothing is rounded in and completed. They are loose and flying, like a silken scarf torn and waved by unsteady hands.'

'What art did you find in America?'

'What you might expect in a new country. The art idea is not strongly rooted in their character. The Catholic religion has fostered a love for Madonnas and altar studies. The vast sweeps of prairie, the grand mountain and landscape scenery, the tumbling falls of Niagara, than which nothing is grander in the world, have not, as one might have thought, impressed an artistic sentiment. The fact is that art-love has not yet a permanency in America. That has got to be created. There are some magazines and periodicals that make very nice pictures and print them, but that kind of picture, while requiring some skill, is not art. It is elementary only.'

'And the literature?'

'There is, it seems to me, the foundation for an excellent school of literature in the States. It is marked by many signs of promise. It is too clannish, however. There are half a dozen or so who are active workers in the field of literature who monopolize the seats in its highest places. These are Mr. Howells, James, Aldrich, Mrs. Burnett, Mrs. Stuart Phelps, Cable and one or two others.'[4]

'And do you not think they are entitled to their high position?'

'Most assuredly, for if they were not they could not hold it. There are among them, as a leaven to their protective system of maintaining the best places, a goodly number of women, who share their honors.'

'Are you going back to America?'

'Not I, indeed.'[5]

'They made it pretty warm for you, did they not?' asked a friend.

'I was very comfortable. But there begins the music.' Mr. Wilde came forward from the mantelpiece, and taking the arm of his brother Willie sauntered out of the lounging room into the large hall of Raleigh House, where a smoking concert was just beginning.

The half-dozen who had gathered about him in the manager's lounging parlor were his acquaintances and friends. Among them was *The Times* correspondent. When Mr. Wilde had gone a gentleman said: 'I fear Oscar is very much embittered by the loss of his money. The fact is, they got nearly $7,000 from him, and one check only did he succeed in stopping. A chap calling himself A. J. Drexel's son called on him, wanted him to see a picture by Millet, led him into a confidence game and then, when he remonstrated, he was thrown out. The whole story was told by a friend of his to a British Consular officer, from whom I have it. Then he was very much involved in the Langtry esclandre.

He had espoused her too warmly and made some enemies by trying to bring her into a dinner party. He was curtly written to and told that the dinner would be postponed.'

1   Wilde went to Paris for three months at the end of January, without his brother William Charles Kingsbury 'Willie' Wilde (1852–1899).
2   There were reports that the conman introduced himself to Wilde as the son of the American banker Anthony Joseph Drexel Sr (1826–1893).
3   Wilde had attended a dinner at New York's Lotos Club on 28 October 1882. In a speech he criticised the American press, saying that he had more than once met with interviewers 'whose ideas of painting had evidently derived from the chromos in the stationers' shop windows, their ideas of sculpture from the figures in front of tobacconists' shops, and their ideas of architecture from the local jail'.
4   Frances Hodgson Burnett (1849–1924) was an English-American author whose best-known works are *Little Lord Fauntleroy* (1885–1886) and *The Secret Garden* (1911). Her first novel, *That Lass o' Lowrie's*, was published in 1877. Elizabeth Stuart Phelps (1844–1911) was an American author of spiritual novels and, like Wilde, an advocate for clothing reform. George Washington Cable (1844–1925) was an American novelist. In 1880 he published his first novel, *The Grandissimes: A Story of Creole Life*.
5   Wilde sailed on the SS *Britannic* for New York on 11 August 1883.

'Paris Gossip', *The Chicago Daily Tribune* (Chicago, IL), 17 Apr. 1883, 7

Paris, April 2.—(Special Correspondence.) Have you quite forgotten the memorable visit paid to the City of Chicago last year by that astonishing and eccentric young man, Oscar Wilde? Or does an amused smile still flit over some Chicago faces as they conjure up his esthetic image and think of the novel theories, sartorial and artistic, which he expounded in America? In either case Oscar is, with all his absurdities (and perhaps a good deal on account of them), a sufficiently interesting character to deserve reverting to now and then, as occasion offers; and, the occasion having offered itself to me several times lately in Paris, I took it. I had various reasons for doing so. First and foremost, a very natural desire to see a man who had so audaciously run the gauntlet of popular prejudice and convention; secondly, professional curiosity—a wish to learn something about the work on America which rumor said he had come to Paris to write, far from the madding crowd of adoring virgins that beset him in his native Kensington; and thirdly—but the two reasons I have given already are sufficient.

He has been here for at least two months already, but curiously enough has attracted very little attention. Not a single French paper has, so far as I have heard, thought it worth its while to send a man to interview him, and though he has been seen daily on the Boulevard de Capucines and in the Avenue de l'Opera his coming and going have made no more stir amongst the Parisians than if he had been a mere Roumanian Minister or a Turkish Pasha. From this my intelligent readers, even though they should not happen to have crossed the briny ocean, will at once perceive that Paris is a very much more cosmopolitan and blasé city than New York or Chicago.

To some extent, no doubt, this absence of excitement may be accounted for by the comparative quiet and simplicity of the esthete's demeanor here. Having no particular object to gain by cutting any ultra-esthetic capers on the boulevard, and, wishing to be allowed to work at his book and his plays undisturbed, he has put away much of his bombast and absurdity for a season; dropped the kneebreeches, discarded all thought of lilies or sunflowers, trimmed his hair carefully, and, in short, has discreetly toned himself down into something not *very* unlike the objectionable and detestable bourgeois against whom he points so much satire.

At home, however, that is to say, in his rooms at the Hotel Voltaire, and at night, when, responsive to the invitations liberally showered upon him by the Americans and English in Paris, he condescends to shine at a stray soirée or dinner, he becomes the Oscar you have seen and I had read of—a glorious creature, all harmonious color and intensity; a gentle dogmatist, a High Priest, and Prophet of the Beautiful. The other day, for instance, when I called upon him, I found him lounging luxuriously in an arm-chair and attired in a green velvet jacket, salmon-colored neckcloth, burnt sienna 'inexpressibles,'[1] red silk stockings, and pumps. At the back of his head he had artfully disposed a tiger or a leopard skin, and round him, strewn about with a great appearance of elaborate disorder, were fifteen or twenty half-read and half-cut yellow-covered novels.[2]

He rose with real though languid courtesy, and begged me to be seated. I must say his face pleased me. Effeminate it is, of course, but decidedly clever and refined. His conversation, of which I had heard so much, pleased me less. He seemed to have an almost insuperable difficulty in being natural, and the tritest remark set him pompously digressing for full five minutes. 'I believe you frequent the same café as I do?' was, for instance, replied to by an exhaustive dissertation (suspiciously like a bit of an old lecture) on the important part the café played in the social economy of the Greeks. Gradually, however, I led him from the ancients to the moderns, and at last we fell into what I found a very enjoyable, gossipy discussion of America. Mr. Wilde spoke of the land of liberty in a kindly and almost a regretful tone; vowed he had learned much from his short trip from the Atlantic to the Pacific, and hinted that the day might not be far distant when he would return to the West. But he had no illusions about the reception he might expect there. 'Even Sarah Bernhardt,' said he, 'would not have any success if she were to go back.[3] See how indifferently it has fared with Rossi,[4] and many another.'

Soon after I made some reference to the book he was supposed to be writing and inquired what scope and character he intended to give it. 'Well,' he replied, 'it will probably be issued in two volumes, and be ready this year. As to its character, I shall not go into very deep criticism. Neither shall I say much about Boston jails and Philadelphia sanitation or things of that sort, which are, of course, of no importance. I shall try to set down what I have heard Americans say of life and art—and I have heard much that was of deep interest—and I shall especially consider what life is to young men in America, what they can hope to do there, and what they do.'

'You must have found yourself very little in sympathy with America and Americans, surely?' I remarked after a pause.

'Oh, no,' condescendingly replied the generous Oscar. 'I feel an interest in—er—all humanity. Even in Chicago I found much—much—of intensest interest—beauties—wonderful beauties. One day as I sojourned in that city I came upon—er—the water-works. A sort of—er—castellated atrocity, with pepper-box turrets and absurd portcullises.

How came they (thought I, with amazement)—how came they to erect this hideous building in this most modern and utilitarian of cities? I must have a closer look at this horror. Perchance I shall find some beauty even here, I murmured, for we cannot live without Beauty, you know. We can do without food and—er—things of that sort, but not without Beauty… Then it occurred to me that perhaps I might discover this Beauty I had sought for in vain so long in—American machinery. A wheel is in itself a very beautiful object. All the noblest forms of the ceramic art are derived from the potter's wheel. And yet in England I had always found machinery such a pitiful and ugly thing; a jumble of cranks and cogs and petty pieces, you know, without a touch of grandeur about them. So I entered that castellated horror at Chicago, and there at last I came upon a wheel—the wheel of the Chicago Water-Works—a mighty, majestic, unutterably harmonious wheel. I saw the beauty and the poetry of America in that revolving wonder; and I said to myself if ever America produces a great musician let him write a Machinery Symphony. He could have no more worthy subject.

'But of course they never will have a great musician out there,' continued Oscar, dropping from the clouds to earth with singular suddenness, 'until they have abolished the shrieking steam whistle. Their tympanums have all been ruined by those whistles.'[5]

We left Chicago at this point and drifted into art. Oscar professed immense admiration for much of the decorative art he had seen in America, and spoke in glowing terms of Chase, 'who has done more for art in his country than anyone living,' said he, and Lafarge, 'who has made quite a new departure in the art of manufacturing stained-glass.' Tiffany's centrepieces, too, he pronounced 'finer than anything of the sort we can show in England.' And he regretted very much that art was such a rarity in America still despite the example set by these three reformers, Chase, Lafarge, and Tiffany.[6]

'But, after all,' he went on, 'the stage will afford Americans the greatest scope. The actor's art is the best for them, because it is the most democratic.'

This brought us to a discussion on transatlantic actresses, one or two of whom appear to have made a deep impression upon our young esthete. From this again we rambled on to American women in general, and American love, on which subject I found Oscar rather shy of expressing an opinion for some time. Why, I know not. He said at last, however, that he thought American love on the whole a very innocent, boy-and-girlish, brotherly and sisterly affair.

'You do not seem to believe in its being profound,' said I, half hoping to hear a burning confession. 'Well, no,' replied Oscar, with a smile. 'You see there can be no question of deep love where it is of the slightest consequence to a man whether he catches his train or loses it. Every one is anxious to catch trains in America, you know.'[7]

And now, fair American maidens, I leave the esthete to your tender charity.

1   i.e., trousers.
2   French novels were often published in yellow paper covers.
3   Bernhardt had toured America in 1880–1881. She embarked on a further eight successful American tours between 1887 and 1917.
4   Ernesto Rossi (1827–1896) was an Italian actor.
5   'Personal Impressions of America': 'I fail to see why these whistles could not be set to very beautiful notes of music. It might not be possible to treat the hearers to a symphony of Beethoven's played by them—I have to acknowledge that would be *too* elaborate—but at least the whistle might play some form of musical sound somewhat less harrowing.'
6   William Merritt Chase (1849–1916) was an American painter and teacher. John La Farge (1835–1910) was an American painter, muralist, and stained glass window maker. Louis Comfort Tiffany (1848–1933) was an American artist and designer, best known for his work in stained glass.
7   'Personal Impressions of America': 'There was an absence of romantic unpunctuality in America, everybody seems in a hurry to catch a train, it was a sort of national amusement. This is a state of things which is not favourable to poetry or romance. Had Romeo or Juliet been in a constant state of anxiety about trains, or had their minds been agitated by the question of return-tickets, Shakespeare could not have given us those lovely balcony scenes which are so full of poetry and pathos.'

'Oscar Wilde's Ambition', *New-York Tribune* (New York, NY), 12 Aug. 1883, 12

'Mr. Wilde?' said the clerk at the Brunswick Hotel to a *Tribune* reporter yesterday. 'Yes, there he is sitting on that bench.' The reporter gazed in the direction indicated, but thought the clerk must have been mistaken.

Wilde photographed with short hair by Sarony (1883).

In place of the rather gaunt, long-haired and sallow-faced Oscar of a few months ago, he saw a rosy-cheeked, cherry-faced individual whose close-cropped hair was almost hidden in the shade of a broad-brimmed, peaked felt hat. But on drawing close Mr. Wilde's identity became apparent, and holding out his hand he gave a cordial greeting. He had only been in the city for a few hours, having arrived on the *Britannic* early in the morning.

'I suppose I am looking well,' assented he; 'you see a sea voyage does one a tremendous lot of good. Besides the invigorating air there is the absence of all petty annoyances such as inquisitive callers, letters that have to be answered and—'

'Interviews?'

'Oh, no, I really think that is too bad. I never object to talking with newspaper men, and, in fact, generally enjoy it. What have I been doing since I left America? Resting chiefly. As soon as I reached the other side I went to Paris and, shutting myself up there, I devoted myself to writing a new play which I have with me here. Its scene is laid in Europe in the sixteenth century. I stopped in Paris till the Salon was opened and then went to London.[1] I was so importuned by the students of the

Royal Academy to give them a lecture on painting, that I consented, and I guess what I told them must have roused the ire of their several preceptors and instructors, to whom my ideas are as "caviar to the general." Then everyone was always asking me my opinion of America, so I lost patience and told them to wait till they heard my lecture on America. I was in for it then, you see, and had to lecture in London. I had heaps of offers for the provinces, of course, but I only repeated it five or six times, for I had to hurry to America.

'Now, I suppose you want to know what I have come over for specially. Well, first and foremost, it is to superintend the production of *Vera*, but there is a motive behind that. Last year I told the people of America, or rather as many as would come to hear me, what my views of art were. This year I want them to see those ideas put into practice. In *Vera* I am making a bold experiment. I am trying to see whether the love of an abstract idea cannot be made as dramatically interesting as the love of an individual. I am trying, too, whether the hoarse cry of the yearners after liberty, which rose above the din around the barricades in Paris, and still is heard not quite drowned by the drum-taps of the Russian soldiery as they beat at the executions of the Nihilistic martyrs, whether that hoarse, harsh cry, which has never ceased in Europe for ninety years, cannot be reduced to music, and thus become a work of art. That my scene is laid in Russia is a mere accident, due to the fact that Russia is the only country where tyranny is ever grinding the people, and where that dull, unromantic, unemotional Philistine "middle class" does not exist. In Russia there are only two degrees—the masters and the slaves.

'Now for the first time I am really on my trial before the American public. Anyone can talk about art, but to talk well one must be able to do well. It is only the creator who can analyze his own creations. There are few exceptions to this. Edgar Allan Poe carried the analytical faculty to the utmost, and thus became the exquisite critic as well as the original creator. Keats was an analyst. Byron was not, and to this most of his shortcomings are due. But I must not bore you. I can only add that I shall take the greatest pains to have my costumes and setting as harmonious as I can, though the question of expense has hampered me materially. Miss Prescott seems thoroughly enthusiastic, and if anyone can make my play a success, I am sure she will.'

1   Wilde was spotted at the Paris Salon in May in the company of Whistler, who was exhibiting his portrait of his mother.

'Mr. Oscar Wilde's Hair', *The New York Herald* (New York, NY), 12 Aug. 1883, 10

Oscar Wilde arrived in New York yesterday on the steamer *Britannic*. He sat in the lobby of the Brunswick Hotel late in the afternoon. A *Herald* reporter was received courteously and had a long chat with Mr. Wilde, who spoke with the peculiar ladylike drawl which is familiar to all who have heard him.

'I see you've had your hair cut,' observed the reporter.

'Oh, yes,' said the poet, 'to the amazement of Europe I cut off my locks. I never had my hair cut in my life until last March.'

'Do you really mean to say that people abroad were amazed?'

'Positively amazed, I assure you. They have not quite recovered. It was a bold act.'

'How did it happen?'

'It's rather interesting I think. You see, I was in the gallery of the Louvre in Paris, and I saw the bust of a young Roman Emperor. It was very beautiful, indeed. As soon as I saw that the young Emperor had his hair cut short, I wanted to be like him.'

'Are you?'

'So far as the hair is concerned, I think I am. I got a hairdresser—and the French hairdressers are artists—to come with me to the Louvre and I showed him the young Emperor's bust. He cut my hair after the fashion he saw there—as nearly as he could. I afterward found that the bust represented Nero, one of the worst behaved young men in the world, and yet a man of strong artistic passion. I thought it just suited my case.

'Speaking of my hair,' he resumed, 'the trouble is that people mistake the forms of art for the principle. There is only one principle in art and yet millions of forms. The majority of people think that one cannot admire art unless one's hair falls below one's collar. I want to show them that they are mistaken. I wore my hair long because I think that long hair is beautiful when it is properly cut.'

'Cut off?'

'No, when it is properly trimmed; but so is short hair.'

'You have given up knee breeches?'

'For the present, yes. You see, one's taste changes; and, besides, one must suit one's trousers to the cut of one's hair. I think there is really a strong desire among young men to wear knee breeches, but it requires great courage to begin—it does, indeed. But they were invented for a period when people wore wigs. We cannot wear short breeches and short hair. That would be absurd.'

'Don't you find it hard to get knee breeches on?

'Not very. Then they are so comfortable, and they give play to the grace and joy and poetry of one's physical being.'

'Have you changed your opinion about the ugliness of the Atlantic ocean?'

'No; I must still quarrel with the Atlantic. It is not beautiful at all. There are no objects to give it distance; nothing but gray, gray sky and gray, gray sea. It is simply monotonous.'

'Mr. Labouchère says in *Truth* that your lecture on America was a failure, and that your audience laughed at you. Is it true?'[1]

'Labouchère made a most brilliant attack on me. It was a rare, brilliant thing, and do you know he is one of the most able men in England and has a great future before him. But the lecture charmed the English people and was well received. To call anything published in Labouchère's paper "truth" is only a bit of fun on his part. Everybody knows that. It is the pride of the paper that nothing published in it is consistent with fact. If it took Labouchère three columns to prove that I was forgotten, then there is no difference between fame and obscurity.'

'Have you written any new poems?'

'Yes, I will publish a new volume before Christmas.'[2]

In conclusion, Mr. Wilde said that he would not make a comparison between the artistic tastes of Londoners and New Yorkers, because such a comparison would not be fair. He said that he was more than ever convinced that the French art imported into the United States after the Revolution was suited only for a king's court and not for the people of a republic. It should be costly or it would not be pretty. The Americans were, he said, going back to the real, simple art which flourished in the colonial days. This, he said, was the only genuine American art, and would be the art of the Republic in the future.

Mr. Wilde has grown quite plump. He wore a black slouch hat, tight trousers, a black waistcoat and coat and white cuffs rolled back. He said he was accompanied on his voyage from England by several old classmates, who were going West to rid the country of wild animals, if they could find any to shoot at. He will be in the city for two weeks, and will then visit several watering places, after which he will go home.

1   Labouchère had been supportive of Wilde during the 1882 tour, but his review of 'Personal Impressions of America' was scathing: Wilde was an 'effeminate phrase-maker' who had lectured 'to empty benches at the height of the season'.

2   Wilde did not publish a second volume of poetry.

'Oscar's Opinion of "Vera"', *Philadelphia Press* (Philadelphia, PA), 22 Aug. 1883, 3

The first appearance of Mr. Oscar Wilde as a dramatic author, which event took place at the Union Square Theatre last night,[1] seems to have been taken advantage of by numerous dramatic critics to make an onslaught that would daunt anyone but the placid Oscar himself, who comes up smiling this morning. Shortly after 9 o'clock the newly-fledged dramatist was met on Fifth Avenue by a reporter for the *Mail and Express*. Oscar looked jaunty, dressed in a short seersucker coat, light trousers and a small straw hat.

'What are your impressions of the first night of *Vera?*' inquired the reporter.

'I consider that the play was a success. Of course it has some faults, but I will correct them. For one thing, *Vera* is too long. I shall cut it judiciously. The first night of a play is nothing more or less than a full-dress rehearsal, and the audience is always a peculiar one. Last night the actors did not act so well, because it was a first night. But, take it altogether, I was quite satisfied. When I have altered the play and shortened the last act a great deal; it will be more successful.'

Marie Prescott photographed as Vera by Sarony (1883).

'The critics seem to be unanimous in speaking of *Vera* as a failure.'

'Ah, well, now, I make it a rule, you know, never to take seriously what newspaper writers say. Oh, dear, no, not at all. If people like my play, why they will go to see it; that's all there is to it. Otherwise all the papers in the country cannot make them come, you know. Besides, I was surprised to see people come out in this hot weather.'

'Will you remain here to improve the play?'

'I shall stay for a few weeks to see how it goes after pruning. I think that it is just that people who were there last night should come again next week to note the improvement, don't you know.'

'Did the actors portray the characters to suit you?'

'Yes, indeed. Mr. Lamb in particular was very good; very good, indeed. Mr. Boniface looked splendid, and Mr. Morrison was exceedingly fine. Miss Prescott was too nervous. She will surprise the public after that wears off. Why, bless me, she acted much better at rehearsal. But she did do some fine work last night, and several of her speeches she gave in a manner to win applause. Yet she gave the same speeches infinitely better at rehearsal. But, as I said before, a first-night audience is an abnormal one, composed mostly of actors and critics. They do not make a play. It is the mere passer-by, who drops into the theatre, who makes a play successful.'

'The critics say there is too much poetry in the play?'

'I presume they think so. Well, the last act does pass into poetry and the prose becomes rhythmic. That is in the nature of things. One could not for a moment imagine the balcony scene from *Romeo and Juliet* rendered in prose. Always passion passes into music at a certain altitude.'

'If *Vera* is a success, will you write another play to afflict a long-suffering public?'

'*Vera* is a success,' said Mr. Wilde, smiling blandly. 'You ask if I will write another play. I have one already written. It is in my room. Come up and I will read it to you.'

The reporter excused himself.

'Well, I will tell you, then, that I have a five-act drama, entitled *The Duchess of Padua.* The period is of the fifteenth century, and the scene is laid in Italy. It is in blank verse and prose mixed. The prose is the comedy portion, and the blank verse is the dramatic parts. I have not yet offered it to a manager.[2] Goodbye; I shall go to a rehearsal shortly,' said Mr. Wilde, as he started down Fifth Avenue.

1   The play opened on 20 August and closed on 25 August.
2   Wilde had written *The Duchess of Padua* for the American actress Mary Anderson (1859–1940), but she disliked the script and declined to accept it.

'Oscar Wilde's Views', *The Morning News* **(Paris, France), 20 Jun. 1884, 1**

Mr. Oscar Wilde is in Paris, on his wedding tour,[1] 'too happy to be interviewed,' as he himself pleaded in a letter that would have melted any heart but that of a representative of *The Morning News.* He was seen at the Hôtel Wagram, stretched on a sofa amid a heap of books, in a room overlooking the spacious Gardens of the Tuileries.

'You are reading, Mr. Wilde?'—not exactly a brilliant opening: but how to begin.

'Yes, I am dipping; I never read from the beginning, especially with novels. It is the only way to stimulate the curiosity that books, with their regular openings, always fail to rouse. Have you ever overheard a conversation in the street, caught the fag end of it, and wished you might know more? If you "overhear" your books in that way, you will go back to the first chapter, and on to the last naturally, as soon as the characters "bite."'

'Huysmans and Stendhal are, I see, in your collection.'

'Stendhal, of course;' and Mr. Oscar Wilde held up *Le Rouge et le Noir* as some people hold up their Bibles. 'As for Huysmans, this last book of his is one of the very best things I have seen.'[2]

'You go to Stendhal again and again?'

'Yes; and he is one of the few. For my part, I think the most exquisite thing in reading is the pleasure of forgetfulness. It is so nice to think there are some books you cared for so much at a certain epoch in your life and do not care for now. There is to me a positive delight in "cutting" an author and feeling I have got beyond him.'

'And do you extend that observation to persons?'

'Undoubtedly; so we all do only I would make it a positive satisfaction instead of a regret. Why should we not joyfully admit that there are some people we do not want to see again? It is not ingratitude; it is not indifference; they have simply given us all they have to give.'

'You do not feel in that way about Paris, I suppose? You were here last year for a long time, and this season brings you here again.'

'No; it is not easy to exhaust the message of Paris, especially when Sarah Bernhardt is playing.'[3]

'You have seen *Macbeth*?'

'Over and over again; there is nothing like it on our stage, and it is her finest creation. I say her creation, deliberately, because to my mind it is utterly impertinent to talk of Shakespeare's *Macbeth* or Shakespeare's *Othello*. Shakespeare is only one of the parties; the second is the artiste through whose mind it passes. When the two together combine to give me an acceptable hero, that is all I ask. Shakespeare's intentions were his own secret; all we can form an opinion about is what is actually before us.'

'And Sarah satisfies you?'

'There is absolutely nothing like her. She brings all her fine intel-

Sarah Bernhardt as Lady Macbeth (1884).

ligence to the part, all her instinctive and acquired knowledge of the stage. Her influence over Macbeth's mind is just as much an influence of womanly charm as of will—with us they only accentuate the last. She holds him under a spell; he sins because he loves her; his ambition is quite a secondary motive. How can he help loving her? She binds him by every tie, even by the tie of coquetry. Look at her dress; the tight-fitting tunic and the statuesque folds of the robe below.

'The whole piece is admirably done. Richepin's translation is perfect in its way.[4] He has put it into rude, majestic prose, the very language of the epoch, as one might conceive it—it is almost literal in parts. Intelligent minds have worked over the whole play in this French rendering. The very ghost is Elizabethan. Remember, in Shakespeare's day ghosts were not shadowy, subjective conceptions, but beings of flesh and blood, only beings living on the other side of the border of life, and now and then permitted to break bounds. The ghosts of the Porte-Saint-Martin are men; you could pinch them and run them through and through; they are not mere things of gauze, like our English stage figures of the kind, elaborated, apparently, from some programme of the Psychical Society.'

'You have seen the *Maître de Forges*?'[5]

'Not here; we have it in London, you know.'

'And London is not "shocked?"'

'Oh, London is improving; and besides it will take anything from the French. Of course, if an English writer had done anything of the sort, there would have been one loud shriek.'

'So you might consider yourself a Frenchman—if you meant to go on writing plays?'

'In one respect, certainly; for the sake of the interpretation. What a gulf there is between the character as you conceive it and the character as it comes out on the stage. I admit, after what I said just now, that the author has no right to complain where the result is artistic; but with us that is so often not the case. I speak from experience: I shall never forget the two hours and a half I passed in the playhouse at New York on the first night of my piece. It was the sharpest agony of my life.'[6]

'But you will write another play of course?'

'Undoubtedly; but just now I am laying myself out for a novel.[7] Plays and novels, I think, ought to go together in a man's practice, if only to make one bear in mind what I consider the cardinal principle of all good style, that writing is something meant to be said aloud—to be spoken, in fact. With the multiplication of books we have got into the habit of merely writing for the eye, and that is fatal to all rhythm and music. Shakespeare's music came naturally from his habit of writing for the voice and the ear. I care little for archaism, for the nice choice of words of this or that epoch; please the mind through the ear—that is the all in all.'

'You have seen the Salon?'

'Yes; I have seen the work of "the trade," matchless work a good deal of it; if you like but still that.'

'And Sargent's portrait?'[8]

'Oh, that is altogether on a higher level: like everything he does, it shows the influence of his fine nature and fine taste. Who but he would have ventured to outline that head as he has done, and yet you feel that was just the way to treat it. It is a pictorial reminiscence of the earlier grand art.'

'Will he succeed in England, do you think? He is going to paint there.'

Portrait of Madame X (1884) by John Singer Sargent.

'Beyond question. England is in a better condition to understand him than France. There is more individuality with us, less of that respect for tradition, good tradition though it be. Everybody there is a law unto himself. Even in such a thing as costume we revive the earlier styles or invent new ones, just because we think them good. He may treat his sitters according to his fancy; he will be sure to find people ready to judge him and them on their merits.'

'So his Salon picture is the one righteous work that saves the city?'

'Not the one; you forget the Whistlers. Was anything more beautiful ever done than the portrait of the child—more tender and simple and finely true? It ought to be a revelation to the art world on this side.'[9]

1   Constance Mary Lloyd (1858–1898) and Wilde were married at St. James's, Paddington, on 29 May 1884.

2   Marie-Henri Beyle (1783–1842) was a French novelist who wrote under the pen name Stendhal. His novel *Le Rouge et le Noir* (1830) is a Bildungsroman that follows the protagonist Julien Sorel's attempts to rise from poverty to the Parisian elite. Charles-Marie-Georges Huysmans (1848–1907) was a French novelist and art critic who wrote as Joris-Karl Huysmans. Wilde refers to Huysmans's *À rebours* (*Against the Grain* or

Against Nature; May 1884), in which the Duc Jean Des Esseintes, the last scion of a noble family, renounces society and becomes a recluse. It inspired the 'poisonous' book that corrupts Dorian Gray.

3   Bernhardt was playing Lady Macbeth at the Théâtre de la Porte Saint-Martin.

4   Jean Richepin (1849–1926) was a French poet and dramatist.

5   *Le Maître de forges* (*The Ironmaster*; 1882) is a novel by Georges Ohnet (1848–1918) about a rich ironworker whose aristocratic wife treats him coldly because of his inferior beginnings. Wilde had seen the adaptation by Arthur Wing Pinero (1855–1934) at London's St James's Theatre.

6   Wilde refers to the staging of *Vera; or, The Nihilists* at New York's Union Square Theatre on 20 August 1883. On the first night the play began at about 20:00 and ended at 23:45, so Wilde's estimate of 'two hours and a half' is rather low.

7   Wilde's only novel, *The Picture of Dorian Gray*, did not appear until July 1890.

8   John Singer Sargent (1856–1925) was an American artist. His portrait of Virginie Amélie Avegno Gautreau (1859–1915) was exhibited at the Paris Salon under the title *Portrait de Mme* ∗∗∗ (later retitled *Portrait of Madame X*). Gautreau, a Parisian socialite, was immediately identified as the model. The public was shocked by the portrait, and particularly by the loose shoulder strap on Gautreau's dress, which Sargent would later repaint as more securely fastened. Sargent moved from Paris to London and, as Wilde predicted, was successful there, though he would concede that *Madame X* was 'the best thing I have done'.

9   Wilde refers to Whistler's *Harmony in Grey and Green: Miss Cicely Alexander* (1872–1873), exhibited in Paris as *Portrait de Miss Alexander*.

'Mr. Oscar Wilde Interviewed in Glasgow', *Evening News and Star* (Glasgow, UK), 22 Dec. 1884, 4

'Good evening,' said Mr. Wilde, with a pleasant smile, as he shook hands with our representative in the smoking-room of the Central Hotel last night. 'Just draw your chair in here.' Mr. Oscar Wilde is a young man, tall and well formed, with a pleasant face and a heavy head of dark curling hair. There was nothing extraordinary in his dress. He wore a plain orthodox evening suit, with the cuffs of his shirt turned up in order to give his hands free play. He chatted with our representative quite freely.

'This reminds me of being in America,' said Mr. Wilde, throwing himself back in his chair with a fragrant cigar in his hand; 'I used to have them (interviewers) coming to my rooms five or six times a day, and I rather liked it. By the way,' he asked, 'how long is it since you commenced your interviews?' Our representative explained that the *Evening News* had interviewed all the distinguished people who had visited the city within the last six months. 'Yes,' said Mr. Wilde. 'I think it is a capital feature of the paper. It gives a man an opportunity of saying and explaining things which he could not do as satisfactorily in an ordinary speech.'

'Now,' said Mr. Oscar Wilde, 'what do you want me to talk about—dress?[1] Well I think all ugly dress has been made and worn by the most useless people in the world, and all beautiful dress by people who had something to do and knew how to do it. The only well-dressed people are the classes like the fisher people and the peasants. In the peasant, the dress has been without a change for centuries. The French workman and the English ploughboy of the present day wear respectively the short tunic, and the long tunic of the thirteenth century—the dress they wore—once adorned kings. I do not mean, of course, that the king should adopt the peasant's costume, but the principle—comfort, utility—ought to be the same. Why,' continued Mr. Wilde smiling, 'when I was in France I wore a blouse for three months, and I was never more comfortable in my life.' Naturally we come now to tight lacing. 'I say at once that the shoulder is the natural place from which to hang anything. Nature gives no opportunity to suspend articles of clothing from the waist, and it has therefore to be compressed. I am quite sure that the reason of tight lacing is not so much the desire to have a tiny waist as the necessity there is for some strong compression in order to keep the clothes on at all. Yes, as you may say, small waists and tight lacing are fashionable, but fashion is folly, and it has always been the greatest enemy of art. The waist, naturally, is a very delicate and very beautiful curve, not a triangle. I know a famous actress who has a beautiful waist simply because she never makes it unnaturally small. I mean Miss Ellen Terry. She does not make herself like an hour-glass. Then, there is Sarah Bernhardt, she never compresses her waist, and the result is she shows a figure with the most beautiful lines imaginable. The same remarks' continued Mr. Wilde, 'apply also to the foot and

Wilde admired Ellen Terry for her decision not to follow the fashion for constricting corsets. She is pictured here in Japanese dress.

the hand. A foot is not beautiful because it is small, but just as it is in proportion to the rest of the figure. And so also with the hand. A hand is not beautiful because it is small, but just as it is in proportion, and as its lines and curves are clearly shown. To crowd a hand into a glove many sizes too tight for it does not make the hand look smaller. It really makes it apparently larger—a shapeless, useless mass. This is not beauty, for beauty consists in the sense of power that it gives you, and a tightly-gloved hand is of no practical use at all. Beauty does not go by size. If you go to China you will get both the smallest foot and the smallest hand, and consequently the ugliest.'

'But,' protested our representative, 'you speak against modern dress, and hold up the Greek costume as the most perfect of all, yet do not advocate its adoption. What would you have us do?'

'Why,' replied Mr. Wilde, 'take their principle—comfort and utility. No good is got by imitation, but we can follow their principles. The principles of Greek art are beauty of line and symmetry and proportion. These are principles that are eternal. You ask if reform in dress is progressing? Look at the societies and institutions we have in London. Apart from them there is Jaeger, who began by simply having two houses for the sale of sensible articles of dress. Now he has several large shops in the West End, and they are always crowded. His woollen dresses are more comfortable than you can imagine—cool in summer, and warm in winter. I wear mine constantly in London. Others are buying them, too, for people wouldn't keep their shops open if they weren't selling their goods.[2] And now,' said Mr. Wilde, 'I want you to let me say something about the land question. In consequence of the land coming to be the property of private persons, most towns are becoming spoiled. The immense price which has to be paid for land necessitates people building monstrously high houses. The houses of our great towns are so absurdly high that the sunlight is never able to enter. The proper proportions should be fixed by law as they are by art—they ought never to be higher than the width of the street. As it is, they shut out the light of the sun. In London, for instance, they have pulled down Northumberland House in Trafalgar Square, and such an enormous price has been asked for the land that the people who bought it have erected unusually high houses, with the result that the sun-light will only be able to enter the street for one hour during the day. Consequently, the streets will always be grim and dark. There ought to be none of this. In every town there should be trees and gardens, places for pretty walks, and open spaces here and there. The fact, however, that the land is in the hands of private individuals prevents all this. They want what they can get out of the property, and consequently, our towns are not what they ought to be—a combination of town and country. Moreover,' continued Mr. Wilde, 'we can never have any beautiful architecture in these narrow streets, and if we had we could not appreciate it. How can you see a beautiful building by standing on the other side of the street? You are too close to it. Even if you want to look at a picture you must stand back from it.

'Do I paint? Well, sometimes—for my own pleasure. When I am travelling I find it easier and more pleasant to use my sketch-book than keep a diary.

'I think,' continued Mr. Wilde, 'the whole face of England has been changed within the last ten years. You could not enter the humblest house now without finding something pretty about the room. In decorative art, ornament should be suggested either by the manufacture or the material. Nobody, for instance, would think of painting on a mat. In the case of the material, take the difference between wrought iron and cast iron. Wrought iron, which is beaten out at the anvil, gives us delicacy of curve and beauty, and immense strength. If you have a cast-iron ornament in the round, you would require to have three or four times the bulk. The best form of ornament is that suggested by the material. You ought to look also at the utility of a thing. The use of a mirror is that people should see themselves in it, and that it should reflect things. To paint anything on a mirror is, of course, to spoil its use. The beauty of a jug or vase is simply the beauty of its curves and the utility of it. The ornament ought never to interfere with it. To stick on it, for instance, great roses as big as life, and twice as natural, is to spoil entirely its beauty, and make it useless. In this way we get no beauty and no utility. The Greeks, in decorating a vase, would mark it first with circles to show the curves, then round the neck, and then perhaps put a little leaf ornament to emphasise its delicacy. Apart from the question of decoration, we should consider the value of ornaments. Once a thing like an ornament ceases to be useful, we demand from it the highest possible beauty. Coming short of this, it falls under the double damnation of being useless and ugly. Art is primarily a question of construction, use, and proportion. Art is not ornamentation—a thing can be quite beautiful without an atom of ornament. In the present day people are always imagining that art means decoration, and so covering everything with foolish designs. An "ornament" is a dangerous thing, because when a thing is useless we demand from it the highest beauty. Bad ornaments are the worst things in the way.

'You want me back to dress—low-necked dresses? Well, if a person wears a dress from the shoulder to shoulder a harsh line is produced, which at once diminishes the height. No dress of the kind is beautiful. A well-constructed dress ought to go right up to the neck, and hang from the shoulders—not by the ridiculous things called shoulder straps. Apart from the question of health, there ought to be an equal temperature over the whole body, whereas the most delicate part of the body is neglected, and left exposed. Wherever you find anything ugly, either in dress or in anything else, you may be quite certain that some mistake has been committed—that somebody has been impractical. Ugliness is thus a sign by which we may judge that a mistake has been committed.

'I think,' said Mr. Wilde, incidentally, 'people who wanted to go to the theatre, could have supper afterwards. Undoubtedly, the best time to appreciate art is before eating.

'Yes,' concluded Mr. Wilde smiling, 'I have discarded my knee-breeches. I found them a little too tight, both at and above the knee. Knickerbockers would, I think, be better. They are comfortably loose above the knee, and tight enough below it not to allow of the air passing up. What, are you going now? Well, good night,' and our representative left.

1   Wilde first gave his new lecture 'Dress' in late September or early October 1884.

2   Dr Gustav Jaeger (1832–1917) was a German naturalist who, for health reasons, advocated wearing wool rather than fabrics made from plant fibres. A shop bearing Jaeger's name was opened in central London in February 1884.

'Oscar Wilde', *The Montgomery Advertiser* (Montgomery, AL), 31 Jan. 1886, 3

DUNFERMLINE, SCOTLAND, Jan. 10.— Oscar Wilde was in Dunfermline a little while back, and lectured on 'Dress' to a very large audience.[1] In this country, as was the case in the States, he draws well as a lecturer. While here he was the guest of Mr. and Mrs. Kenneth Mathieson, Jr., a charming newly married couple who have a delightful home. They have fine literary tastes, and had several friends at their house to meet Mr. Wilde. It was my good fortune to be one of the number, and a more enjoyable evening I do not remember to have spent. Socially Mr. Wilde is a most agreeable gentleman. And he is an ardent friend of America. When he learned of my connection with Montgomery, he immediately asked about the late Mrs. Henry D. Clayton, whom he knew as Miss Allen, and whose recent untimely death was so profoundly regretted throughout Alabama. When I told him of her death he was greatly shocked, and expressed the deepest regret. 'She was a beautiful woman,' he said, 'I may say she was perfect,' and he went on to speak at length of her many charms. 'I thought Miss Allen,' said he, 'and a young lady in California, and one in Boston, were the most beautiful women I saw in America, and your American women are marvellously lovely. There is a spirit and a dash, and withal a delicacy, about them charming to behold.' Mr. Wilde was warm in his praises of our country, and he was quite enthusiastic about the Southern people. He had been delighted with a visit to Mr. Jefferson Davis, at Beauvoir, and referred to the famous chieftain as 'that grand old man living with his books and fighting battles with his pen that he was powerless to win with his sword.' He referred at length to other distinguished Americans whom he had met, among them being Mr. Beecher, Mr. Whittier, Harriet Beecher Stowe, Mark Twain, Mr. Pendleton and Mr. Bayard, for all of whom he entertained a lively appreciation.[2] In reference to Bret Harte, he said: 'Why did your government remove him from the consularship at Glasgow?[3] I think you should pay him a good salary to represent American literature in London. He is a great pet at all the clubs; we are all very fond of him. He is a very charming companion.'

Mr. Wilde, like many other of his countrymen, cannot appreciate or comprehend the social gulf between the white and black races in the States. He thinks that political equality should beget some measure of social equality; which opinion seems very absurd to an American. And upon this point, strange to say, the unthinking millions in this country have an idea that there are no social distinctions of any nature in the Land of the Free. They suppose that men who meet upon a common level at the ballot-box do not change their relation when they come to the drawing room. As they see it, the social and political world of America blend in the utmost harmony, and the man who has the right to aspire to the Senate, carries a passport to the parlors of the upper-ten thousand, which he can use if he has but one coat to his back and no learning in his head.

Mr. Wilde had a colored valet whom he picked up in New York, and he never saw a servant his equal for intelligence and reliability. This model valet always carried his master's cash, and with great satisfaction the poet lecturer related that whenever he desired a little pocket change, he had to go to his colored valet for it. But something he couldn't understand, was why his valet was not permitted to travel in the sleeping-car with the master. Once in North Carolina, his servant came into the car to bring some books, when the conductor peremptorily ordered him out.[4] 'We British know nothing of good servants,' he said. 'The colored people of the United States are the model servants of the earth.

'But,' said Mr. Wilde, 'I have no quarrel to make with Southern people on the race question. They are a high-minded, intelligent, hospitable, Christian people; they are simply delightful. Richard Henry Wilde, the Southern poet, was my blood relation, and my family had other kins-people who emigrated from the old country to the South.[5] So I feel that the Southern people are, to some extent, my own people.

'Take America as a whole,' continued Mr. Wilde, warming up on what was evidently a pleasant subject, 'and it is a grand country. It is a marvel of progress and development. New York is a garden of delight, Boston is unsurpassed, New Orleans is most charming. Madison Square is one of the most beautiful spots I ever beheld; and, do you know, the statue of Farragut in New York is a finer work of art than anything of the kind we have in London.[6] A desire to live in New York is not an unworthy ambition of any man.'

Something was said about the statement of a leading London journal to the effect that England is becoming Americanized. 'So it is,' said Mr. Wilde, 'and to me it is far from being a cause of regret. The world will probably become Americanized some day, which is so much the better for mankind. The Americans are so far-sighted, shrewd and energetic. There was one thing that struck me very forcibly: your people are born orators. Any and every man can speak well in public. Just before Matthew Arnold left home for his lecturing tour of the States he asked me if I had any advice to offer him. 'Commit your lectures to memory,' said I. 'If you use manuscript the people won't listen to you. They are all orators.' And after Mr. Arnold reached New York he felt obliged to employ a teacher and go through a regular course of study in elocution. It would strike you as a trifle odd that an Englishman of such conspicuous ability as Matthew Arnold should feel called upon to study that which is taught to all your school boys before they are taught to read!'[7]

1   Wilde lectured in Dunfermline on 10 December 1885.
2   John Greenleaf Whittier (1807–1892) was an American poet and abolitionist. Harriet Beecher Stowe (1811–1896) was an American author and abolitionist, best known for her novel *Uncle Tom's Cabin* (1852). Samuel Langhorne Clemens (1835–1910), better known by his pen name Mark Twain, was an American lecturer, humourist, and author. There is no evidence that he and Wilde met in America in 1882, though they lunched

together in Bad Nauheim in 1892. George H. Pendleton (1825–1889) and Thomas F. Bayard (1828–1898) served as United States Senators. Wilde met both men in Washington in January 1882.

3   Bret Harte (1836–1902) was an American writer of short stories and poetry. He took up the role of United States Consul in Glasgow in 1880. In 1885 he settled in London.

4   When a rail employee at Atlanta realised that one of the sleeping car tickets he had sold to Wilde's agent was intended for Wilde's valet, he requested the return of the ticket. Wilde refused at first but, upon being warned that his valet would be mobbed when the train passed through Jonesboro, he returned the ticket. Either Wilde is mistaken in locating the story in North Carolina, or he is recalling a different incident.

5   Richard Henry Wilde (1789–1847) was a Dublin-born lawyer who served as a Member of the House of Representatives from Georgia. His best-known poem is the posthumously published 'Hesperia', 'a nationalistic poem in four cantos'. Wilde also refers to his uncle, Judge John Kingsbury Elgee.

6   David Glasgow Farragut (1801–1870) was an admiral in the United States Navy. A bronze statue of him by Augustus Saint-Gaudens (1848–1907) was dedidated in Madison Square Park in 1881.

7   Matthew Arnold (1822–1888) was an English poet, critic, and inspector of schools. Wilde listed him among the 'very few masters' of English prose. Arnold's 1883–1884 tour of North America was promoted, as Wilde's had been, by Richard D'Oyly Carte.

'Oscar Wilde's Hair Cut', *The Brooklyn Daily Eagle* (Brooklyn, NY), 20 Oct. 1889, 14

The Oscar Wilde who made himself famous in America a few years ago is not the Oscar Wilde of today. The long hair has been cut and is now short and curly. The knee breeches have been put away carefully, the lackadaisical air is no longer worn, and the Oscar Wilde of London today is a straight, strong, broad-shouldered, athletic fellow, with no nonsense about him and an evident determination on his face to make fame and money. The Wilde craze, so far as England is concerned, is over. Mr. Wilde will question this—yet there are thousands of people, men and women, who believe that Wilde did much good in his late crusade, and he has still a very respectable following, but nothing like what one would be led to believe from a perusal of the satirical Gilbert's *Patience*.

I saw Oscar on Fleet Street today, and would not have known him had not an English friend pointed him out to me. He looked as English in his dress as in his manner, and conducted himself as thousands of other broad-shouldered young fellows whom you will find at Oxford or Cambridge, or in the big commercial houses of London and Liverpool. He was looking in the window of a second hand book store. He carried an armful of papers and a thick blackthorn stick in his hand. There was nothing about him to attract attention. He might perhaps be picked out of a crowd for a professional man. In a recent newspaper article it was reported that Mr. Wilde had grown very stout and very inartistic looking in the matter of dress. This does him a great injustice. As all the world knows, he has an artistic cast of countenance, and his proportions are massive. He is not a favorite among men. Englishmen seem to look upon him as something of a curiosity. Women take more kindly to him. He is chiefly known now by his contributions to magazines, work in which he is most assiduous. *Punch* calls his latest article 'Oscar Wilde's Mad Fancy.'[1] His time is entirely occupied. He lectures now and then, writes special articles occasionally, does a book review once in a while, and every other day spends a couple of hours or so editing the *Ladies' World*, or the *Woman's World* as he now calls it, and performs the difficult task of managing a large staff of feminine contributors in a masterly fashion.[2] He frequently drops in at the Lyric Club, although he belongs to half a dozen others in London, and it was there over a cigarette and a straw drink that your correspondent had a brief chat with him.

'Your school of aestheticism, Mr. Wilde' I began, 'seems to have died out?'

'Oh, no,' was the quick rejoinder, 'it has not. There does not seem to be the interest in aesthetic matters that there was some years ago, but the school has not died out—not by any means.'

'Then the progress has been satisfactory to you?'

'Oh, yes, yes,' was the reply, 'perfectly satisfactory;' and then he added after a puff at his cigarette, 'perfectly; how could it be otherwise?'

'It was said in a leading newspaper not long since that you had grown tired of what was called "the aesthetic fad" and did not desire to be identified with the movement any longer.'

To this view of the matter Mr. Wilde offered a distinct, implicit and somewhat contemptuous denial—one of those denials which are far better expressed by looks and gesticulations than by words. It meant that such an idea was ridiculous. 'Of course things change,' he said. 'They have their various stages, they develop, and require different treatment. But I have not changed, as my articles in the late magazines on the subject will show.'

'Has the progress of aestheticism been more marked in this country or America?'

'Oh, it is difficult to draw any hard and fast lines where the change everywhere has been so great,' was the reply. 'For the same reason it is perhaps hard to note the advance. Everything is different and no comparison can be drawn. Both countries have made satisfactory progress.'

'Do you think the poor people have benefited equally with the rich in the development of artistic grace?'

'Well, of course, the rich can have their artistic hangings, their fringes, their tapestry and very many things which the poor cannot have. Still, they have gained much recently. They have their People's Palace, their music and the like, and this all through our endeavors.[3] I think on the whole you may safely say that the common people have benefited very much.'

'What are some of the benefits afforded by the Renaissance school?'

'Look at color. The new colors in dress, in tapestries and in fringes. It is beautiful.'

'What about dress?'

'Well, you may change the Englishman's religion, but you must not change his dress. In other countries it is different. In your own it is different. No court dress, no traditional uniform which extends everywhere in this country. There is, of course, some hope for a change of beauty in America.'

'Speaking of America, American people took well to your plans, did they not, and your visit there was agreeable?'

'Quite so,' replied Mr. Wilde, 'the Americans are charming people. They treated me very generously.'

'Do you think the Americans adopted your ideas with more eagerness than the English people?'

'No; I did not imply that. I like the Americans. It is a pleasure to lecture to them. The American audience is all attention. It sees your ideas and it grasps your points at once. The people are smart, quick-witted, and if they like a thing they warmly express their approbation.'

'You lecture occasionally now, Mr. Wilde?'[4]

'Yes,' was the reply, 'and I have received a great many letters from all parts of America and from England on the subject. None of these letters are of much importance. Many of them contain words of hearty praise. These I remember. There are a few others not so pleasant, but I have forgotten them.'

He lighted a fresh cigarette, crossed his legs in a comfortable sort of way, was lost in silence for a moment, and when he spoke his thoughts were apparently running on literature. He introduced the subject by saying that a nation had only one way of expressing its better instincts. 'England expresses hers through her literature, Greece did the same, and the literature of these two nations stands forth incomparable,' he said.

'And America?'

'Oh, America expresses hers by energy. What marvelous workers the Americans are. No wonder they all make money so rapidly. Yours, indeed, are a wonderful people.'

He rose to go. He explained that he had to dine out, which he does very often, by the way, and that he had first of all to see his mother and wife.

1   This is a reference to Wilde's story 'The Portrait of Mr. W. H.', which is about the identification of the dedicatee of Shakespeare's sonnets as the boy actor William Hews.

2   Wilde edited *The Woman's World* between 1887 and 1889.

3   The People's Palace was opened in 1887 as an educational and cultural venue for the East End of London.

4   Wilde had by this time ceased lecturing.

'The Censure and "Salome"', *The Pall Mall Gazette* (London, UK), 29 Jun. 1892, 1–2

The Lord Chamberlain has declined to authorize the representation of Mr. Oscar Wilde's French play, *Salomé*, so the *première* will probably be given in Paris instead of London.[1]

I should show (writes a representative of the *Pall Mall Gazette*) but small appreciation of Mr. Wilde's courtesy were I to describe the piece, or do more than refer incidentally to a conversation that would have appeared in this column on the eve of the first performance had *Salomé* been licensed for representation. I may, however, be permitted to say that, judging from what I saw at rehearsal, Art has suffered by the Lord Chamberlain's action, for with such interpreters as Mdme. Sarah Bernhardt and M. Albert Darmont there was no danger that the author's dignified treatment of the Biblical story would be degraded.[2] I have had the advantage of reading a great many forbidden plays, for in Paris the Censure is applied more frequently than in London, and I have no hesitation in saying that in nine cases out of ten the prohibitive measure is a mistaken policy. It is not pretended that there is any religious or moral gain to compensate for the wrong done to Art. Diametrically opposed standards seem to be set up by the Censure in passing judgment on religious and social dramas. If Justice does not suffer every time some monstrous injustice is handled by the playwright, why should Religion suffer when the acts of its oppressors are made the subject of artistic treatment by the dramatic author? The public can be trusted to save Religion from insult.

This is, of course, but the expression of my own opinion. It was with these thoughts running in my mind that I called on Mr. Oscar Wilde yesterday to beg him to modify an earlier interview he had given me in such particulars as might be important in view of the Lord Chamberlain's decision.

'Personally,' said Mr. Wilde, 'to have my *première* in Paris instead of London is a great honour, and one that I appreciate sincerely. The pleasure and pride that I have experienced in the whole affair has been that Mdme. Bernhardt, who is undoubtedly the greatest artist on any stage, should have been charmed and fascinated by my play and should have wished to act it.'

I could not help feeling that Mr. Wilde's pride was justified. It is the fashion today to write single-rôle pieces for Mdme. Bernhardt. The talents of several authors have been almost exclusively devoted to the task of fitting the talents of the artist. *Salomé* is not a one-rôle drama: it was not written for Mdme. Bernhardt; indeed, it had been in manuscript nearly six months before it was submitted to her.

'Every rehearsal,' continued Mr. Wilde, 'has been a source of intense pleasure to me. To hear my own words spoken by the most beautiful voice in the world has been the greatest artistic joy that it is possible to experience. So that you see, as far as I am concerned, I care very little about the refusal of the Lord Chamberlain to allow my play to be produced. What I do care about is this, that the Censorship apparently regards the stage as the lowest of all the arts, and looks on acting as a vulgar thing. The painter is allowed to take his subjects where he chooses. He can go to the great Hebrew and Hebrew–Greek literature of the Bible and can paint Salomé dancing, or Christ on the cross, or the Virgin with her child. Nobody interferes with the painter. Nobody says painting is such a vulgar art that you must not paint sacred things. The sculptor is equally free. He can carve St. John the Baptist in his camel-hair, and fashion the Madonna or Christ in Bronze or in marble as he wills. Yet nobody says to him sculpture is such a vulgar art that you must not carve sacred things. And the writer—the poet—he also is quite free. I can write about any subject I choose. For me there is no Censorship. I can take any incident I like out of sacred literature and treat it as I choose, and there is no one to say to the poet, "Poetry is such a vulgar art that you must not use it in treating sacred subjects." But there is a Censorship over the stage and acting, and the basis of that Censorship is that, while vulgar subjects may be put on the stage and acted, while everything that is mean and low and shameful in life can be portrayed by actors, no actor is to be permitted to present, under artistic conditions, the great and ennobling subjects taken from the Bible. The insult in the suppression of *Salomé* is an insult to the stage as a form of art, and not to me.'

'I understand that Mdme. Bernhardt's engagements will not allow her to play *Salomé* at an invitation performance. We shall not see your play in London, then?'[3]

'I shall publish *Salomé*.[4] No one has the right to interfere with me, and no one shall interfere with me. The people who are injured are the actors; the art that is vilified is the art of acting. I hold that this is as fine as any other art, and to refuse it the right to treat great and noble subjects is an insult to the stage. The action of the Censorship in England is odious and ridiculous. What can be said of a body that forbids Massenet's *Hérodiade*, Gounod's *Reine de Saba*, Rubinstein's

Judas Maccabaeus, and allows *Divorçons* to be placed on any stage?[5] The artistic treatment of moral and elevating subjects is discouraged, while a free course is given to the representation of disgusting and revolting subjects.'

'How came you to write *Salomé* in French?'

'My idea of writing the play was simply this: I have one instrument that I know I can command, and that is the English language. There was another instrument to which I listened all my life, and I wanted once to touch this new instrument to see whether I could make any beautiful thing out of it. The play was written in Paris some six months ago, where I read it to some young poets, who admired it immensely. Of course there are modes of expression that a French man of letters would not have used, but they give a certain relief or colour to the play. A great deal of the curious effect that Maeterlinck produces comes from the fact that he, a Flamand by grace, writes in an alien language.[6] The same thing is true of Rossetti, who, though he wrote in English, was essentially Latin in temperament.'

During this part of our interview the correspondent of the *Gaulois* was present. The conversation was consequently carried on in French, and my colleague remarked on the admirable way that Mr. Wilde spoke the language. This elicited from him a splendid tribute to Paris, 'the centre of art, the artistic capital of the world.'

'If the Censure refuses *Salomé*,' said Mr. Wilde, for at the time of my first interview the decision of the Lord Chamberlain had not been announced, 'I shall leave England and settle in France, where I will take out letters of naturalization. I will not consent to call myself a citizen of a country that shows such narrow mindedness in its artistic judgments.'

My colleague of the *Gaulois* made a movement of surprise…

'I am not English, I'm Irish, which is quite another thing.'

'To continue the story of *Salomé* —'

'A few weeks ago,' said Mr. Wilde, 'I met Mdme. Sarah Bernhardt at Mr. Henry Irving's. She had heard of my play and asked me to read it to her. I did so, and she at once expressed a wish to play the title-rôle. Of course it has been a great disappointment to her and to her company not to have played this piece in London. We have been rehearsing for three weeks, the costumes, scenery, and everything has been prepared, and we are naturally disappointed. Still all are looking forward now to producing it for the first time in Paris, where the actor is appreciated and the stage is regarded as an artistic medium. It is remarkable how little art there is in the work of dramatic critics in England. You find column after column of description, but the critic rarely knows how to praise an artistic work. The fact is, it requires an artist to praise art; anyone can pick it to pieces. For my own part, I don't know which I despise most, blame or praise. The latter, I think, for it generally happens that the qualities praised are those one regards with the least satisfaction oneself.'

Just as I was taking leave of Mr. Oscar Wilde the conversation went back to the question of prohibition:—

'What makes the Lord Chamberlain's action to me most contemptible, and the only point in which I feel at all aggrieved in the matter, is that he allows the personality of an artist to be presented in a caricature on the stage,[7] and will not allow the work of that artist to be shown under very rare and very beautiful conditions.'

1   After the London production was cancelled Bernhardt promised Constance Wilde that she would 'have a great success in *Salomé* and I assure you that the French public will be very proud to have the premiere of that admirable play'. *Salomé* would not be staged until 1896, and then with Lina Munte (c. 1850–1909) in the lead role.

2   The French actor Auguste Albert Darmont (1863–1913) had been cast as Jokanaan (John the Baptist).

3   The Lord Chamberlain could prohibit public but not private, invitation-only performances.

4   The French-language edition of *Salomé* was published in February 1893.

5   Jules Émile Frédéric Massenet (1842–1912) was a French composer. His opera, *Hérodiade*, which told the story of Salomé and John the Baptist, was first performed in Brussels in 1881. Charles-François Gounod (1818–1893) was a French composer whose opera, *La reine de Saba* ('The Queen of Sheba'), premiered in Paris in 1862. Anton Grigoryevich Rubinstein (1829–1894) was a Russian pianist and composer who wrote several operas on biblical themes, including *Judas Maccabaeus*. All three of the operas mentioned were censored by the Lord Chamberlain; *Divorçons* was not.

6   Maurice Maeterlinck (1862–1949) was Flemish but wrote in French.

7   Wilde refers to *The Poet and the Puppets*, a parody of *Lady Windermere's Fan* by Charles Brookfield (1857–1913) and James Mackey Glover (1861–1931) that premiered on 19 May 1892. Charles Hawtrey (1858–1923) played a version of Wilde.

William Theodore Peters, 'Oscar Wilde at Home', *The Sunday Inter Ocean* (Chicago, IL), 16 Dec. 1894, 31[1]

'It is necessary to have an interior where one never is,' observed the wicked old Duke, in that witty play, *Paris Fin de Siecle*.[2] Nothing if not paradoxical, Mr. Oscar Wilde has a most attractive home at No. 16 Tite Street, and it was there that his charming wife presented me to him. Mrs. Wilde receives during the season on Wednesday afternoons, in a drawing-room decorated in white and harmonizing shades of blue and green. If one has the privilege of being admitted to it, the 'interior' of No. 16 Tite Street is well worthy inspection, for apart from its aesthetic beauty it contains many interesting literary and artistic souvenirs. In Mr. Wilde's study, which is littered with books, pamphlets, and manuscripts, a place for everything and nothing in its place, a veritable paradise for a man of letters, I remarked hanging upon the wall the original manuscript of Keats' 'blue' sonnet and looking calmly down from its pedestal, beautiful and 'forever young,' a life-size bust of the Hermes of Praxiteles.[3] Near by, on a chair, stood a clever imitation of an old Elizabethan painting by Mr. Charles Ricketts, a portrait of the 'incomparable Mr. W. H.'[4] Leaning against the wall, on the floor was a nude study of a woman by Mr. Charles Shannon.[5] 'What does Cook think of it?' asked Mr. Wilde with a twinkle in his eye.

In the drawing-room is a full-length portrait of the author of *Lady Windermere's Fan*, by Mr. Harper Pennington;[6] an etching by Whistler,[7] and a good reproduction of Bastien le Page's portrait of Bernhardt, underneath which is a note in uncertain English by the divine one to Mr. Wilde.[8] Here is also to be seen a portrait of Lady Mount Temple and a graceful drawing by Mr. Graham Robertson of Miss Ellen Terry.[9] The room is filled, but not overcrowded, with bibelots, silver dragee-boxes, silver photograph frames, flowers, rare first editions, pretty lamps, silken cushions—all the usual adjuncts of a smart London drawing-room.

Mrs. Wilde sits on a low couch by the fire, pouring out tea from an old Georgian teapot with a malachite green handle. Cyril, the elder of her two sons, a fine little boy, is perhaps aiding his mother in dispensing hospitality to her guests. Mr. Oscar Wilde has named the two characters in his essay on 'The Decay of Lying' after his two children,

Constance Wilde née Lloyd, photographed shortly before her marriage to Oscar Wilde.

Cyril and Vivian.[10] Mrs. Wilde, who is one of the London beauties, has a blooming complexion and an abundance of gold-brown hair. She is always tastefully and modishly dressed. On the first night of *Lady Windermere's Fan* she made a very attractive picture in one of the stage boxes, wearing a blue silk gown copied from the style of dress worn by Henrietta Maria in Van Dyck's portrait.[11]

It is easy to be seen that among Mr. Wilde's most ardent admirers not the least is his wife, whose devotion is indeed charming. She has made a complete collection of his journalistic work in a large scrap book, in which I noticed an appreciative review of one of Mr. Richard Le Gallienne's earlier books and an article on Mrs. Brown Potter's and Buffalo Bill's first season in London.[12] In this paper he says: 'Formerly we sent the Americans the pilgrim fathers; now at length in revenge they send us every spring the pilgrim mothers.' 'Mr. Wilde hates journalistic work,' said Mrs. Wilde. I was likewise permitted to turn the leaves of a very interesting book of autographs, which contains specimens of the writings of almost every living famous English author, artist, statesman, actor, and actress, most of whom Mrs. Wilde has personally known. Among these I observed the 'sentiments' (in prose or verse) of Mr. Henry Irving, Miss Ellen Terry, Mr. Burne-Jones, Mr. George Meredith, Mr. Ruskin, Mr. Archibald Balfour, and Miss Marie Corelli.[13]

Late in the afternoon, but before his wife's guests have departed, a step is heard on the stair, the portiere is pushed aside by a large, smooth, white hand, and Mr. Oscar Wilde, in a fashionable frock coat and irreproachable trousers, his silk scarf fastened with the very latest style of pin, wearing a 'carefully thought out buttonhole,'[14] and carrying a pair of spotless gloves, enters his wife's drawing-room smiling.

He seats himself before the open fireplace on an elegant lacquered settee, upholstered with blue silken cushions (a present from Mrs. Bloomfield Moore).[15] Cyril offers him a plate of tea-cakes and a cup of freshly made tea.

Some one remarks on the vigor and beauty of his eldest little boy, who is truly a handsome child, reminding one, in spite of his chocolate-colored jersey suit and stockings, of Andrea Verrochio's boy with the dolphin in the Ducal Palace at Florence.[16]

'Yes,' replied Mr. Wilde, 'he is filled with the wine of life and he will suffer superbly.'

Mr. Wilde having recently returned from France, I ventured to ask him about his play of *Salome* which Mr. Pigott had prohibited in England on account of the chief character having been taken from the New Testament.

'It is not yet ready for publication,' Mr. Wilde answered. 'I have brought it back in order to put a few more little gilt things in it—a few more little Oscarisms.'

From *Salome* the conversation naturally drifted to the Jewish question.

'The Jews are a wonderful race,' said Mr. Wilde. 'They are the only people who have ever appreciated the romance of commerce.'

Speaking of a mutual acquaintance, a young American painter, he said: 'Yes, yes, he has talent, but at present he is too troubled about life.'

'What a pity it is,' I said, 'that no artist, however great, ever "arrives" altogether. There will always be some one who will deny his right to exist as an artist.' 'You are mistaken in that,' replied Mr. Wilde. 'No audience can be exclusive enough. The most exclusive audience will always include some one who ought not to be there.

'It is for the artists to ask the questions, and for the others to answer them.

'There is the genius and the artist. The genius, like Keats or like Chatterton, who gives birth to some great book and then dies;[17] the artist, like Shakespeare, who begins by writing such poorly constructed comedies as *Love's Labour's Lost* and the *Comedy of Errors*, and then becomes gradually more and more of a sublime artist, until he finally produces a *Hamlet* and a *Tempest*.'

'It is sinning against art,' I observed, 'for an artist to conceive of a work and not to produce it.'

'Ah, yes,' he answered, 'there is a certain poem that I have in my mind (*The Sphinx*) which I mean to have sumptuously published in gold and purple.[18] I could not help thinking what a curious thing it would be if I died before it was written without ever having produced it. I am such a Hedonist I have to shut myself up or else go away by myself in order to write; but I find the country life by wood and stream more complex than life in town.'

Then the inevitable question rose to my lips: 'And what do you think of America?' I asked.

Mr. Wilde turned upon me fiercely.

'I do not think of America,' he replied, 'any more than I think of my school Latin prose exercises.'

Whereupon I bowed my adieus and departed.

If not always as clever in his talk as the conversations in his comedies, at least it cannot be denied that Mr. Wilde is an amusing man, in spite of the accusation that like Moliere he takes his own wit where he finds it. But, to echo Jean Jacques Rousseau, 'Better a man with paradoxes than a man with prejudices,' or, as Trublet said, 'To select well among old things is almost equivalent to inventing new ones.'

1   William Theodore Peters (1862–1905) was a Brooklyn-born poet and actor. His article appears to be based on a visit to the Wildes' home in mid-August 1892.

2   An 1890 comedy by French dramatists and journalists Ernest Blum (1836–1907) and Raoul Toche (1850–1895).

3   The Hermes of Praxiteles is a statue that was discovered among the ruins of Ancient Olympia shortly after Wilde visited the diggings in 1877.

4   Wilde commissioned English artist Charles Ricketts (1866–1931) to paint

the portrait as a frontispiece. Its present location is unknown.

5   Charles Haslewood Shannon (1863–1937) was an English artist and the partner of Charles Ricketts. The painting referred to here is *Ashtoreth*, which was exhibited at the Grosvenor Gallery in 1888. Wilde referred to the nude as 'dangerous to chambermaids'. It was considered lost until it emerged at auction in 2017.

6   R. G. Harper Pennington (1854–1920) was an American artist. *Lady Windermere's Fan* (1892) was Wilde's first society comedy.

7   The Wildes owned three of Whistler's etchings of Venice.

8   Jules Bastien-Lepage (1848–1884) was a French naturalist painter. His painting of Sarah Bernhardt (1879) won him the cross of the Legion d'Honneur.

9   Georgina, Lady Mount-Temple née Tollemache (1822–1901) was a close friend of Constance Wilde's. Walford Graham Robertson (1866–1948) was a British painter, illustrator, and author.

10   The Wildes' second son was christened, and preferred, Vyvyan, but his parents usually spelt his name 'Vivian'.

11   Anthony Van Dyck (1599–1641) was a Flemish artist. He painted many portraits of Queen Henrietta Maria, the wife of Charles I, in several of which she wears blue silk gowns.

12   Richard Le Gallienne (1866–1947) was an English poet whom Wilde befriended in 1888. Cora Urquhart Brown-Potter (1857–1936) was an American actress who made her stage debut in 1887 in Brighton. William Frederick 'Buffalo Bill' Cody (1846–1917) was an American bison hunter and showman. He brought his Wild West Show to London in 1887.

13   George Meredith (1828–1909) was an English novelist. Peters is mistaken in naming Archibald Balfour (1840–1922), a British businessman: Constance's autograph book was inscribed by Arthur James Balfour (1848–1930), the Conservative politician and future Prime Minister. Marie Corelli (1855–1924) was a popular English novelist. An edition of the autograph book has been published by the Oscar Wilde Society (2022).

14   Cecil Graham to Lord Darlington in *Lady Windermere's Fan*: 'My dear fellow, what on earth should we men do going about with purity and innocence? A carefully thought-out buttonhole is much more effective.'

15   Clara Jessup Bloomfield-Moore (1824–1899) was an American philanthropist, poet, and philosopher.

16   *Putto with Dolphin* by Andrea del Verrocchio (1435–1488), a Florentine sculptor, was commissioned c. 1470.

17   Thomas Chatterton (1752–1770) was an English poet, known for forging the works of an imaginary fifteenth-century poet.

18   Wilde had begun writing *The Sphinx* in 1877–1878 and continued working on it in Paris in April 1883. It was finally published in June 1894 in gilt vellum boards and printed in black, red, and green ink.

Percival H. W. Almy, 'New Views of Mr. Oscar Wilde', *Theatre* (London, UK), Vol. 23, Mar. 1894, 119–127

A rambling fishing village on the western shore of Torbay, with a rugged range of cliffs sloping down to the water's edge—such is Babbacombe.

An old-world place, with its cluster of decaying cottages at the cliff's foot, the thresholds of which are washed by the incoming tides; with its deeply indented harbour, its tiny fleet of boats, its chaos of tattered nets and broken oars, its everlasting odour of ozone and fish and tar—an old-world place it is—or *was*. For that ubiquitous spirit, *Modernity*, has found Babbacombe out, and in its dilettante attempts to improve, has already more than half destroyed the air of quaintness that so long brooded over the little village, and Babbacombe the quaint is fallen—is fallen.

But still it is a lovely spot. Nothing can destroy the beauty of its situation—the grandeur of its coasts—the placid azure of its bay. It is a dwelling place for a poet still, and it was here that I sought and found the poet Oscar Wilde.

He was spending a few weeks at 'Babbacombe Cliff,' a picturesque old manor house of 16th century date, whose mullioned windows glance down across a wooded slope within murmuring distance of the sea.[1]

I found him seated at an open window, for although the month was December, the air of this delightful place is mild as that of the Riviera.

Luxuriously ensconced in a deep armchair, with eyes slightly elevated, and head thrown carelessly back, his appearance suggested the idea of indolence or ennui, but it was the abstraction of a thoughtful mind, rather than the inertia of a vacant one that produced this result. Poetry is from within; it is produced by the action of external scenes and circumstances on the sensitive plate of a poet's soul. Hence the most important action of a poetic mind consists of absolute passivity—a complete abandonment of the soul to the inspiration of chance or surrounding influences. It was in such a mood that Oscar Wilde seemed to be indulging at the moment of my entry; he was as one who waited for inspirations. He rose as I approached, and I had an opportunity of making a mental note of his chief personal characteristic. I never saw a face so garrulous of the inner mind; it is such as is best described as a 'speaking countenance'—one that cannot keep a secret. In manner

Wilde photographed by Ellis & Wallery
(1892).

he is refined, not without a suspicion of aestheticism, and there is an
engaging charm in his personality that would win him many friends
and not a few disciples.

He plunged at once into poets and poetry. 'A glorious passion is
poetry.' Keats is his favourite; 'he is the greatest artist of them all.' He
is prepared to admit, however, that there is 'often more colour than
congruity in the creations of that remarkable genius; with ability so
great and judgment so immature, this is naturally to be expected.' I find,
although he did not mention the fact, that the celebrated letter from
Keats to Fanny Brawne, in which the poet recants his late rhapsodies
with regard to the sex, was, in 1885, purchased by Mr. Wilde for £18.[2]

Shelley is 'a magnificent genius,' but as far as his own personal
taste is concerned he prefers Keats. He likes a poet that 'walks on the
ground;' Shelley is 'too ethereal.'

He has no great regard for the Brownings—there is too much effort
with them. Mrs. Browning is 'a dear good soul,' but he allots her a
very secondary place. Her rhymes are shocking. 'She rhymes "moon"
with "table"!' he exclaimed. He wishes *Aurora Leigh* had been written
in prose.[3]

Robert Browning is too diffuse. It is a pity he did not concentrate more. 'I can revel in four of the closely compressed lines of Herrick,'[4] Mr. Wilde observed, 'but I cannot tolerate dross in poetry.' Poetry should be absolutely without a moral. 'That is a great thing in its favour,' Mr. Wilde writes, in a letter now before me, of a poem of which it had been stated that it did not strive to inculcate any particular moral. 'A poet should not think.' 'Poetry is not the place for thought; we must have beauty, and beauty and thought are incoalescent.' He recalled that passage in 'The Excursion,' in which the poet,[5] discoursing of the effects of natural beauty on the soul of the youthful herdsman, says:—

'They were his life;
In such access of mind, in such high hour
Of visitation from the living God
Thought was not; in enjoyment it expired.'

Thought and beauty cannot occupy the mind at the same time.

Mr. Wilde is not a great Shakespearean; he likes Ford and Marlowe, and Jonson and Massinger, and the Elizabethan dramatists generally, but he does not rave over Shakespeare.[6]

Lady Windermere's Fan has sometimes been paralleled with *The School for Scandal*; it is, therefore, interesting to know what are Mr. Wilde's opinions of Sheridan. He is by no means enthusiastic over the author of *The Rivals*. 'I do not rate Sheridan very high,' he writes in another letter; 'I consider Congreve far beyond him.'[7]

Milton is sometimes heavy; but *Paradise Lost* is 'undoubtedly the grandest organ-music we have.' 'Very sober' is Thomson. There is one line in 'The Seasons,' however, that he greatly admires—that in which the poet compares the colour of the wallflower to iron-rust; 'the simile is perfect.'[8]

The life and fate of Chatterton is 'the most tremendous tragedy in history.' Wordsworth is sometimes fine; but, as a whole, 'The Excursion' is 'Decidedly tedious.' Tennyson is 'a supreme artist.' 'The music of Swinburne is perfect.' 'What all-seeing eyes William Morris has!' Austin Dobson is 'very delightful'—'you *must* get Austin Dobson.' 'The other Austin is vulgar—"The Season" execrable.'[9] 'There is not enough fire in William Watson's poetry to boil a tea-kettle.'[10]

He wishes that it were always possible to convey poetry to the mind by some means other than print. 'Print is by no means the proper purple for Poetry to show herself in,' he says.

The conversation turned to prose writers. He is a great novel reader. Amongst English novelists, he prefers George Meredith. *The Egoist* is 'a terrible book for human nature. Every sentence tells—every line is an arrow in one's own soul.'[11] R. L. Stevenson is very fine.[12] Some people would rather have Rider Haggard; 'that is because they are insane.'[13] The two are not to be compared. 'Rider Haggard writes like a man playing football, and as long as he confines himself to blood and bruises he does well; but immediately he begins to moralise, he gets outside his natural sphere and becomes absurd.' He is not enthusiastic over Scott.[14] He is able to read Thackeray's *Esmond*.[15] Charlotte Brontë is 'often quite charming.'[16] *Robert Elsmere* 'everyone should read.'[17]

He is thoroughly steeped in French literature. Indeed, he is more conversant with French than with English, and spends some months of each year in France. The French novel is 'a miracle.' 'They have brought the art of fiction to a point beyond which human genius cannot go.'

The English stage is in 'a shocking condition;' this is rather the fault of the public; 'nothing but comedy and farcical comedy go down with an English house; the French are far ahead of us in matters theatrical.'

On matters of English history he discoursed much and curiously.

He likes the Puritans 'for their thoroughness;' they are the only people he would burn—'they really deserve burning—it is a great honour to a man to burn him.' But 'when the faith of the Puritan begins to broaden, that which constituted his greatest charm is gone; he is no longer a Puritan, and forthwith he becomes unworthy of the honours of faggot and stake.' There is much in the character of the Stuart Kings that he admires. William III he detests.[18] 'Kings ought not to be "ower gude."'[19] His ideal king is 'a man of high artistic sensibilities; one who can write beautiful poetry; who can appreciate good music; who is charmed with the beauties of painting and sculpture.' 'Not one who goes about with a swallow-tail coat on, laying foundation stones and doing little goodnesses.' 'In matters of taste' our present Royal Family is 'shockingly deficient.'

Theology was the next subject touched upon. He reads Theology every day; 'the history of Theology is the history of madness.' He much laments that religious literature is of so poor a quality. Dante is the only Christian writer of supreme merit. Wordsworth's was the religion of nature rather than the religion of Christ; he is pantheistic rather than Christian. 'I do not altogether believe in bringing children up on the Bible,' Mr. Wilde observed. By the time they arrive at an age to appreciate the Book, it has lost, to them, much of its charm. Anyone taking up the Gospels for the first time at or about the age of 18 would be enchanted. '"What a marvellous personality!" they would exclaim, "what a remarkable story!" But when their infancy has been surfeited with it, their manhood revolts at it. Their eyes have become blind by gazing at the sun before their minds are strong enough to comprehend and appreciate its vastness and meaning.' He has a profound admiration for the character and personality of Christ, but he cannot accept the doctrine of his Divinity; 'it would place too broad a gulf between Him and the human soul.' I suggested that the humanity of Christ bridges over the gulf that his Divinity creates, but in his opinion such bridgement is not adequate for the purpose. It is in the milder aspects of the Christ character that he most delights: teaching the poor, tending the sick, discoursing of a marvellous and ideal Faith with a few uncultured fishermen on the margin of Galilee. 'In His utmost humanity, He approaches nearest the Divine.' Those scathing words that He uttered at Jerusalem on the eve of His betrayal—in which, in the divine consciousness of innocence and right, He hurls anathema and defiance in the teeth of the Pharisees who were clamouring for His blood, Mr. Wilde considers rather as an outburst of spleen consequent upon the disappointment of cherished hopes and the defeat of a high and generous ambition. He discovered a certain partiality for the Pharisees; 'they were the repositories of all the learning and culture of their times.'

'Creeds are very personal things,' continued Mr. Wilde. 'Most of us believe in the great cardinal religious doctrines. That God made the Heaven and the Earth, and is the preserver and ruler of all things, few of us are prepared to deny: but when it gets beyond that, it becomes a merely personal matter.' 'The same reasoning applies to matters of secular history: Henry VIII reigned, granted; but if we proceed further, if we commence to tell how he reigned and to pass judgment on his commissions, omissions, and permissions as a King, we get out of history into personal opinion.' 'History ends with a few bare facts; Religion with a few undeniable Doctrines—beyond that all is invention.'

'Prayer is a splendid privilege, but it is the utmost presumption for a man to expect or suppose that his petition will be granted.' 'What a funny world it would be, to be sure, if the Almighty answered every prayer that is offered up to him! As though the All-Father does not know what is best for us!'

From Theology to Thieves is a long leap. But it is like the man to take it. He feels 'considerable sympathy' with Burglars. 'In nine cases out of ten they only take what we really do not want.' 'That only may be accounted a loss that is something gone from our own persons, or that it is impossible to do without.' 'The loss of a finger *is* a loss; the loss of our last guinea is a loss; but the loss of a thousand pounds when we have a hundred thousand in the bank is *not* a loss.' Burglars broke into the house of a friend of his and made off with all they could lay their hands to. Mr. Wilde called; everybody was in hysterics. He administered to them the consolations of this unique philosophy; he assured them that inasmuch as human nature is constituted to be capable, in certain contingencies, of dispensing with silver spoons and Japanese curiosities, a visitation of burglars is really a matter of very small moment indeed. 'Now, had someone fallen downstairs and broken a limb, it would have been a reasonable cause for distress; but really, silver spoons! Japanese curiosities! what good are they?'

He is 'very sorry Smugglers have gone out of fashion.' 'What glorious places the creeks and caves of Babbacombe would be for smuggling enterprise, and what a pity it is that such fine natural advantages have to be disregarded.' Adam Smith (he believes it is) somewhere says that 'if it had not been for Smugglers in the last century, the commercial property of this country would have become extinct!'[20]

Pirates, too, are 'very fine fellows.' It was they who established the maritime reputation of England. What was his friend Sir Francis Drake, but a pirate?[21] 'Every profession in which a man is in constant danger of losing his life has something rather fine about it.' He would 'infinitely rather' see one of his boys a smuggler 'than a grocer serving up sugar, or a stock-broker baiting traps for people, and keeping himself secure beyond the reach of law.'

Beggars are remarkable people. He greatly wonders that no one has undertaken to write the history of beggars. He is sure the subject is full of capabilities. 'The life of an Italian beggar is one of the jolliest that can be imagined.' 'They have no need of homes who can live in the open air; their only requirement is food.' 'The climate of England is a great hardship to the poor of this country.'

He likes Jews. He has many friends among the Hebrews. He thinks Spinoza a very fine character. He seems to have some doubt as to whether Spinoza was really the founder of the Pantheistic sect.[22]

The conversation drifted into politics. 'We are all of us more or less Socialists now-a-days,' he remarked. 'Our system of government is largely socialistic.' 'What is the House of Commons but a socialistic assembly?' 'I think I am rather more than a Socialist,' he added, laughingly; 'I am something of an Anarchist, I believe; but, of course, the dynamite policy is very absurd indeed.'

'What a perfect fiasco is our system of penal administration!' 'To punish a man for wrong-doing, with a view to his reformation, is the most lamentable mistake it is possible to commit.' 'If he has any soul at all, such procedure is calculated to make him ten times worse than he was before.' 'It is a sign of a noble nature to refuse to be broken by force.' 'Never attempt to reform a man,' he said; 'men never repent.'[23]

He loves true ignorance. He has not much faith in our modern system of educating everybody. 'A truly ignorant and unsophisticated man is the noblest work of God.'[24]

And so he reasoned on; the range of subjects, the diversity of interests, that his conversation represented was truly surprising. He does not weary with profundity, nor bore with unnecessary detail. No armchair lecturer he. Like a bee, he flits from flower to flower, just tastes the sweets and passes on. His style is fluent and animated, like a sort of gentle insistence not infrequently found in men of strong mind. He avoids hackneyed terms and commonplace phrases; his words are choice and ready; he takes the lead in all topics of discussion, and initiates all new departures in the conversation. His opinions are convincingly expressed, but not oracularly delivered. His conversation is entirely free from that ipse-dixitical 'cocksurishness' so often assumed by people on pedestals. I noticed one peculiarity: he makes very frequent use of one or two select words—'artist' is one, 'culture' another, 'fascinating' another, and so on.

To accurately gauge the character of the man is a task for which I feel myself incompetent. Words are to him a means whereby he may disguise his own personality. He never allows us to see the real emotions of his heart; his object seems to be to cast a glamour over us with the brilliance of his mind; he appears to sacrifice sentiment on the altar of analysis. He is a moral acrobat of a most extraordinary description. He stands before us a sane, plain gentleman of the nineteenth century, but in a moment, 'Εια άγε!'[25] he is on his head, gazing up at us solemn as a Sphinx, declaring that up to this moment humanity has been labouring under a ridiculous delusion, that *this* is the natural gait of a man, and that God Almighty never ordained that he should go otherwise. He is so solemn, so composed, so self-possessed, wonder seizes us—is the man schooling us in a great fact, or fooling us with a great farce!

1   Babbacombe Cliff was the home of Lady Mount-Temple. Wilde rented it between December 1892 and February 1893. Almy's interview appears to have been published after a delay.

2   Keats's letters to Fanny Brawne were sold at Sotheby's on 2 March 1885. Wilde's poem 'Sonnet on the Sale by Auction of Keats' Love Letters' was published in January 1886.

3   Elizabeth Barrett Browning (1806–1861) was an English poet, married to Robert Browning. She described her epic poem *Aurora Leigh* (1856) as 'a novel in verse'.

4   Robert Herrick (1591–1674) was an English poet and cleric.

5   William Wordsworth.

6   All the men named were English playwrights who worked during the late sixteenth- and early seventeenth-centuries.

7   Richard Brinsley Sheridan (1751–1816) was an Anglo-Irish playwright. His plays include *The Rivals* (1775) and *The School for Scandal* (1777). William Congreve (1670–1729) was an English playwright. He is best known for the Restoration comedy *The Way of the World* (1700).

8   James Thomson (1700–1748) was a Scottish poet and playwright, best known for his sequence of poems, *Seasons* (1726–1730). Wilde refers to a line from *Spring*: 'The yellow wallflower, stain'd with iron-brown'.

9   Henry Austin Dobson (1840–1921) was an English poet. Alfred Austin (1835–1913), an English poet who served as Poet Laureate from 1896 until his death, wrote *The Season: A Satire* (1861).

10   William Watson (1858–1935) was an English poet who wrote celebratory and political poems. Wilde had been annoyed by Watson's comic poem about Wilde's intention to leave England for France in the wake of the censorship of *Salomé*.

11   Meredith's *The Egotist* (1879) is about a self-absorbed knight who cannot understand why the various women whom he pursues do not want to marry him.

12   Robert Louis Stevenson (1850–1894) was a Scottish novelist, best known for his adventure novels *Treasure Island* (1881–1882) and *Kidnapped* (1886) and his gothic novella *Strange Case of Dr Jekyll and Mr Hyde* (1886).

13   Henry Rider Haggard (1856–1925) was an English writer of adventure stories and novels, including *King Solomon's Mines* (1885).

14   Sir Walter Scott (1771–1832) was a Scottish novelist, poet, and historian. His novels include *Rob Roy* (1817) and *Ivanhoe* (1819).

15   Thackeray's *The History of Henry Esmond* (1852) tells the story of a colonel in the service of Queen Anne, and has him participate in a number of historical events of the English Restoration.

16   Charlotte Brontë (1816–1855) was an English novelist, best known for *Jane Eyre* (1847).

17   *Robert Elsmere* (1888), an immensely popular novel about the religious struggles of an Oxford clergyman, was written by Mrs Humphry (Mary Augusta) Ward (1851–1920). In 'The Decay of Lying', Wilde has his character Vivian remark that '*Robert Elsmere* is of course a masterpiece—a masterpiece of the "genre ennuyeux [tedious type]"'.

18   William of Orange (1650–1702) invaded England in 1688–1689, deposed James II of England and Ireland (who was also James VII of Scotland), and thereafter reigned as William III of England, Scotland, and Ireland until his death. James attempted to regain his crown, but was defeated by William's forces at the Battle of the Boyne in Ireland in 1690.

19   Scots dialect, 'too good'. Wilde may be recalling the use of the phrase by James I of Scotland in that king's poetry.

20   Adam Smith (1723–1790) was a Scottish economist and philosopher. He wrote about smuggling in *An Inquiry into the Nature and Causes of the Wealth of Nations* (1776), though did not use the words quoted by Wilde.

21   Sir Francis Drake (c. 1540–1596) was an English privateer and explorer of the Elizabethan era.

22   Baruch Spinoza (1632–1677) was a Dutch philosopher of Portuguese Sephardi origin. He is considered by some to be an exponent of pantheism because of his equating God with Nature, although he complained that his readers took him too literally.

23   Wilde's own imprisonment did not change his attitude. After his release he wrote to the editor of the *Daily Chronicle*: 'It is not the prisoners who need reformation. It is the prisons.'

24   Lady Bracknell in *The Importance of Being Earnest*: 'I do not approve of
       anything that tampers with natural ignorance. Ignorance is like a delicate
       exotic fruit: touch it and the bloom is gone.'
25   εἶα ἄγε, a colloquialism meaning 'come on!'

'Mr. Oscar Wilde's Philosophy', *The New York Herald, European Edition* (Paris, France), 9 Sep. 1893, 1

DINARD, Sept. 7.

Mr Oscar Wilde left Dinard today on the steamer for St. Helier, where he will surprise the audience at the theatre there by appearing unexpectedly at the performance of his play, *A Woman of No Importance.*

I met him on the beach this morning previous to his departure.

'I came to Dinard,' he said, 'upon the advice of Dr. Manley Sims, for seclusion and rest, but I have not found either; and I must go away. Dinard is a delightful spot and filled with most charming people, but for summer life the hours are too late, if one follows the round of gaiety here; and I prefer rest and repose.'[1]

'I am not only engaged in writing a new play, but I am thinking of publishing a book of maxims, called *Oscariana,* which may or may not be acceptable to the thinking world.'[2]

'My idea is that every day should begin a new thought, a fresh idea, and that "yesterday" should be a thing of the past. Forget everything unpleasant in the past, and live for the present and the future.'

'What was your idea when in your book *Dorian Gray* you said, "Beware of women who wear violet?"' I asked.[3]

'Ah!' Mr. Wilde replied, 'I cannot tell you that without giving you the story of my life, and that would take too long. But truly, it is my theory to *beware of women who wear mauve.* It is a dangerous colour, and therefore most attractive, for to be fascinating one must be the least bit dangerous. And apart from this, there are psychological reasons for the warning.'

And now that the apostle of aestheticism has departed there will be a great void, for as a young lady remarked the other evening at the Casino to Mr. Wilde, who was surrounded by a crowd of ladies: 'You remind me of *Patience* and the "twenty love-sick maidens."'

At the balls and dinners given for Mr. Wilde there has been a run on sunflowers for decorations, and today there is scarcely a sunflower left in the gardens of the working classes, for every *soleil* has been plucked to adorn the tables at which 'Oscar' has been a guest.

1   Wilde writes in *De Profundis* of how he had gone to Dinard to obtain 'peace and freedom from the strain' of his friendship with Lord Alfred 'Bosie' Douglas (1870–1975).
2   *Oscariana*, with selections from Wilde's writings made by Constance, did not appear until January 1895.
3   In *The Picture of Dorian Gray* Lord Henry says: 'Never trust a woman who wears mauve, whatever her age may be, or a woman over thirty-five who is fond of pink ribbons. It always means that they have a history.'

F. E. McKay, 'A Clever Dramatist's Eccentric Views', *Kate Field's Washington* (Washington, DC), Vol. 9, 4 Apr. 1894, 220–221

I called lately upon Oscar Wilde at his apartments in St. James's Place.[1] It is here he receives those whom he wants to spare the long drive to Tite Street, where he has a charming house, over whose aesthetic penates,[2] Mrs. Wilde, his beautiful wife, presides.

Mr. Wilde, it is well known, has abandoned his 'Fauntleroy' costumes and now dresses, as he imagines, in *fin-de-siecle* fashion.[3] He wears a long sack coat. It is of gray Scotch cloth. It reaches nearly to his knees. His cravat is enormous. His hair is long and parted on the side. His cuffs are many sizes too large for him and are fastened with links. He wears a golden chain bracelet. Attached to it is a heart-shaped locket. The little finger of his left hand is covered, to the nail, with conspicuous rings.

I asked Mr. Wilde if he will ever go again to America. He said he had not decided. 'I had fully intended to be present at a performance of my comedy, *A Woman of No Importance*, by Rose Coghlan at the Fifth Avenue Theatre,'[4] said he, 'but the dislike I have to be interviewed by inquisitive reporters, who make no allowances for moods, has kept me from making trips. I shall go to France soon. I am content in its atmosphere. It is sympathetic.'

I asked Mr. Wilde how he works.

'I am not able to write a line,' he said, 'unless I feel inspired. In order to evolve anything I consider worthy of myself, I must feel that I am "possessed" of my subject. I seldom write during the day; it is at night, when all is still, dead almost to the writer, that the mind may soar above earthly considerations. In this I follow the maxims of Gustave Flaubert.'[5]

'Does this apply to everyone?' I asked.

'I do not believe in equality,' he replied. 'The world would be far better off if only few were in command and the masses were reduced to slavery—mentally as well as bodily.

'In each century only three or four men should rule; men of genius, and these men should be allowed to do exactly as they please.'

'Why?'

'Because they have genius. That is superior to anything human. It is a subtle something that is a spark of divinity. It should excuse vagaries, faults, weaknesses, even crimes.'

When asked whether he applied his theory to women, too, Mr. Wilde said: 'I like to detect intelligence in men; I do not like to find it in women—their mission in life is to be beautiful—that is all!'

Beautiful women, in Wilde's mind, ought to have the same privilege that men of genius would possess in the ideal world he describes. That is to say, there should be no restraint put upon them. No laws of country, conventions of society or prejudices of class should hamper them.

With regard to the drama, Wilde declares it one of the most wonderful achievements of modern civilization. 'The stage,' he told me, 'should be neither a battlefield nor a mere place for amusement. All plays should contain morals. The stage should not teach a stratum of society, but all humanity. It ought to hold before the public's eyes all the vices. It should not stay there. It should reveal the consequences of an evil life, so that the audience be thoroughly impressed and prevented from doing likewise.

'Before all, and above all, the characters that interpret a play should be true to life. Whether they are types of people the author has met in different epochs of his life or in different countries, he should be permitted to combine them in one drama.'

Wilde says he never writes a line in a play or a book without supposing himself the person he makes talk. This applies with equal force, of

course, to Dorian Gray, Lady Windermere, Mrs. Erlynne, Lord Illing-
worth or 'A Woman of No Importance.'[6]

1   Wilde kept rooms at 10 St James's Place for the purpose of writing and,
     according to testimony in his trials, as a place to meet with young men.
2   In ancient Roman religion the Penates were household gods.
3   *Little Lord Fauntleroy* (1885-1886) is a children's novel by Frances Hodg-
     son Burnett about an American boy who inherits a British title. The little
     lord's costume – a black velvet suit with knee breeches and a lace collar –
     became fashionable attire for children.
4   Rosamond Marie 'Rose' Coghlan (1851-1932) was an English actress. *A
     Woman of No Importance* was first performed in London on 19 April 1893
     and had its American premiere on 11 December.
5   Gustave Flaubert (1821–1880) was a French novelist, best known for
     Madame Bovary (1857); Wilde preferred *Salammbô* (1862) and *The Temp-
     tation of Saint Anthony* (1874).
6   Lady Windermere and Mrs Erlynne are characters in *Lady Windermere's
     Fan*; Lord Illingworth, in *A Woman of No Importance*.

'News From Afar', *The Press* (New York, NY), 8 Jul. 1894, 7

During Beerbohm Tree's absence on tour next autumn the Haymarket will pass into the hands of Lewis Waller, who intends to produce
there a new comedy by Oscar Wilde.[1] In connection with the above
forthcoming production, a characteristic correspondence has passed
by wire between Oscar Wilde and a writer. Lewis Waller is at present
out of town, and in order to obtain particulars about the new play the
writer telegraphed to Oscar Wilde, asking him to grant an interview.
This was the reply, received about an hour or so later:

'Very many thanks, but quite impossible. No one should read newspapers. Oscar.'

A second telegram was sent to the literary esthete, reading: 'Many
thanks for your wire. What should one read?'

'My own books, of course,' was the prompt response.

1   Herbert Beerbohm Tree (1852-1917) and Lewis Waller (1860-1915) were
     English actors and theatre managers. Tree had, in 1893, staged *A Woman
     of No Importance* at the Theatre Royal, Haymarket, creating the role of
     Lord Illingworth. Later that year Waller played Illingworth in the touring

production. In 1894 Waller leased the Haymarket while Tree was touring America: Wilde's third society comedy *An Ideal Husband* was his first production. He played Sir Robert Chiltern.

Gilbert Burgess, 'An Ideal Husband at the Haymarket Theatre', *The Sketch* (London, UK), 9 Jan. 1895, 495

On the morning following the production of *An Ideal Husband* I met Mr. Oscar Wilde as he came down the steps of a club at the top of St. James's Street, and I took advantage of the occasion to ask him what he thought of the attitude of the critics towards his play. 'Well,' he replied, as we walked slowly down the street, 'for a man to be a dramatic critic is as foolish and as inartistic as it would be for a man to be a critic of epics or a pastoral critic, or a critic of lyrics. All modes of art are one, and the modes of the art that employs words as its medium are quite indivisible. The result of the vulgar specialization of criticism is an elaborate scientific knowledge of the stage—almost as elaborate as that of the stage-carpenter and quite on a par with that of the call-boy—combined with an entire incapacity to realize that a play is a work of art, or to receive any artistic impressions at all.'

'You are rather severe upon dramatic criticism, Mr. Wilde.'

'English dramatic criticism of our own day has never had a single success, in spite of the fact that it goes to all the first nights.'

'But,' I suggested, 'it is influential.'

'Certainly; that is why it is so bad.'

'I don't think I quite—'

'The moment criticism exercises any influence it ceases to be criticism. The aim of the true critic is to try and chronicle his own moods, not to try and correct the masterpieces of others.'

'Real critics would be charming in your eyes, then?'

'Real critics? Ah, how perfectly charming they would be. I am always waiting for their arrival. An inaudible school would be nice. Why do you not found it?'

I was momentarily dazed at the broad vista that had been opened for me, but I retained my presence of mind, and asked—

'Are there absolutely no real critics in London?'

'There are just two.'

'Who are they?' I asked eagerly.

Mr. Wilde, with the elaborate courtesy for which he has always been famous, replied, 'I think I had better not mention their names; it might make the others so jealous.'[1]

'What do the literary cliques think of your plays?'

'I don't write to please cliques; I write to please myself. Besides, I have always had grave suspicions that the basis of all literary cliques is a morbid love of meat-teas. That makes them sadly uncivilized.'

'Still, if your critics offend you, why don't you reply to them?'

'I have far too much time. But I think some day I will give a general answer in the form of a lecture in a public hall, which I shall call "Straight Talks to Old Men."'

'What is your feeling towards your audiences—towards the public?'

'Which public? There are as many publics as there are personalities.'

'Are you nervous on the night that you are producing a new play?'

'Oh, no, I am exquisitely indifferent. My nervousness ends at the last dress rehearsal; I know then what effect my play, as presented upon the stage, has produced upon me. My interest in the play ends there, and I feel curiously envious of the public—they have such wonderfully fresh emotions in store for them.'

I laughed, but Mr. Wilde rebuked me with a look of surprise.

'It is the public, not the play, that I desire to make a success,' he said.

'But, I'm afraid I don't quite understand—'

'The public makes a success when it realizes that a play is a work of art. On the three first nights I have had in London, the public has been most successful, and, had the dimensions of the stage admitted of it, I would have called them before the curtain. Most managers, I believe, call them behind.'

'I imagine then, that you don't hold with the opinion that the public is the patron of the dramatist?'

'The artist is always the munificent patron of the public. I am very fond of the public, and, personally, I always patronize the public very much.'

'What are your views upon the much-vexed question of subject-matter in art?'

'Everything matters in art except the subject.'

When I recovered I said, 'Several plays have been written lately that deal with the monstrous injustice of the social code of morality at the present time.'

'Ah,' answered Mr. Wilde, with an air of earnest conviction, 'it is indeed a burning shame that there should be one law for men and another law for women. I think'—he hesitated, and a smile as swift as Sterne's 'hectic of a moment' flitted across his face—'I think that there should be no law for anybody.'[2]

'In writing, do you think that real life or real people should ever give one inspiration?'

'The colour of a flower may suggest to one the plot of a tragedy; a passage in music may give one the sestet of a sonnet; but whatever actually occurs gives the artist no suggestion.[3] Every romance that one has in one's life is a romance lost to one's art. To introduce real people into a novel or a play is a sign of an unimaginative mind, a coarse, untutored observation, and an entire absence of style.'

'I am afraid I can't agree with you, Mr. Wilde; I frequently see types and people who suggest ideas to me.'

'Everything is of use to the artist except an idea.'

After this I was silent, until Mr. Wilde pointed to the bottom of the street and drew my attention to the 'apricot-coloured palace' which we were approaching. So I continued my questioning.

'The enemy has said that your plays lack action.'

'Yes; English critics always confuse the action of a play with the incidents of a melodrama. I wrote the first act of *A Woman of No Importance* in answer to the critics who said that *Lady Windermere's Fan* lacked action. In the act in question, there was absolutely no action at all. It was a perfect act.'

'What do you think is the chief point that critics have missed in your new play?'

'Its entire psychology—the difference in the way in which a man loves a woman from that in which a woman loves a man, the passion that women have for making ideals (which is their weakness) and the weakness of a man who dare not show his imperfections to the thing he loves. The end of Act I, and the end of Act II, and the scene in the last act, when Lord Goring points out the higher importance of a man's life over a woman's—to take three prominent instances—seem to have been missed by most of the critics. They failed to see their meaning; they really thought it was a play about a bracelet.[4] We must educate our critics—we must really educate them,' said Mr. Wilde, half to himself.

'The critics subordinate the psychological interest of a play to its mere technique. As soon as a dramatist invents an ingenious situation they compare him with Sardou.[5] But Sardou is an artist not because of his marvellous instinct of stagecraft, but in spite of it: in the third act of *La Tosca*, the scene of the torture, he moved us by a terrible human tragedy, not by his knowledge of stage methods. Sardou is not understood in England because he is only known through a rather ordinary travesty of his play *Dora*, which was brought out here under the title of *Diplomacy*. I have been considerably amused by so many of the critics suggesting that the incident of the diamond bracelet in Act III of my new play was suggested by Sardou. It does not occur in any of Sardou's plays, and it was not in my play until less than ten days before production. Nobody else's work gives me any suggestion. It is only by entire isolation from everything that one can do any work. Idleness gives one the mood in which to write, isolation the conditions. Concentration on oneself reveals the new and wonderful world that one presents in the colour and cadence of words in movement.'

'And yet we want something more than literature in a play,' said I.

'That is merely because the critics have always propounded the degrading dogma that the duty of the dramatist is to please the public. Rossetti did not weave words into sonnets to please the public, and Corot did not paint silver and grey twilights to please the public.[6] The mere fact of telling an artist to adopt any particular form of art, in order to please the public, makes him shun it. We shall never have a real drama in England until it is recognised that a play is as personal and individual a form of self-expression as a poem or a picture.'

'I'm afraid you don't like journalists?' I remarked nervously.

'The journalist is always reminding the public of the existence of the artist. That is unnecessary of him. He is always reminding the artist of the existence of the public. That is indecent of him.'

'But we must have journalists, Mr. Wilde.'

'Why? They only record what happens. What does it matter what happens? It is only the abiding things that are interesting, not the horrid

Lewis Waller as Sir Robert Chiltern and Julia Neilson as Lady Chiltern in the first production of *An Ideal Husband*.

incidents of every-day life. Creation, for the joy of creation, is the aim of the artist, and that is why the artist is a more divine type than the saint. The artist arrives at his moment, with his own mood. He may come with terrible purple tragedies, he may come with dainty rose-coloured comedies—what a charming title!' added Mr. Wilde, with a smile. 'I must write a play and call it "A Rose-Coloured Comedy."'

'What are the exact relations between literature and the drama?'

'Exquisitely accidental. That is why I think them so necessary.'

'And the exact relations between the actor and the dramatist?'

Mr. Wilde looked at me with a serious expression which changed almost immediately into a smile, as he replied, 'Usually a little strained.'

'But surely you regard the actor as a creative artist?'

'Yes,' replied Mr. Wilde, with a touch of pathos in his voice; 'terribly creative—terribly creative!'

'Do you consider that the future outlook of the English stage is hopeful?'

'I think it must be. The critics have ceased to prophesy. That is something. It is in silence that the artist arrives. What is waited for never succeeds; what is heralded is hopeless.'

We were nearing the sentries at Marlborough House, and I said—

'Won't you tell me a little more, please? Let us walk down Pall Mall—Exercise is such a good thing.'

'Exercise!' he ejaculated, with an emphasis which almost warrants italics, 'the only possible form of exercise is to talk, not to walk.'

And as he spoke he motioned to a passing hansom. We shook hands, and Mr. Wilde, giving me a glance of approval, said—

'I am sure that you must have a great future in literature before you.'

'What makes you think so?' I asked, as I flushed with pleasure at the prediction.

'Because you seem to me such a very bad interviewer. I feel sure that you must write poetry. I certainly like the colour of your necktie very much. Good-bye.'

1   One of these critics was William Archer (1856-1924). See also p. 240.
2   Burgess's reference is to *A Sentimental Journey Through France and Italy* (1768), a novel by Laurence Sterne (1713-1768): 'The poor Franciscan made no reply: a hectic of a moment pass'd across his cheek, but could not tarry'.
3   'The Critic as Artist': 'Whatever actually occurs is spoiled for art.'
4   In *An Ideal Husband* Lord Goring confronts Mrs Cheveley about a bracelet he suspects she has stolen.
5   Victorien Sardou (1831-1908) was a successful and influential French playwright. His works include *Dora* (1877) and *La Tosca* (1887).
6   Jean-Baptiste-Camille Corot (1796-1875) was a French landscape and portrait painter.

[Robert Ross], 'Mr. Oscar Wilde on Mr. Oscar Wilde', *St. James's Gazette* (London, UK), 18 Jan. 1895, 4-5[1]

I found Mr. Oscar Wilde (writes a Representative) making ready to depart on a short visit to Algiers,[2] and reading—of course, nothing so obvious as a time-table, but a French newspaper which contained an account of the first night of *An Ideal Husband* and its author's appearance after the play.

'How well the French appreciate these brilliant wilful moments in an artist's life,' remarked Mr. Wilde, handing me the article as if he considered the interview already at an end.

'Does it give you any pleasure,' I inquired, 'to appear before the curtain after the production of your plays?'

'None whatsoever. No artist finds any interest in seeing the public. The public is very much interested in seeing an artist. Personally, I prefer the French custom, according to which the name of the dramatist is announced to the public by the oldest actor in the piece.'

'Would you advocate,' I asked, 'this custom in England?'

'Certainly. The more the public is interested in artists, the less it is interested in art. The personality of the artist is not a thing the public should know anything about. It is too accidental.' Then, after a pause—

'It might be more interesting if the name of the author were announced by the *youngest* actor present.'

'It is only in deference, then, to the imperious mandate of the public that you have appeared before the curtain?'

'Yes; I have always been very good-natured about that. The public has always been so appreciative of my work I felt it would be a pity to spoil its evening.'

'I notice some people have found fault with the character of your speeches.'[3]

'Yes, the old-fashioned idea was that the dramatist should appear and merely thank his kind friends for their patronage and presence. I am glad to say I have altered all that. The artist cannot be degraded into the servant of the public. While I have always recognized the cultured appreciation that actors and audience have shown for my work, I have equally recognized that humility is for the hypocrite, modesty for the incompetent. Assertion is at once the duty and privilege of the artist.'

'To what do you attribute, Mr. Wilde, the fact that so few men of letters besides yourself have written plays for public presentation?'

'Primarily the existence of an irresponsible censorship. The fact that my *Salome* cannot be performed is sufficient to show the folly of such an institution. If painters were obliged to show their pictures to clerks at Somerset House, those who think in form and colour would adopt some other mode of expression.[4] If every novel had to be submitted to a police magistrate, those whose passion is fiction would seek some new mode of realization. No art ever survived censorship; no art ever will.'

'And secondly?'

'Secondly to the rumour persistently spread abroad by journalists

Robert Ross as a Cambridge undergraduate in 1887, soon after he and Wilde first met.

for the last thirty years, that the duty of the dramatist was to please the public. The aim of art is no more to give pleasure than to give pain. The aim of art is to be art. As I said once before, the work of art is to dominate the spectator—the spectator is not to dominate art.'[5]

'You admit no exceptions?'

'Yes. Circuses where it seems the wishes of the public might be reasonably carried out.'

'Do you think,' I inquired, 'that French dramatic criticism is superior to our own?'

'It would be unfair to confuse French dramatic criticism with English theatrical criticism. The French dramatic critic is always a man of culture and generally a man of letters. In France poets like Gautier have been dramatic critics. In England they are drawn from a less distinguished class. They have neither the same capacities nor the same opportunities. They have all the moral qualities, but none of the artistic qualifications. For the criticism of such a complex mode of art as the drama the highest culture is necessary. No one can criticise drama who is not capable of receiving impressions from the other arts also.'

'You admit they are sincere?'

'Yes; but their sincerity is little more than stereotyped stupidity. The critic of the drama should be versatile as the actor. He should be able to change his mood at will and should catch the colour of the moment.'

'At least they are honest?'

'Absolutely. I don't believe there is a single dramatic critic in London who would deliberately set himself to misrepresent the work of any dramatist—unless, of course, he personally disliked the dramatist, or had some play of his own he wished to produce at the same theatre, or had an old friend among the actors, or some natural reasons of that kind. I am speaking, however, of London dramatic critics. In the provinces both audience and critics are cultured. In London it is only the audience who are cultured.'

'I fear you do not rate our dramatic critics very highly, Mr. Wilde; but, at all events, they are incorruptible?'

'In a market where there are no bidders.'

'Still their memories stand them in good stead,' I pleaded.

'The old talk of having seen Macready: that must be a very painful memory.[6] The middle-aged boast that they can recall *Diplomacy*: hardly a pleasant reminiscence.'

'You deny them, then, even a creditable past?'

'They have no past and no future, and are incapable of realizing the colour of the moment that finds them at the play.'

'What do you propose should be done?'

'They should be pensioned off, and only allowed to write on politics or theology or bimetallism, or some subject easier than art.'

'In fact,' I said, carried away by Mr. Wilde's aphorisms, 'they should be seen and not heard.'

'The old should neither be seen nor heard,' said Mr. Wilde, with some emphasis.

'You said the other day there were only two dramatic critics in London.[7] May I ask'——

'They must have been greatly gratified by such an admission from me; but I am bound to say that since last week I have struck one of them from the list.'

'Whom have you left in?'

'I think I had better not mention his name. It might make him too conceited. Conceit is the privilege of the creative.'

'How would you define ideal dramatic criticism?'

'As far as my work is concerned, unqualified appreciation.'

'And whom have you omitted?'

'Mr. William Archer, of the *World*.'[8]

'What do you chiefly object to in his article?'

'I object to nothing in the article, but I grieve at everything in it. It is bad taste in him to write of me by my Christian name, and he need not have stolen his vulgarisms from the *National Observer* in its most impudent and impotent days.'

'Mr. Archer asked whether, if it was agreeable to you to be hailed by your Christian name when the enthusiastic spectators called you before the curtain.'

'To be so addressed by enthusiastic spectators is as great a compliment as to be written of by one's Christian name is in a journalist bad manners. Bad manners make a journalist.'

'Do you think French actors, like French criticism, superior to our own?'

'The English actors act quite as well; but they act best between the lines. They lack the superb elocution of the French—so clear, so cadenced, and so musical. A long sustained speech seems to exhaust them. At the Théâtre Français we go to listen, to an English theatre we go to look. There are, of course, exceptions. Mr. George Alexander, Mr. Lewis Waller, Mr. Forbes Robertson, and others I might mention, have superb voices and know how to use them.[9] I wish I could say the same of the critics; but in the case of the literary drama in England there is too much of what is technically known as "business." Yet there is more than one of our English actors who is capable of producing a wonderful dramatic effect by aid of a monosyllable and two cigarettes.'[10]

For a moment Mr. Wilde was silent, and then added, 'Perhaps, after all, that is acting.'

'But are you satisfied with the interpreters of the *Ideal Husband*?'

'I am charmed with all of them. Perhaps they are a little too fascinating. The stage is the refuge of the too fascinating.'

'Have you heard it said that all the characters in your play talk as you do?'

'Rumours of that kind have reached me from time to time,' said Mr. Wilde, lighting a cigarette, 'and I should fancy that some such criticism has been made. The fact is that it is only in the last few years that the dramatic critic has had the opportunity of seeing plays written by anyone who has a mastery of style. In the case of a dramatist also an artist it is impossible not to feel that the work of art, to be a work of art, must be dominated by the artist. Every play of Shakespeare is dominated by Shakespeare. Ibsen and Dumas dominate their works.[11] My works are dominated by myself.'

'Have you ever been influenced by any of your predecessors?'

'It is enough for me to state definitely, and I hope once for all, that not a single dramatist in this century has ever in the smallest degree influenced me. Only two have interested me.'

'And they are?'

'Victor Hugo and Maeterlinck.'[12]

'Other writers surely have influenced your other works?'

'Setting aside the prose and poetry of Greek and Latin authors, the only writers who have influenced me are Keats, Flaubert, and Walter Pater;[13] and before I came across them I had already gone more than halfway to meet them. Style must be in one's soul before one can recognize it in others.'

'And do you consider the *Ideal Husband* the best of your plays?'

A charming smile crossed Mr. Wilde's face.

'Have you forgotten my classical expression—that only mediocrities improve? My three plays are to each other, as a wonderful young poet has beautifully said,

> as one white rose
On one green stalk to another one.[14]

They form a perfect cycle, and in their delicate sphere complete both life and art.'

'Do you think that the critics will understand your new play, which Mr. George Alexander has secured?'[15]

'I hope not.'

'I dare not ask, I suppose, if it will please the public?'

'When a play that is a work of art is produced on the stage what is being tested is not the play, but the stage; when a play that is not a work of art is produced on the stage what is being tested is not the play, but the public.'

'What sort of play are we to expect?'

'It is exquisitely trivial, a delicate bubble of fancy, and it has its philosophy.'

'Its philosophy!'

'That we should treat all the trivial things of life very seriously, and all the serious things of life with sincere and studied triviality.'[16]

'You have no leanings towards realism?'

'None whatever. Realism is only a background; it cannot form an artistic motive for a play that is to be a work of art.'

'Still I have heard you congratulated on your pictures of London society.'

'If Robert Chiltern, the Ideal Husband, were a common clerk, the humanity of his tragedy would be none the less poignant. I have placed him in the higher ranks of life merely because that is the side of social life with which I am best acquainted. In a play dealing with actualities to write with ease one must write with knowledge.'

'Then you see nothing suggestive of treatment in the tragedies of every-day existence?'

'If a journalist is run over by a four-wheeler in the Strand, an incident I regret to say I have never witnessed, it suggests nothing to me from a dramatic point of view. Perhaps I am wrong; but the artist must have his limitations.'

'Well,' I said, rising to go, 'I have enjoyed myself immensely.'[17]

'I was sure you would,' said Mr. Wilde. 'But tell me how you manage your interviews.'

'Oh, Pitman,' I said carelessly.[18]

'Is that your name? It's not a very *nice* name.'

Then I left.

1   Robert Baldwin Ross (1869–1918) was a Canadian-British journalist, art critic, and gallerist. He was a close friend of Wilde's and may have been his first male lover. He later served as Wilde's literary executor.

2   Wilde departed for Algiers on 15 January for a two-week holiday with Lord Alfred Douglas.

3   Wilde appeared before the curtain and spoke at the opening nights of *Vera; or, The Nihilists*, *Lady Windermere's Fan*, and *An Ideal Husband*. He was criticised in the press for his speech after *Lady Windermere's Fan*, not only for its boastful tone but because he was smoking when he made it.

4   Somerset House was then the headquarters of various government departments.

5   'The Soul of Man under Socialism': 'The work of art is to dominate the spectator: the spectator is not to dominate the work of art. The spectator is to be receptive. He is to be the violin on which the master is to play.'

6   Macready last appeared in London in 1851. *Diplomacy* opened in London in 1878 and was revived there in 1884 and 1893.

7   See pp. 232–233.

8   Archer thought *An Ideal Husband* entertaining but marred by 'a disproportionate profusion of inferior chatter'.

9   George Alexander (1858–1918) was an English actor and theatre manager who appeared in and produced *Lady Windermere's Fan* and *The Importance of Being Earnest*. Wilde is probably referring to Johnston Forbes-Robertson (1853–1937), Norman Forbes-Robertson's older and more successful brother.

10   Wilde may have had in mind Allan Aynesworth (1864–1959), creator of the role of Algernon Moncrieff in *The Importance of Being Earnest*.

11   Henrik Ibsen (1828–1906) was a Norwegian dramatist. His plays include *A Doll's House* (1879) and *Hedda Gabler* (1891)

12   Victor Hugo (1802–1885) was a French poet, novelist, and playwright.

13   Walter Pater was an English literary and art critic, a classics professor at Oxford, and a mentor to Wilde from autumn 1877. He advised Wilde to turn from poetry to prose, and to moderate references to male–male attraction in *The Picture of Dorian Gray*.

14   Wilde quotes 'Jonquil and Fleur-de-lys', a poem by Lord Alfred Douglas in which a 'shepherd lad' and prince swap roles. Fleur-de-Lys was one of Wilde's nicknames for Douglas. The three plays Wilde refers to are his society comedies – he omits his first two tragedies and *Salomé*.

15   *The Importance of Being Earnest.*

16   The subtitle of the play is 'A Trivial Comedy for Serious People'.

17   Ross quotes Wilde's brief speech after the first performance of *An Ideal Husband*: 'I thank you very much for the charming reception you have given my play. I thank the company for the very careful way in which they have acted it, and I have enjoyed my evening immensely.'

18   Pitman is a system of shorthand developed by Sir Isaac Pitman (1813–1897).

Frank Marshall White [and Robert Batho], 'Oscar Wilde to Write',
The Chicago Daily Tribune (Chicago, IL), 17 May 1897, 2[1]

LONDON, May 16.

Oscar Wilde has broken his long enforced silence. In Reading Prison today he announced to me his plans for the future. The terrible punishment he has suffered has not broken his spirit nor impaired his strength. He will try to live down the shame he has brought on himself and will not flee from his country and his enemies. Frank Harris of the *Saturday*

Review remains his friend through his humiliation and disgrace.[2] These are the questions put to Wilde and his answers:

'Tell me the condition of your health?'

'My health, physically, is good, but my brain is weary.'

'Have you formulated any plans for your future?'

'Yes, and now I am in the hands of a few faithful friends and my own dearest friend. To them I will deliver myself up, and with them chiefly lies my destiny. To them alone will I communicate my dearest desires.'

'But I ask for the public, the myriad admirers of your genius as poet, dramatist, and author. Are they to lose the benefit of your gifts? Is the world to have no more masterpieces from your pen?'

'At present my brain is too weak, too worn, too tired, but the power that is in me will resume its sway. I shall write again soon, but not yet. I am too tired, too distressed.'

'You will write in English or in French exclusively?'

'I will write in English.'

'Do you propose leaving England?'

'Not at present. As I have told you I am in the hands of a few friends. They will decide for a while.'

'Allow me to ask bluntly, you do not intend to efface yourself?'

'I do not. I shall get to work again before long, the moment I feel well enough.'

'And for the present?'

'For the present, thanks to the friends to whom I have alluded, I shall retire into absolute seclusion. I shall see no one, speak to no one but them.'

'When may I tell the public they may expect to hear of you?'

'The public will hear from me through my next work, not before it is ready and not by any other means.'

'Will it bear your name?'

'Most assuredly, as I am at present disposed.'

'Can you not give me some approximate idea of when that will be?'

'No, I cannot tell until I have rested. I do not intend to work until my brain has recovered its balance.'

'And you seek to recover your equanimity in absolute seclusion?'

'In absolute seclusion.'

'Of course, you decline to name the whereabouts of your seclusion?'

'Most assuredly. The place will not, however, be far from London.'

Maj. Nelson, Governor of Reading Prison, here abruptly terminated the interview, as the limit of time under the Home Office regulations had expired.

1   Wilde was convicted of gross indecency on 25 May 1895 and sentenced to two years' hard labour. He was transferred to HM Prison Reading in November. British journalist Robert Batho (1856–1928) and American journalist Frank Marshall White (1861–1906) probably collaborated on the present article, with Batho conducting the interview and White cabling it to his employers in America. Batho had previously interviewed Wilde in 1883 and 1888. White had been in Reading for at least a week, seeking information about Wilde's imprisonment and impending release. An American reporter, possibly White, had written to Major James Osmond Nelson (1859–1914), the governor at Reading, offering to pay any sum for an interview with Wilde. Wilde was appalled by the idea, but may have agreed to an interview prior to his release if Nelson acted as intermediary, perhaps hoping that this would dissuade the interviewers from ambushing him later. He does not appear to have been paid for the interview. On the evening of 18 May 1897 he would be taken to Pentonville Prison. He was released the following morning. That evening, he sailed for France.

2   Frank Harris (1855–1931) was an Irish-American journalist. In April 1897 he visited Wilde in prison and promised to give his friend £500, though the money was not forthcoming.

[Louis Sérizier], 'An Interview with Mr. Oscar Wilde', *Gil Blas* (Paris, France), 22 Nov. 1897, 3

The scene is Dieppe, where the English novelist spent the last beautiful days before departing for Naples, which he has chosen, we believe, as a winter resort.[1]

A group of young Parisian poets and literary men surrounds Oscar Wilde, who responds with a good humour tinged with irony or bitterness to the rather indiscreet questions that we ask him.

Oscar Wilde is fluent in colorful, modern French, with a light British accent that is not without charm.

Although he denies that he is English and prides himself on his Irish origins and his Catholicism, one would have to be blind not to immediately recognise at first sight, from his physical appearance, an authentic representative of the Anglo-Saxon race. His height, portly build, the grey blue of his eyes, his fair hair, and the powerful jaw that rounds off the lower face leave no doubt about it.

When he laughs—he often laughs, with the laugh of a contented ogre—his teeth appear: dreadful, long, wide, with the gaps filled with gold.

Wilde, quite the fatalist, wears, on the little finger of each hand, a ring set with an emerald. These gemstones, engraved with cabalistic symbols, are from an Egyptian pyramid. He attributes to the emerald of the left hand the cause of all his happiness, and that of his misfortunes to the emerald of the right hand. To my observation—logical enough, I think—that he should have ridden himself of the evil ring, he replied in a changed voice: 'It takes misfortune in life to live happily.'

Besides, green is Oscar Wilde's favourite colour: he advocates it and says it is the symbol of Hell. He has a very special idea about Hell. He says that Heaven is made for the good people, the honest bourgeois and, in general, for all the mediocrities who ignore the new Desires. The good Lord is good. He is merciful, he is too merciful; Saint Peter allows easy entry, but Satan demands much more from his followers: with him formalities are required.

'To enter Paradise, you only have to knock once, but you have to knock three times to enter Hell. Trust me, love green, love Hell: the colour green and Hell are made for thieves and artists.'

Oscar Wilde loves France, because she alone is for freedom of speech, because she helps the weakest, and she alone aspires towards justice. Asked if we could stage for an English public French vaudeville pieces so mediocre that it would be pointless to name them, he said (and I state his opinion for the benefit of those authors who work for the export market): 'We can stage anything for the English, anything... except *Tartuffe!*'[2]

However, his soul is devoid of resentment; he confesses that he has experienced a Redemption through his sentence and his two years of hard labour, which he poetically calls his Exile. 'It is always the sin of pride that wrecks men: I had climbed too high and now I will wallow in the mud.' He is very grateful for the French Press which has so warmly argued for his cause. His gratitude goes especially to those who took up his defence without knowing him. To hear him, what he regrets most is that he was unable to attend the performance of his *Salomé* at the Théâtre de l'Œuvre during his imprisonment. He speaks with good grace of the two years lost to him and in his remarks about his fellow prisoners, whose state of mind he set out to define. He does not seem to have suffered much physically, but his great torture must have been that of the mind and the heart; he had to go through all the phases and anxieties of the night of the soul, which Huysmans speaks of befalling St. John of the Cross. When we asked him to talk about all he suffered during his imprisonment, he replied with horror in his voice: 'Excuse me, I never talk about that.'

To see him so cheerful, so lucid, so quick with the repartee, we ended up forgetting the terrible trials he had gone through.

He is very familiar with modern literary movements and their proponents, to the extent that he confounded us: he quoted from the young up-and-comers whom we hardly knew by name.

Wilde was, as we all know, very close to Verlaine,[3] whom he considers to be one of the most magnificent writers of the nineteenth century, as much for his poetic work as for the changes he wrought and for the aesthetic talks Wilde had with him at the Café François I, under the benevolent eye of the ineffable Bibi-la-Purée.[4] He would like Poor Lélian's statue to be erected not in the Luxembourg nor in the street, but in one of the cafes where Verlaine spent his life, so that his image would be sheltered from the weather, especially from the rain that the poet feared so much:[5]

It rains in my heart as it rains on the city.[6]

'The hero's statue must be on the battlefield of his life,' he told us, when speaking of this subject.

As for Mr. Stéphane Mallarmé, Mr. Oscar Wilde prefers this poet when he writes in French—we all know that Mr. Mallarmé also writes in English—'because at least in French Mallarmé is incomprehensible; Alas! in English he is not.'[7] And Wilde adds, perhaps to remedy his harsh criticism: 'Incomprehensibility is a gift, not everyone has it. Poor Moréas doesn't have it, but does Moréas really exist?'[8]

And, upon our assertion that the poet Moréas really existed in the flesh, Wilde added with a smile: 'I always thought he was a myth.' And he quoted us two or three other French writers whose existence had always seemed to him a legend, perhaps even a hoax.

The author of *The Picture of Dorian Gray* praises *Aphrodite* without reservation, and, as we drew a parallel between the novels of Pierre Louÿs and *Salammbô*,[9] he interrupted us, with a sort of ecstasy in his gaze: 'Nothing is as beautiful as this book!... And the Goncourts, what artists![10] and proud, and conceited, and jealous, justifiably, of their fame!...'

By and by, Oscar Wilde ceased his criticisms, and spoke instead of his own projects, of his books. He will write one directly in French; then, he will do as Mallarmé did, and translate it into English. He told us about the theatre he dreams of, the plays he wants to write, and the unparalleled worship he dedicates to the 'princess of beautiful gesture and attitudes,' Sarah Bernhardt, on whom he counts to embody one of his heroines.

He then told us, with verve, the scenario of an ironic play in three scenes, which he projected but gave up writing, at least for the moment.

Here we give him the floor:

'The Gospel often speaks of the sick whom Christ healed; nowhere in the holy books is there any mention of what happened to them afterwards. This is a gap that the imagination of a short story writer or a playwright should try to fill.

'Here is my idea:

'In the first scene, we see a young man crowned with roses getting drunk on wine. Christ passes by and reproaches him for his intemperance. The young man recognises him and, paying homage to him, says: "Master, I am the paralysed man whom you healed."

'Christ arrives, in the second scene, in a place where another man is engaging in debauchery with courtesans. He blames him for his vice. The man recognises him and, bowing down, says to him: "Master, I am the leper whom you healed."

'Then Christ, very sad, goes to the desert (third scene) and, seeing a young man who was crying, says to him softly: "Why do you weep?" And the young man, recognising him, replies: "Master, I was dead, and you resurrected me!"

'But,' added Oscar Wilde, in closing, 'I don't think I will follow through on this project because one has to respect the majesty of Christ.'

1   Wilde arrived in Dieppe by 13 September and left for Paris on or about
     15 September. He and Lord Alfred Douglas rented a villa near Naples.
     By December Douglas had departed; Wilde was back in Paris by mid-
     February 1898.
2   The eponymous character in Molière's comedy *Tartuffe* (1664) is a hyp-
     ocritical religious devotee. Wilde appears to be accusing the English of
     hypocrisy.
3   Paul-Marie Verlaine (1844–1896) was a French poet.
4   André-Joseph Salis (1848–1903), known as Bibi-la-Purée, was a French
     actor and iconic figure of bohemian Paris.
5   Verlaine's nickname for himself was Pauvre Lélian. A public subscription
     to fund a monument to Verlaine was announced in February 1897. A
     statue was unveiled in the Jardin du Luxembourg in 1911.
6   The opening of Verlaine's poem, 'Il Pleure dans mon Cœur', or 'It Rains
     in My Heart'.
7   Stéphane Mallarmé (1842–1898) was a French symbolist poet.
8   Jean Moréas (1856–1910) was a Greek symbolist poet and art critic who
     wrote mostly in French.
9   Pierre Louÿs (1870–1925) was a French writer and the dedicatee of the
     French edition of *Salomé*. His first – and, at the time this interview was
     given, his only – novel *Aphrodite: Ancient Manners* (1896) is about a sculp-
     tor who attempts to win the love of a courtesan by committing theft and
     murder for her.
10   Edmond (1822–1896) and Jules de Goncourt (1830–1870) were French
     authors and brothers.

**[Clifford Millage], 'The Late Oscar Wilde', *The Daily Chronicle*
(London, UK), 3 Dec. 1900, 5**

PARIS, Sunday Night[1]

About three weeks ago I was scouring Paris to discover the address of a
M. Sebastian Melmoth for the purpose of verifying a statement that he
had been unjustly deprived of certain dramatic rights of authorship.[2]
At length a French literary friend informed me that the object of my
search was lying ill at a little hotel in the far-off Rue des Beaux Arts.
To save time he had called upon him in my name. M. Melmoth was
Oscar Wilde. On the same evening I received a letter in answer to my
petit bleu. I instantly answered this in person. The once brilliant and
adulated poet-playwright, though in bed, looked well in the face. The

Wilde photographed in Rome in the spring of
1900, possibly by Robert Ross.

first part of the conversation on his side was a mixture of defiance and
bitterness. I did my best to console him, and he suddenly burst into
tears. I felt deeply moved as he told the sad tale of blight and misery
through which he had passed. Men who had been the recipients of
sterling generosity had betrayed him and trodden him under their feet.
Perhaps there was some justice in his wailing.

Then he turned to religious subjects, and muttered almost savagely,
'Much of my moral obloquy is due to the fact that my father would not
allow me to become a Catholic. The artistic side of the Church and the
fragrance of its teaching would have curbed my degeneracies. I intend
to be received before long.' He spoke almost smilingly of his operation,
saying that it would cost him £40, adding that he owed nearly 2,000f.
to the hotel.

The operation in question was intestinal, and then symptoms of cere-
bral meningitis set in.[3] Leeches were applied to the ears, but the patient
sank away rapidly. Two kind friends, Mr. Robert Ross and Mr. Turner,
nursed him, whilst Father Cuthbert Dunne, one of the British Catholic
chaplains from the Avenue Hoche, administered the customary rites of
the Church.[4] Oscar Wilde tried to articulate the prayers which accom-
pany Extreme Unction, and his death bed was one of repentance.

Tomorrow morning the funeral service will take place at the Church St. Germain des Prés, after which the body will be interred in the Bagneux Cemetery. A small cross will surmount the grave, with the following inscription:— 'Ci gît Oscar Wilde, Poéte et Auteur Dramatique. R. I. P.'[5]

1   2 December. Wilde died at 13:50 on 30 November of meningoencephalitis secondary to chronic right middle-ear disease.

2   Millage wrote to Wilde on 5 November on *Chronicle* stationery asking for an appointment to discuss Wilde's new play. Wilde had written the scenario for a play he called 'Love is Law' and sold it to a number of people, including Frank Harris, who based his script for *Mr. and Mrs. Daventry* upon it. Harris's play was staged in London between 25 October 1900 and 23 February 1901. Harris was obliged to pay off the other claimants and withheld most of Wilde's fee. Wilde wrote several letters to Harris demanding payment.

3   The operation was conducted on 10 October and was probably a radical mastoidectomy.

4   Reginald 'Reggie' Turner (1869–1938) was an English journalist. Cuthbert Dunne (c. 1868–1950) was an Irish-born Passionist priest.

5   The inscription on Wilde's gravestone at Bagneux read: '† | OSCAR WILDE | OCT. 16TH 1854—NOV. 30TH 1900. | VERBIS MEIS ADDERE NIHIL AUDEBANT | ET SUPER ILLOS STILLABAT ELO-QUIUM | MEUM. [After my words they spake not again; and my speech dropped upon them.] | JOB XXIX, 22. | R. I. P.' Wilde's remains were transferred to Père Lachaise Cemetery in 1909.

ACKNOWLEDGEMENTS

I thank the many people who made this collection possible. Firstly, if Matthew Hofer and Gary Scharnhorst had not compiled and published a bibliography of interviews in their *Oscar Wilde in America: The Interviews*, I could not have begun to contemplate beginning research for *Oscar Wilde: The Complete Interviews*. Merlin Holland allowed me to quote from Wilde's letters and provided useful pointers. John Cooper identified many interviews and I thank him for sharing his materials and for his invaluable support and encouragement. I am indebted to John Cooper and Matthew Sturgis for enlightening discussions about Frank Marshall White and Robert Batho's article, and to Robert Whelan, Joseph Donohue, and Matthew Sturgis for their comments on William Theodore Peters's article. My translation of Louis Sérizier's interview from the French was improved by the astute comments of Doriane Nemes and LibriVox volunteer Sonia (of course, I remain responsible for any errors).

I am also grateful to the many librarians, historians, and archivists who searched their collections on my behalf.

IMAGE CREDITS: 11, 187, oscarwildeinamerica.org; 23, Yale Center for British Art, Paul Mellon Collection; 24L, 34, 44, 55, 71, 78, 119, 122, 137, 147, 151, Library of Congress; 24R, J. Paul Getty Museum; 42, 82, 197, Wikimedia; 51, William M. Quinlan; 63, Art Institute of Chicago; 84, 85, 200, Folger; 89, Newberry Library, Chicago; 172, 220, 251, National Portrait Gallery, London; 192, Houghton Library, Harvard University; 195, Paris Musées. All others, author's collection.

SELECTED BIBLIOGRAPHY

My chief source for facts about Wilde's life is *Oscar: A Life* (Head of Zeus, 2018) by Matthew Sturgis. Wilde's correspondence is collected in *The Complete Letters of Oscar Wilde* (Fourth Estate, 2000) edited by Merlin Holland and Rupert Hart-Davis. Wilde's North American lecture tours are documented by John Cooper on his website oscar-wildeinamerica.org; the tours of Great Britain and Ireland, by Geoff Dibb in *Oscar Wilde: A Vagabond with a Mission* (Oscar Wilde Society, 2013). Dibb is also my source for 'Personal Impressions of America'. Quotations from 'The English Renaissance' are taken from the *Miscellanies* volume of *The Collected Works of Oscar Wilde* (Methuen, 1908), edited by Robert Ross.

References to Wilde's works are to the Oxford English Texts edition of Wilde's *Complete Works*, or, where necessary, to the Oxford World's Classics 2025 edition of *The Importance of Being Earnest and Other Plays*, edited by Kate Hext. References to Shakespeare's works are to *The New Oxford Shakespeare: Modern Critical Edition* (2016).

I expand on some of the topics in the interviews in this volume in my publications Marland, R. (2021) Imitatio Neronis: Oscar Wilde's 'Neronian Coiffure', *The Wildean*, *59*, 3–56; Marland, R. (2021) Oscar Wilde at the Nebraska State Hospital for the Insane, *Notes & Queries*, *68*, 328–331; Marland, R. (2021) Oscar Wilde on the husbands of beautiful women, *Notes & Queries*, *68*, 331–332; Marland, R. (2022) On Sarah Bernhardt's cancelled production of Oscar Wilde's *Salomé*, *Notes & Queries*, *69*, 350–354; Marland, R. (2024) John Donoghue's 'Requiescat' plaque, *The Wildean*, *64*, 3–67; and Marland, R. (2026) *Oscar Wilde's First Tragedy: The Composition, Production, and Reception of Vera; or, The Nihilists*, Little Eye.